# INTERPRETING THE INDIAN

# Interpreting the Indian

*Twentieth-Century Poets
and the
Native American*

## Michael Castro

Foreword by Maurice Kenny

*University of Oklahoma Press
Norman and London*

ISBN: 0-8061-2351-6
LC: 90-50684

Permission acknowledgments may be found on page 211.

*to my mother & father*

# ♦ *Contents* ♦

"A Change of Worlds": Foreword by
    Maurice Kenny      vii
Acknowledgments      xv
Preface      xi
1    Early Translators of Indian Poetry      3

    The Early Ethnologists      7
    *The Indians' Book*      8
    Indian "Poetry"      11
    Other Early Twentieth-Century Native
      American Literature      12
    Early Poet-Interpreters      13
    The Spiritual Connection      15
    Early Interpretations of Indian Poetry      16
    The First Anthology      19
    *Path on the Rainbow* as a Contribution
      to American Poetry      20
    Indian Poetry and Imagism      22
    Early Approaches to Interpretations by
      American Poets      25
    Characteristics of Indian Poetry      32
    Austin's "The American Rhythm"      38
    Critical Responses      42

2    The Indian as a Symbol: Vachel Lindsay,
      Hart Crane, and William Carlos Williams      47

    Vachel Lindsay      49
    Hart Crane's "The Bridge"      55
    William Carlos Williams      59

3    Translating Indian Consciousness:
       Lew Sarett and John G. Neihardt      71

       Lew Sarett      73
       John G. Neihardt      79

4    Toward a New Poetry and a New Man:
       Charles Olson's Projective Verse      99

       Olson's "The Kingfishers" and the
       Backgrounds of Projective Verse      102
       "Projective Verse" and "Postmodern" Man      107

5    Jerome Rothenberg: New Forms from Old      115

       Convergence of the Primitive and the Modern      117
       Native American Forms and a
       New Modern Poem      124

6    Gary Snyder: The Lessons of
       Turtle Island      137

       Being in Nature      139
       "Original Mind"      146

7    Snyder and the Emergence of Indian Poets:
       Restoring Unity      153

       The 1970s: An Uprising of Indian Writers      155
       Native American Consciousness      165

Notes      175
Bibliography      191
Permission Acknowledgments      211
Index      213

# "A Change of Worlds"

## Foreword by Maurice Kenny

And when the last Red Man shall have perished, and the memory of my tribe shall have become a myth among White Men, these shores will swarm with the invisible dead of my tribe, and when your children's children think themselves alone in the field, the store, the shop, upon the highway, or in the silence of the pathless woods, they will not be alone. In all the earth there is no place dedicated to solitude. At night when the streets of your cities and villages are silent and you think them deserted, they will throng with the returning hosts that once filled them and still love this beautiful land. The White Man will never be alone.

    Let him be just and deal kindly with my people, for the dead are not powerless. Dead, did I say? There is no death, only a change of worlds.—Chief Seattle, in *Indian Oratory*, ed. W. C. Vanderwerth, pp. 121–22

This October Sunday morning I sit watching out the window. The southern sun passes over the slopes. I am aware of the ghosts on those old towers—and not merely in the names of these great mountains hewn and formed by glaciers, and whittled by time and winds, and more recently by loggers and miners. Iroquois, Algonquin, and probably Abenaki once homed to these valleys and slopes. Ghosts remain. Spirits are under the great white pine and the tamarack, or in the ripple of the flowing creeks. The brown bear knows, as he sniffs for honey; the wolf, who only recently returned in small numbers; the red-tailed hawk and the rarely sighted eagle; the speckled trout; the winds and the rising sun. They know these ghosts persist and observe the villages grow and develop as more fast-food and mini marts crowd these hollows along the lake shores. Chief Seattle spoke of the lack of solitude: there is no solitude here in these Adirondacks. The invisible dead chant a morning song, an evening prayer. Listen. It is not the wind among the conifers; it is the voice of the dead rising in unison through their living children.

Recently Mohawk traditional chief Tom Porter, speaking to a congress of Native American writers in Saranac Lake, New York, confided to his listeners that "one day our children will speak to the world." That, too, is happening: Karoniaktate is writing his poems not far from here on the St. Lawrence River at Akwesasne; Elizabeth Woody, far away in Oregon, is also composing poems; and in the more central section of the land, the Indian Territory of Oklahoma, Lance Henson, Joe Dale Tate Nevaquaya, and Charlotte DeClue are penning their poems and telling stories with Patricia Mousetail Russell. If you listen you can hear their pens scratch the paper. If you listen *here* you can detect the shuffle of feet in the rabbit dance, the drum. The drum rams the ears, and the rattles shake. A voice chants over the autumnal morning of the eastern sky. Mountains vibrate. A resilient whisper greets the rising sun. These ghosts appear mortal to the listener.

I cannot but believe that Michael Castro, poet, teacher, editor, and critic, has stood somewhere on a high place, perhaps the Cahokia Mounds in Illinois, or on the shores of the great Mississippi lowlands, and attuned his hearing to these voices rising out of the earth. Castro, once a disenfranchised student of the 1960s, has listened to many voices and has, indeed, interpreted them in the essays in *Interpreting the Indian*. He has not necessarily dared the anthropologist's path and interpreted, critiqued, the "Indian" voice, but has sharpened his critical astuteness to interpret those American voices that have stolen, borrowed, or rendered traditional literatures and concepts of Native Americans. He interprets the voices of the twentieth century—voices who had lost contact with their European heritage and faith in their contemporary institutions of government and religion, and who realized that America had lost touch with the earth itself, from which rise national literatures, life-codes, and spiritual consciousness.

Seeking alternatives himself, Michael Castro investigated a body of American literature and found it, in part, at fault, and at times belligerently inaccurate in stealing Native American "myths" (to use Seattle's word) and destroying these "myths" through lies, theft, and renderings from original languages when the renderer had no thorough fluency in those ancient tongues. Nevertheless, Castro found that these attempts reveal a real hunger for unity with inner and outer nature, and for an art indigenously American.

Others have sought faith or spirit through communication with the earth on seeing its destruction by "the White Man," knowing that European religion, having risen originally from the Middle East, no longer served. Feeling not merely a genuine concern but a deeply rooted hunger for spirit, they have turned in many ways and finally have gyrated to Native American spirituality. Some seek a return to European tribalism and an ethnicity through rituals and ceremonies of the Native Americans.

Castro has no fear of the clay gods. He removes them from the high pedestals where former critics had positioned them. In fact, he nearly returns their clay to dust. Vachel Lindsay, Hart Crane, Lew Sarett, and the estimable John Neihardt, among others, are discovered to be, if not fraudulent, certainly in error. Critic Castro is somewhat kinder to William Carlos Williams, Gary Snyder, and Jerome Rothenberg—all three of whom have made serious borrowings. At least, according to Castro, they did not make mockeries of the Pocahontas legend or turn a "medicine person" into "Doctor Mohawk," or childishly assess the once-free buffalo as did the barnstorming bard Vachel Lindsay. Or climb the Brooklyn Bridge howling for Americans to march west across the continent upon this magnificent bridge—a true work of art built in part by Iroquois ironworkers—and strike out for new conquests. Crane's vision, in his most difficult, barely accessible poem, *The Bridge,* is certainly "all American" as Whitman would have declaimed, but shows an immediate lack of concern for American history and no understanding or sympathy with either the earth or the First Peoples' place upon it.

It seems a shame that *Interpreting the Indian* has no space to interpret the writings of the classic American authors other than with quick strokes. Surely thefts and lies also can be found in Whitman, himself, Emerson, Longfellow, Whittier, James Russell Lowell, Cooper, Parkman, and more modern authors such as Walter D. Edmonds, in his contrivance *Drums along the Mohawk;* Edmund Wilson, who broke a promise to the People of the Longhouse in *Apologies to the Iroquois,* an infraction of ceremony; and the many anemic, biased, and historically inaccurate biographies of the great Native American leaders. Surely Castro has contemplated these materials seriously. He might still take Robert Penn Warren to task for his abominations of Chief Joseph in the collection of poems of the same name, which could easily be labeled a mock epic, or tour de force in cliché, because the high-romantic noble hero reads bloodless, shorn of human frailty. But these are subjects for another book of essays.

In the last chapter of *Interpreting the Indian,* Castro mentions a handful of contemporary Native American writers— N. Scott Momaday, whose Pulitzer Prize in 1969 definitely opened established but closed doors; Leslie Marmon Silko; James Welch; Vine Deloria, Jr.; Simon J. Ortiz; among others—and their successes and contributions. Essays might now be written on the contributions of Janet Campbell Hale, Elizabeth Cook-Lynn, Joy Harjo, Peter Blue Cloud, Duane Niatum, Gerald Vizenor, Roberta Hill Whiteman, and Lewis (Little Coon) Oliver. Other essays might deal with the successes of Charles Eastman, D'Arcy McNickle, and the eminent Canadian Mohawk E. Pauline Johnson, sometimes referred to as the grandmother of modern Native American literature. As young authors are born and develop, more such essays will be needed. Hopefully, Native Americans will gain both readership and prominence because of the quality of their creativity and not because *New York Times* headlines are written and smeared with their blood.

The casual reader today, the student and scholar, need not read the dishonest thievery of Vachel Lindsay, the self-serving transformations of Hart Crane, the translations of Mary Austin, nor the reminders by Gary Snyder of the value and inheritance of the earth and spirit, or by Jerome Rothenberg of the importance of tribal ritual to get to the heart of Native culture—prayer, song, and chant. These works are more meaningfully read as expressing lacks and needs—

American yearnings. The translations of these Native arts are now rendered, voiced, by Native American artists themselves such as Ray Young Bear, Nora Dauenhauer, Rokwaho (Daniel Thompson), Salli Benedict, Nia Francisco, and others. And the "white shaman" of whom Geary Hobson and Silko wrote so eloquently in *The Remembered Life,* and whom Castro also discusses, this sham has more or less been put out of business. Native Americans are quite capable of defining themselves. They have learned once more to value their arrows, to sharpen the points, and to reinforce their strength. Michael Castro's examination of the literary borrowings is a valuable reminder to Native People to hold their arrows ever more closely, to cherish and respect not only these arrows of the arts, but to continue the *adowe,* thanks to the Creator for the miraculous gifts of these incredible arrows.

*Interpreting the Indian* reinforces the fact that American literature simply is not American if it excludes the Native American chanters and writers who support and enrich it, who perhaps are even a strong post or two of its very foundation.

Presently I sit at the window of my sun porch–studio, viewing a particular range of the Adirondacks. The ghosts remain on the slopes, peaks, and in the valleys. They tell me these old mountains are maturing still. The great elm tree just to the right of my window is also maturing. When I rise each morning, the range and tree remind me that Seattle's ghosts are not only vividly here on the slopes and rivers, but that they, too, are developing the arts of both peace and war, of survival through law and literature, and that they will continue to compose and sing the old into new in the history of humankind. I am pleased this continuum is strong and healthy, this glorious creativity among the young Native American poets and storytellers.

*Saranac Lake in the Adirondacks*

# ◆ *Acknowledgments* ◆

I would like to thank Donald Finkel, Richard Hazelton, and Carter Revard for their help in the development of this study from its inception to completion. Many others have offered valued support and encouragement at various stages along the way, among them Bob Dyer, Jim Ruppert, Nancy Lankford and her staff at the Missouri Historical Society, Hilda Neihardt Petri, Beth Hadas, and the scholars, writers, and teachers who taught each other at the MLA sponsored Native American Literature Conference in the summer of 1977. I am especially grateful to Gary Snyder and Jerome Rothenberg, who consented to interviews. Without the aid of all of these interested, interesting, and generous people, the project would not have been completed.

# ◆ *Preface* ◆

This book is about America, Americans, and Native Americans. Particularly it is about twentieth-century poets who have sought to bring their notions of the three together to create something new—new poetry, new consciousness, a New World. I hope it will strike readers close to home—readers concerned with America and her poets' search for rootedness and roots, their attempts to dig in and come to terms with what Charles Olson referred to as America and Americans' "spatial nature."

The book evolved out of a complex of personal influences, many of which were typical to poets whose formative years occurred during the Vietnam War era and its aftermath. Some of these factors are worth sketching in here, for they establish some of the important cultural connections that stimulated the most recent wave of interest by twentieth-century American writers in Indian materials. During the late sixties and early seventies, the author was experimenting as a primarily oral poet with the jazz musicians of the Human Arts Ensemble in St. Louis. Though this performance activity was not initially related to an interest in Native American cultures and poetries, the subsequent discovery of these cultures' rich traditions of mixed-media-performance poetries, linked to the social and spiritual needs of community, soon helped to establish that interest.

But other factors were also involved. Interest in things Indian evolved for me, as for many poets of my generation, naturally—conditioned by the cultural turmoil, politics, and poetics that involved us. Younger poets here, as elsewhere during this period, tended to think of themselves as "tribal" and "communal." We saw ourselves as "counterculturists," and were active in the antiwar movement. We were reading poems in public—in many cases, before we had published any. We were collaborating with other artists in "intermedia situations." We were developing our own communities and educating one another by reading aloud our own poems, and those of the "real poets" we liked, in social and political contexts. For many of us, such communal activities were more relevant than formal classroom study to our felt needs and actual development as poets. Allen Ginsberg, Charles Olson, and William Carlos Williams had pointed us toward a poetics rooted in the rhythms of body and breath and the music of the human voice talking American speech. For us, the actual involvement in physical, oral poetics distinguished our own evolving aesthetic sharply from what was being promoted in the academies; it linked us, however superficially, with the poetries of tribal peoples.

Politically and culturally we identified with these peoples. Their historical oppression caused by America and the West we saw as paralleling the contemporary plight of the Vietnamese peasant with whom we sympathized; and more directly, we sensed that each of us was, in more subtle ways, a victim of the same oppressive consciousness. Our political-cultural stance, like that of the poets we took as our teachers, was anti-Western. We reject the destructive qualities of America and Western civilization—the lack of respect for human and natural life that we saw as responsible for the tragedy of Vietnam. We saw poetry as a form of resistance to this brutality, a guerilla war waged on the field of consciousness against the isolation and alienation that numbed society's managers to the suffering inflicted by corporate legions. Gary Snyder had established for us the poet's ancient responsibility as a representative of nature. And nature—human and otherwise—we saw, with Snyder, as under unnatural fire. Poetry was a place to plant and nourish an alternative consciousness—one supportive of the human spirit and the spirit of life that wed man to nature.

We saw our work as paralleling that of contemporaries in other fields, especially the singer-songwriters whose poetry moved us—Bob Dylan, John Lennon, Donovan (and their ancestors: American rock, blues, and folk artists like Chuck Berry, Robert Johnson, and Woody Guthrie)—as well as the jazz musicians, calling up unknown, indigenous music from feelings and breath. We saw ourselves, with these artists, as building a community of like souls, with mansions spiritual as well as political. My generation's deep need for community and communion, crucial to our sense of poetry, also underlies the work of many of the earlier poets discussed here.

As the sixties flowed into the seventies and the war ended, we dwelt more on the spiritual aspects of this "revolutionary" consciousness. Contributing to this process, for many of us, was the availability of literature by and about Native Americans and other tribal peoples. This literature helped us to see revolution as a cyclical process involving a return to understandings and values once widely held by people in America. For me, Jerome Rothenberg's anthologies of tribal poetries, *Technicians of the Sacred* (1969) and *Shaking the Pumpkin* (1972), were most important in this process, particularly as it related to poetry. The poems collected there, along with Rothenberg's commentaries, helped me see my own work as an oral poet experimenting with intermedia performance as a kind of return for renewal to an ancient human tradition and to the sources of poetry itself. Similarly, the efforts to create "alternative" spaces in which poetry could breathe—readings, radio programs, publications—seemed somehow the richer, for they appeared akin to ancient American tribal forms in the way they sought to serve the spiritual needs of community. Rothenberg suggested a "convergence" of modern poetry with "primitive" poetics and thought, and it is this perception that led to the current work.

Following Rothenberg's lead, and my own sense of curiosity about why so many of my contemporaries were basing their poetry and spiritual outlook on Indian models, I have sought to trace the line of American poets in this century whose work has in one way or another "interpreted" the meaning of the Indian for American poetry and life. I hoped in the process to learn more not only about poets who were of interest, but about "Indian consciousness" itself. The many texts and people I have had the good fortune to encounter along the way may have contributed to this end, but ultimately, and not surprisingly, this study reveals something more about the white American psyche. Readers have always, I think, read with fascination about the Indian precisely because they sense that they are discovering previously unknown aspects of themselves. Since first contact, the literary treatment of the Native American by white writers has, in fact, been more revealing of white culture than red.

This mirroring has been true of Indian-related literature from its inception. But *what* the white culture understands or reveals about itself through the Indian is not necessarily static. A part of what is new in this book is that the twentieth century has been a time of significant change in many non-Indians' perceptions of Native Americans (and themselves), and of a need for new "translations" based on new "texts." At the heart of this change is modern Americans' need for relatedness—to other people, to the land they live on, and to nature itself. In order to understand better how modern poets have "related to" the Indian, then, it would be useful here to briefly consider the earlier "text" or reading, the generalized image of the Indian before the change took place.

Prior to the twentieth century, literary approaches to the Indian were dominated by two apposing and distancing stereotypes, the "brutish savage" (Caliban) and the "noble savage" (Uncas), each serving underlying psychic needs of Western culture. The brutish savage stereotype is shaped by the common prejudices of Western "civilized" people who see tribal, "natural" people as inferior. It achieved philosophical expression in the Calvinist thought so pervasive in early American society. John Calvin himself had written of man in his natural state, "So depraved is his nature that he can be moved or impelled only to evil." This view held that man, without the controlling and inhibiting structures of civilization, was inherently a base creature. Many European writers, usually having little or no contact with actual Indian people, viewed the red man through this lens. A passage from Edward Waterhouse, a British writer of the seventeenth century, suggests the specific elements and scope of the brutish savage image. Waterhouse describes the Indian as "by nature sloathful & idle, vicious, melancholy, solvenly, of bad conditions, lyers, of small memory, of no constancy or trust . . . by nature of all people the most inconstant in the world, sottish & soddaine, never looking what dangers may happen afterwards, lesse capable than children of sixe or seaven years olde, & lesse apt & ingenious." Such a litany of abuse made white, "more advanced" people look good by comparison. When the image persisted into the nineteenth century, it served to reinforce one of the driving myths of our culture—the myth of progress—as well as the social Darwinism that often supported it.[1]

The brutish savage stereotype is evident in early European explorers' preoccupation with finding "cannibals." Columbus projects it in his journals, where he records without skepticism wild hearsay stories of "men with one eye and others with dogs' noses who ate men." The brutish savage occurs prominently in a variety of American literary sources: in "captivity narratives,"[2] initially published by Puritan clerics and later developed into a popular, if pulpy, literary genre; in the Indian figures populating the gothic novels of Charles Brockden Brown; in the histories of Francis Parkman; and very noticeably in the popular journalism of the nineteenth century. Emerson, surprisingly, seems to telescope the Indian through this lens, writing to Longfellow: "the dangers of Indians are, that they really are savage, have poor, small sterile heads—no thoughts."[3] Melville satirizes such prevalent social attitudes in *The Confidence Man,* in the chapter "On the Metaphysics of Indian-Hating," in which he suggests how these imaginary views actually dehumanize and dechristianize the white man and enable him to sanction the most awful atrocities against the Indian. As Melville indicates, the brutish savage stereotype, which reduced the Indian to a kind of vermin best eradicated, neatly gloved the genocidal hand of government, as it cleared the way to America's "manifest destiny." The brutish savage stereotype represented a chauvinistic affirmation of the "progress" of Western civilization—and a *moral* rejection of what was *different* in Indian cultures, i.e., Native American attitudes toward religion, nature, sexuality, and property.

Opposed to this image in pre-twentieth-century literature was the familiar stereotype of the noble savage. Popularized by Montaigne, Dryden (who coined the term in his long poem *Almanzor*), Rousseau, and other European writers with little if any firsthand knowledge of the red man, the term and concept were often employed rhetorically to criticize and satirize European societies. It supposed that humans in the "natural" state, rather than being nasty and brutish, were basically good, and that what corrupted such goodness was the influence of civilization itself. Not only naturally good, the noble savage was naturally dignified, poetic, serene, generous, essentially egalitarian, economically stable, and living in harmony with nature. In contrast, the civilized person appeared insecure, materialistic, selfish, warlike, oppressed and depressed by brutalizing class differences, and essentially out of touch with or opposed to nature.

The idea of the noble savage has been traced back by Boas and Lovejoy to Greek antiquity.[4] In the sixteenth and seventeenth centuries, it thrived in the popular voyage books, where it was used to promote settlement and commercial exploitation of the New World. It is central to the "Indian Death Song" poetry of the eighteenth and nineteenth centuries, of which Philip Freneau was a prominent practitioner; to Longfellow's immensely popular *Song of Hiawatha,* which can be seen as an epic culmination of that tradition; and to the widely read Leatherstocking novels of James Fenimore Cooper. Like the brutish stereotype, the noble one incarnated a central cultural myth—that of the Golden Age, in which the noble savage was pictured as living Adam-like in a higher (because unfallen) stage of development than his civilized counterpart.

The noble savage stereotype is akin to the views of the Indian held by many of the modern poets we will discuss, both in its sense of the inadequacies of Western man, and in its accompanying sense that the Indian possessed qualities we lack and need. But unlike most modern approaches, the noble savage convention was ultimately depressing and hopeless—for it accepted the "march of civilization" and the demise of tribal man and all associated with him as inevitable; it viewed Western man's fallen condition as irrevocable. Like the brutish savage stereotype, it thus often served to rationalize, however ruefully, a quasi-genocidal Indian policy. And just as much as the brutish savage stereotype, it tended to dehumanize and abstract the Indian, picturing him largely in terms of his difference from us, and in terms of his death.

Each of these stereotypes, then, set the red man at a chilly distance from the white. Each carried strong feelings about these differences—negative and hostile in the one, and positive and nostalgic in the other. But neither image contained the "real" Indian, or brought from actual Native American attitudes, expression, and lifeways anything of special value to white America.

Fittingly, one of the first American writers to break away from such distancing imagery was the grandfather of modern American poetry, Walt Whitman. In *Song of Myself* (section 39 in the "Deathbed Edition" of *Leaves of Grass*), a poem which can be seen as the American epic of the fully developed man, Whitman casts doubt on the assumption that underlies both the brutish and noble stereotypes: the assumption that the Indian is "civilized man" in an earlier state of development:

> The friendly and flowing savage, who is he?
> Is he waiting for civilization, or past it and mastering it?

Whitman's question suggests that the "savage" may be a model for a "new man" he hoped would emerge from the American experiment with democracy. He sensed, embodied in the red man, an egalitarian spirit and freedom implicit in nature and the American continent itself:

> Behavior lawless and snowflakes, words simple as grass,
> uncomb'd head, laughter, and naivete,
> Slow stepping feet, common features, common modes and
> emanations,
> They descend in new forms from the tips of his fingers,
> They are wafted with the odor of his body or breath, they
> fly out of the glance of his eyes.

Whitman anticipated the approach of "poets to come" in his view of the American Indian as a vital resource, in touch with the spirit of the American continent and offering, for an emerging American consciousness and identity, "new forms" of language and life-style. In writing of the Indian, he adopts imagery not of distance and decline, but of merger and renewal:

> Wherever he goes, men and women accept and desire him,
> They desire he should like them, touch them, speak to them,
> stay with them.

The poets we shall discuss extend and develop these seed-like perceptions found in Whitman. Their writings tend to lack the degree of cultural smugness and security that stood behind the earlier stereotypes. They see in "Indian consciousness" a resource that can renew and revive an insecure American cultural identity—one that can connect us to the spirit of the land we inhabit and from which we have historically been alientated, and can open us to aspects of ourselves that define our full human identity.[5]

Like Whitman in "Passage to India," they envision a time when "Nature and Man shall be disjoin'd and diffused no more." Reorienting Western man's relationship to place and to the nature surrounding him and within is, as we shall see, a central underlying theme for many of the twentieth-century poets attracted to the Indian. Their various efforts at interpreting the red man might be understood collectively as an ongoing healing ceremony, seeking to restore a harmonic relationship to "place" (that is, locality, but also one's interior landscape, continent, universe), and thus to establish wholeness in an ailing American psyche. These writers ultimately seek, through the Indian, to address the spiritual, psychological, and physical survival needs of our century.

In important ways, the intense interest in the Indian on the part of many twentieth-century poets can be seen as inevitable, a natural function determined by time and place. As Gary Snyder told me in a 1979 interview, it

> grows out of their sense of place, and sometimes direct acquaintance with some of the old time people around, or the use of old anthropological collections. It grows with these people; and, on another level, a genuine attraction to the symbolism, the archtypes, the language of old tales. . . . Part of it is that it's the twentieth century and not the nineteenth century. The process of time, with an

ocean between you and the mother continent, naturally makes it more and more remote. You become more and more conscious that you are where you are.[6]

As Snyder suggests, a variety of factors are involved in this phenomenon: the availability of reliable information about Indians in anthropological studies and the writings of Native American authors; a desire for familiarity with the mythopoeic archetypes indigenous to the continent; a growing sense of the interdependence of identity and place; and direct personal acquaintance with Indian peoples. The importance of this last factor should not be overlooked. It distinguishes many twentieth-century writers from earlier ones, imbuing their work with a sense of nuance and humanity rather than stereotypical ideology. Poets like Mary Austin, John G. Neihardt, Charles Olson, and Jerome Rothenberg each emerged from periods of direct contact with Indian peoples personally and creatively renewed, and their writings tended to reflect and generalize this experience. These and other poets have interpreted the Indian as a guide to our understanding "where we are" and how to survive and thrive here.

Roles have been reversed in this century. The red man has come to teach the white. The Native American has come to represent to many of our poets a key to self-discovery; to "contact" (to use William Carlos Williams's term) with the forces of nature, inside and out, from which we have been too long estranged; and to our poetic and cultural renewal.

In 1975 I wrote a poem called *The Kokopilau Cycle*, based on stories surrounding the hump-backed flute-player, a culture hero of the Pueblo peoples of the Southwest.[7] Kokopilau's stick figure is found etched on cliff faces and boulders throughout the West. With his antennae pressing forward toward the future, his dancing feet connecting him to the energies of the American earth, his flute in touch with his own inner nature and breath, and his humped back from which he scatters seeds to an emerging world, Kokopilau can be seen as an apt glyph for this study. For the Pueblo tribes, he is an alien being (from the Pleiades) yet a model—a figure associated with renewal.

For us he can become an image of the New Man in the New World that American poets attracted to the Indian have ultimately sought to create.

The sampling of poets discussed in the following chapters is designed to represent, and not to cover exhaustively those twentieth-century poets attracted to the Indian. I have tried to select poets whose work has been most influential and innovative and who, taken collectively, would suggest the varied and ongoing nature of such approaches. The study concludes with a discussion of contemporary Native American poets to open a perspective on "Indian consciousness" which the reader might care to pursue further, and which, I hope, sheds further light on the whole.

# INTERPRETING THE INDIAN

I have naturally a mimetic temperament which drives me toward the understanding of life by living it. If I wished to know what went into the patterns of the basket makers, I gathered willows in the moon of white butterflies and fern stems when these were the ripest. I soaked the fibers in running water, turning them as the light turned, and did my ineffectual best to sit on the ground scraping them flat with an obsidian blade, holding the extra fibers between my toes. I made singing medicine as I was taught, and surprised the Friend-of-the-Soul-of-Man between the rattles and the drums. Now and then, in the midst of these processes I felt myself caught up in the collective mind, carried with it toward states of super-consciousness that escape the exactitudes of the ethnologist as the life of the flower escapes between the presses of the herbalist. So that when I say that I am not, have never been, nor offered myself, as an authority on things Amerindian, I do not wish to have it understood that I may not, at times, have succeeded in being an Indian.

Mary Austin, *The American Rhythm*

The first quarter of the twentieth century was a period in which Americans rediscovered the Indian, largely through his "poetry." This chapter traces the development of that renewed interest by examining the attempts of ethnologists, poets, and anthologists to interpret the meaning of "Indian poetry," both through literary translations and through attempts to identify the significance of those translations for American literature, cultural identity, and consciousness. Of necessity, it will also discuss the nature and characteristics of Native American poetry itself.

The central figure in the movement to bring Indian poetry to non-Indian Americans was Mary Hunter Austin, who pioneered the exploration of Indian consciousness in this century as a poet, playwright, essayist, and anthologist. Austin was one of the most active and influential of the early twentieth-century writers who redefined the meaning of the Indian for American culture. Through she is regarded as a minor poet today, Austin's efforts were extremely important in stimulating many of her contemporaries to consider the Indian's relevance to American cultural identity, poetry, and poetics, and in anticipating the concerns of more talented and influential poets later in the century. The fullest statement of Austin's ideas in this area is found in her essay "The American Rhythm" (1923), a discussion of which concludes this chapter. But before we can proceed with our examination of the varied approaches to American Indian poetry that culminate in "The American Rhythm," we must identify what Austin and others recognized as the central characteristic of that poetry and the cultures that produced it: what I term *holistic awareness*. Holistic awareness is, in a sense, what this book is really about: the quality that, more than any other, has made Indian poetry and cultures attractive and important to Americans in this century. By *holistic awareness* I mean the Indian's sense of oneness with the earth and with the creatures on it; the term suggests also the oneness, within each person, of body, mind, and spirit and the sense of overall oneness of material and spiritual reality.

What Austin claims to find among Indian peoples has been found elsewhere by American writers; strong parallels can be discovered, for example, in nineteenth-century transcendental

5

writings. Unlike Emerson or Whitman, however, Austin did not go to India but to the Indians; her claims are for the experience of peoples who have lived in America for thousands of years, rather than for German and Hindu philosophies. The growth of these values and perceptions from American soil makes them especially important for modern poets in search of mythopoeic roots or the spirit of place. Sitting under the Bo tree with Buddha is one thing; sitting in the sweat lodge with Black Elk quite another, as far as feeling at home in America is concerned. The breakdown of spiritual norms, the alienation of the individual from land, work, and self, give urgent importance to the healing properties and the unifying forces that have been claimed for Indian literature by Austin and others. To Austin and the writers discussed here, Indians are not the colorful exotics seen by nineteenth-century Americans confident of the power and coherence of their new culture. Instead they are the only genuine indigenous source of desperately needed poetic and personal values. On a literary level, Austin's and other writers' attention to Indian awareness can be seen as answering Emerson's call for a uniquely American poetry. On a social level, it anticipates and parallels the ecological thinking of people who have lately come to see over-dependency on thechnology as destructive and unnatural. On a spiritual level, it parallels the modern quest for wholeness of the self articulated in the work of Jung and many others working in various disciplines throughout the century.

In "The American Rhythm," Austin concentrates on the expression of holistic awareness in Indian poetry. She explores its significance from several different angles, each of which anticipates the approaches of later poets. Essentially, Austin proposes that American poets study Indian poetry to acquire a broader consciousness, an awareness more in tune with nature and place, and that they study its forms, imagery, and compositional techniques as an alternative model for a new American poetry. She predicted that the holistic awareness implicit and explicit in Native American poetry would be paralleled in the form and content of an emerging American poetry, a poetry characterized by its intimate relationship to the American landscape and environment; by its open form, based on the organic rhythms of body and mind; by an increased reliance on nonlinear, nonrational modes—a tendency toward the incantatory, imagistic, and spatial; and by the poetry's increased tendency to bring people together to experience collectively community and communion.

Though Austin's direct influence is limited today, her predictions are responsive to the literary leanings and longings of her times and to the literary and psychological temper of the twentieth century. Better and more influential poets who followed her have, in their own ways, emphasized and explored the very awareness and qualities to which she first pointed. The holistic awareness of the Indian has become an important resource, model, and theme for American poets.

## The Early Ethnologists

The Indian's holistic awareness is reflected in all areas of his culture. It was first recognized and cited by American poets in the ceremonial chants, spells, and personal power songs that, following Austin, we now call "Indian poetry." Widespread attention to this body of literature is a fairly recent development. Not until the late nineteenth century did the first American anthropologists begin systematically and carefully recording and translating Indian chants and songs. Ethnologists like Washington Matthews ("The Mountain Chant: A Navajo Ceremony," 1887), James Mooney ("The Sacred Formulas of the Cherokees," 1891; *The Ghost Dance Religion,* 1896), Francis LaFlesche and Alice Cunningham Fletcher ("A Study of Omaha Indian Music," 1893), and Frances Densmore *(Chippewa Music,* 1910 and 1913) are among the first and greatest recorders and translators. Their work was an important resource for poets and interpreters like Austin, and their translations, extracted from original scholarly contexts, are still anthologized today; in fact, they are more widely read now than at the time of their original publication.

The ethnologists published almost exclusively for a specialized scholarly audience, mainly in journals like *American Anthropologist* and the bulletins of the Bureau of American Ethnology, Smithsonian Instition, and American Folklore Association. Unlike later poet-interpreters of Indian poetry and culture, the ethnologists did not seem to think that the material they were translating had any particular relevance to the development of a new American poetry and identity. Rather, they saw themselves as either antiquarians or social scientists, scrupulously preserving for history the traditions and literatures of dying cultures. In doing so, however, they were consciously countering the stereotype of the Indian as an unsophisticated, barbaric savage. The work of the many anthropologists who studied Native American tribal people between 1880 and 1920 tended to establish that Indians were indeed capable of quite sophisticated thought as well as of complex, ingenious means of expression. As the antiquarian Daniel G. Brinton wrote in *Aboriginal American Authors* (1893), "the languages of America have every whit as high a claim on the attention of European scholars as the venerable documents of Chinese lore, the mysterious cylinders of Assyria, or the painted and figured papyri of the Nilotic tombs." Brinton, who developed his respect for the Indian mind through studying Indian languages, wrote the first literary criticism on Native American poetry in an essay of that title published in 1890.

### The Indians' Book

Still, it was not until 1907, with the publication of Natalie Curtis's *The Indians' Book,* that the ethnological discovery of the rich variety of Indian poetry was introduced, almost unwittingly, to a popular audience. The book was intended as a collection of Native American myth, music, and song. Curtis was a musician and musicologist who, during the 1890s, had studied at the National Conservatory of Music in New York as well as in Europe. While visiting her brother in Arizona just after the turn of the century, she became fascinated with local Indian life and lore and began collecting and recording Indian songs, myths, and music. In 1903 she began to collect materials in earnest for *The Indians' Book,* traveling by train, wagon, and horseback to visit tribal peoples in remote locations all over the country. Scholarly curiosity motivated her, but she also felt that such a book would be of inestimable value to the Indian peoples themselves. She hoped "that this their own volume, when placed in the hands of their children, might help to revive for the younger generation that sense of the dignity and worth of their race which is the Indians' birthright, and without which, no people can progress."[1]

Such a noble aim, Curtis found, ran contrary to the policies of Indian agents and missionaries who, in their efforts to acculturate Indian peoples, tended to suppress Indian languages and traditions. On more than one occasion Curtis's efforts were frustrated by the refusal of these masters of the Indians' fate to cooperate. She confronted this problem by enlisting the support of President Theodore Roosevelt.[2] Roosevelt's enthusiastic backing facilitated the necessary cooperation by government authorities and encouraged native informants, who would otherwise have feared repercussions, to participate in the project.

Curtis's problem in gathering materials underscores a long-standing and inherent contradiction in American governmental policy. On the one hand, traditional Indian cultures were being stamped out in a variety of ways by the policies of the Bureau of Indian Affairs (BIA), which autocratically ruled reservation life. The most visible and brutal of these policies was forcibly separating Indian children from their families and sending them often hundreds of miles away from the reservations to BIA-run boarding schools where Indian languages and customs were prohibited and Indian identity destroyed. Opposing this practice was the government's support of the efforts of the ethnologists who were preserving, in the name of knowledge, the very traditions that the BIA was wiping out. Roosevelt's support for *The Indians' Book* was a benign gesture toward supporting a positive Indian image and self-concept, and it did enable Curtis to get on with her project, but it did little to soften the overall governmental oppressions.

As did many of her fellow ethnologists, Curtis came to see her work as a labor of love. She was warmly received by Indian peoples who offered her their friendship and trust and gave her the name *Tawa Mana* ("Song Maid"). Curtis reciprocated by giving full credit to her collaborators on the title page of *The Indians' Book:* "The Indians are the authors of this volume. The songs and stories and theirs; the drawings, cover design, and title pages were made by them. The work of the recorder has been but the collecting, editing, and arranging of the Indians' contributions." Containing more than 150 songs from seventeen different tribes representing the eastern forest dwellers, the Plains and Great Lakes regions, the northwestern coast dwellers, and the peoples of the desert Southwest, the book is a rich sourcebook of American Indian cultures. It is arranged in sections containing explanations of the myths, legends, customs, and traditions of each tribe followed by texts of songs that are an integral part of the tribal lore. Following earlier ethnological models, Curtis presents the songs within a descriptive and explanatory context that makes their meaning more intelligible. She includes transcriptions of each song's melody in Western musical notation and, following the ethnological convention of the time, presents each song's lyrics in three forms: a phonetic transcription of its original language, a literal translation into English, and a free, poetic translation.

Not only a work of scrupulous scholarship, *The Indians' Book* was also artistically packaged and highly readable. But its most striking quality was the "poetry" of the translated songs. Curtis herself observed this in a note on her transcriptions: "the songs in this book are written after a new manner in that corresponding musical phrases are placed one beneath another like lines of verse. The system makes the form of the song to flash before the eye like the form of a stanza of poetry." Roosevelt also was struck by the book's "poetry," observing in a note to Curtis that was later printed as the frontispiece to most editions: "These songs cast a wholly new light on the depth and dignity of Indian thought, the simple beauty and strange charm of a vanished elder world—of Indian poetry." Roosevelt's public enthusiasm for *The Indians' Book* and the attention he called to its inherent poetry helped spread its popular reputation and encouraged a curiosity about and a positive attitude toward the recently conquered Indian population.

The book was reviewed widely and most favorably. *The Dial* recommended it at the top of a list of "Miscellaneous Holiday Books," stating, with the unthinking racist chauvinism and condescension typical of the times, that "to most white readers this book will be a revelation of the vaguely stirring genius and the art, mystic in its intent, spontaneous in its symbolism, of a child race."[3] *The American Review of Reviews* praised the book highly, quoting Curtis's argument that it not only contained materials of exotic interest but also added something essential and otherwise missing from the American spirit:

> We are a people of great mechanical and inventive genius, but we are not naturally song-makers, poets, or designers. Can we afford to lose from our country any sincere and spontaneous art inpulses, however crude? The undeveloped talents native to the aboriginal American are precisely those in which the Anglo-Saxon is deficient.[4]

Here we have the first major statement of the theme that has characterized twentieth-century writers' interest in the Indian: that the red man represented in some way the missing aspects of the American self. Curtis went further, suggesting that there was something renewing for American art itself in the indigenous song of the Native American: "the folk music of any land is a soil from which genius draws sustenance for fresh growth, and the stimulus to the creative mind through contact with this native art should give America a new and vigorous art impulse." Poets like Austin and the others who followed came to Indian poetry seeking such a renewal.[5]

*Indian "Poetry"*

Despite the richness of its Indian materials and Curtis's accurate commentary on its ethnomusicological dimension, *The Indian's Book* became best known as a collection of Indian poetry, and this circumstance presents us with our first serious problem, both in seeing clearly what we are naming and in giving it the right name. Curtis herself, like virtually all her ethnologist colleagues, was precise in calling a song a song, as it were. But others used the term *poetry,* which is misleading because it applies a literary name to the chants, charms, and songs of an almost exclusively oral tradition. Nor is the misnaming trivial, for it carried an entire set of misconceptions with it. The motivation of these compositions is not the creation of an aesthetic artifact, as the term *poetry* would imply to an English-speaking audience of the twentieth century. Rather, the motive is magical. An Indian singer or chanter does not merely seek to entertain or to please; he wants to effect change in himself, in nature, or in his fellow human beings. The word is understood and used as an instrument of power.

The word in Indian songs is also, more often than not, combined with meaningful gestures, music, pictorial or plastic arts (for example; sand paintings, masks), or dance. Its contexts are essentially mimetic, dramatic, and ceremonial. Ethnologists like Curtis were careful to describe the circumstances and the "accompanying acts" of each poem or song and to make clear that it was not originally intended, as poetry is, for contemplation by a silent reader. When poets began interpreting or "re-expressing" (Austin's term) Indian poetry, they, like the ethnologists, tended to realize that the nonverbal components of a given work were inseparable from the verbal ones and that they were crucial to the song's overall power. Unlike the ethnographers, however, poets reinterpreting Indian poetry rarely resorted to explanatory commentaries. Instead, they tended to exercise considerable freedom as translators, seeking to capture in their interpretations the hidden meanings and spirit of the originals. That is, they often tried to build into the words the nonverbal components of meaning, converting chants to lyrics. Often, as we shall see, the intent and meaning of the original were ultimately distorted or lost in the translated version.

## Other Early Twentieth-Century Native American Literature

The attention given to the Native American by ethnologists and poets was not an isolated literary activity. *The Indians' Book* was only one of many significant and widely read books that followed the end of the Indian wars and the domestication of the Native American on government-controlled reservations. History, autobiography, fiction, and drama—as well as poetry—were all well served by the appearance of works largely based on careful scholarship and on close contact with Indian peoples rather than on stereotypes. One that preceded Natalie Curtis's work was Helen Hunt Jackson's *A Century of Dishonor* (1881), which exposed the hypocrisy and brutality of America's Indian policy. Jackson's novel *Ramona* (1884), dealing with California mission Indians, also enjoyed popularity and drew sympathetic attention to its subject. In 1890

Adolph Bandelier published his novel *The Delight Makers*. Based on his close contact with the Pueblo peoples of the desert Southwest, the book, still in print, is essentially accurate in its cultural detail, and quite readable. George Bird Grinnell, Frank S. Linderman, and Charles Lummis each published popular collections of tribal stories and myths before the turn of the century. These were followed by collections written by Indian writers—Gertrude Bonnin's (Zitkala-Sa's) *Old Indian Legends* (1901) and Charles A. Eastman's (Ohiyesa's) *The Soul of the Indian* (1911). Eastman's *Indian Boyhood* (1902), the first major Indian autobiography of the century, enjoyed considerable popularity. It was followed by the widely read *Geronimo, His Own Story* (1906, and still in print), edited by S. M. Barrett; *Goodbird the Indian* (1914), edited by Gilbert L. Wilson; Joseph K. Griffis's *Tahan: Out of Savagery into Civilization* (1915); and Eastman's *From the Deep Woods to Civilization* (1916). Eastman, a Santee Sioux and a physician who had studied medicine at Boston University, became a national celebrity, toasted by Roosevelt and the great men of his age as an American success story.

Even American theater reflected the contemporary revival of interest in the Indian. In 1911 Mary Austin's play, *The Arrow Maker,* was a smash hit on Broadway. Its plot involved the preposterous imposition of non-Indian women's-rights issues onto a plot focusing on a main character closely modeled after a Paiute *chisera* or medicine woman whom Austin had known personally. More authentically Indian were the names, costumes, scenery, dances, and songs, all of which had been carefully researched. The choreography was directed by Big Eagle, an Indian of Winnebago and Paiute parentage. The play's audience was impressed less with the complex and sentimental plot than with what the *New York Times* called its "splendid scenic display."[6] All this activity reflected a public hunger for information concerning the "real Indian" and further attracted American readers and writers to the red man.

*Early Poet-Interpreters*

Though in touch with the Indian-related literature of their times, most of the early poets who interpreted the Native American drew their inspiration from firsthand contact with

Indian peoples. Typically, this firsthand contact resulted from the chance circumstances of the poet's life. Austin, for instance, discovered the Paiute and Shoshone as neighbors in 1888 when she moved from Illinois to homestead with her mother in the California desert of Tejon County. John G. Neihardt established his first friendships with Plains peoples among the Omaha when he worked as a general factotum for J. J. Elkin, whom Neihardt later described as an "Indian skinner," trading with the reservation people near Neihardt's home in Bancroft, Nebraska. Lew Sarett worked his way through Northwestern University as a summer hunting and fishing guide around the Great Lakes, where he befriended and swapped stories and songs with many Chippewa. These three poets' formative contact with Indian peoples took place during the same turn-of-the-century years when Curtis was gathering materials for *The Indians' Book.* This coincidence is partially attributable to a general spirit in America of interest in the Indian and the related available literature but is more related to the Indians' sudden accessibility. They were *there,* nearby—domesticated on the reservation; at least partially acculturated; available; able, often anxious, to converse intelligently in English with genuinely friendly and interested whites. Once they discovered and befriended the Indian, these poets found, usually to their astonishment, a wealth of literary material. Most often it was revealed to them informally, in the normal course of relations. In a few instances sacred material normally kept secret from outsiders was revealed. Black Elk's sharing of his sacred vision with Neihardt is the most prominent example. This type of information was offered only after a deeply trusting and spiritual relationship had been established and was usually discussed within more formal, even ceremonial, circumstances that emphasized its high seriousness.

Poets such as Austin, Neihardt, Sarett, and others who came later regarded their fascination with the Indian as essential to their being and becoming American poets. These early poets were not interested in being literal translators. They could not have been even if they had wished to, for none possessed the knowledge of Indian languages that some ethnographers had.[7] They were interpreters, trying to bring over to our very different language and culture modes of expression and consciousness that they felt could help Americans better understand Indians and, more important, themselves. The poems of these poet-interpreters tended to be freer translations than those of the ethnographers. Their allegiance was to what each poet conceived as the spirit rather than the letter of the originals. As Austin wrote,

> [I try] to saturate myself in the poem, in the life that produced it, and the environment that cradled that life, so that when the point of crystalization is reached, I myself give forth a poem which bears, I hope, a genetic resemblance to the song that was my point of contact.[8]

"Genetic resemblance" suggests a new creation of varying degrees of similarity to its parent—an apt description, as I shall demonstrate, of many of the poems that resulted. But it also suggests something of deeper significance: the desire of Austin and other twentieth-century poets for intimacy and kinship with the red man.

## The Spiritual Connection

These early poets tell us that they were drawn to the Indian by a deep sense of spiritual affinity. Even before contact with Indian ways, Austin, Sarett, and Niehardt each possessed a somewhat mystical attitude toward the land. Austin and Niehardt derived theirs from powerful insights and visions in childhood;[9] Sarett's came from years of solitary camping and attention to nature and animals. This love and respect for the land helped to establish a special rapport with the Indian people they met. Austin writes in "The American Rhythm": "Better than I knew any Indian I knew the land they lived in. This I hold to be a prime requisite for understanding the originals of whatever description."[10]

Beginning, then, with such a feeling of kinship, the poets, not surprisingly, found themselves profoundly transformed by their contact with Native Americans. Austin and Niehardt are early examples of this phenomenon; Charles Olson and Jerome Rothenberg are more recent ones. Each emerged from a period of intense contact with Indians creatively renewed and committed to sharing the new attitudes and understandings they had developed. In other instances that we shall discuss, such as in certain writings of Hart Crane and William Carlos Williams, poets with little intimate knowledge of Indians have nevertheless used them as a focal image of their own and, by implication, of other Americans' need for personal transformation. A desire for fuller spiritual awareness, including intimacy with the spirit of the land, is at the center of most of the works we shall consider here.

Such conversions are not merely to Indian themes and experiences, but to what I can only call "meaningfulness." This is a hard point to make clear. What I mean is that each of the poets considered here found in the red man's culture not merely a set of new things to talk about but also a healing and an explanation of his or her personal experience or of the American experience in general. Those who focused on Indian poetry and literature—particularly Austin, Olson, and Rothenberg—found themselves changing their approach to American poetics. And as always, a change in style implied a change of being.

In general, these and other poets in this century have turned to the Indian for a variety of reasons. Many have reacted against the limiting rationalism, scholasticism, and egocentrism that periodically pervade the practice of American verse, seeking in Indian poetry the renewing spiritual energy basic to all vital poetries. Some have sought in Indian materials a mythopoeic universe related to America, not to Europe or the Middle East. Others have sought in the holistic perspectives of Indian cultures and poetries a fuller sense of their own humanity, including a cure for the disease of psychological and spiritual alienation afflicting so many in the twentieth century. The Indian has been perceived as the key to the secrets of self and surroundings that have somehow eluded us. These essentially spiritual connections should not be underestimated, for they stand behind virtually all of the literary activity covered in this book.

*Early Interpretations of Indian Poetry*

During the first two decades of the twentieth century, "reexpressions" of Indian verse by American poets began to appear with increasing frequency in literary magazines, often side by side with other early experiments with free verse. They coincided with the general literary interest in things Inian, but they also encountered the coexistent attitude of literary snobbishness and downright racism. Austin, for instance, found her re-expressions returned in 1904 by *The Atlantic,* which had previously published her work extensively, accompanied by an irritated note stating that "there was no excuse for this sort of thing." A year later, *The Century* sent others back with the message, as Austin recounted it, "that if I would admit that I had made them up myself, they would publish them as poetry, but never on the assumption they were Indian."[11] In the view of these publications, the "savage" Indian was incapable of poetry.

Resistance was based on poetic as well as racist grounds. Following the apparent lack of rhyme or regular metrics in most Indian originals (or at least in ethnologists' translations of them), poets' interpretations tended to be written in free verse. At the turn of the century, this practice represented a radical departure from conventional verse forms, one that only began to gain acceptance a decade or more later with the efforts of Ezra Pound, the imagists, and the *vers librists.* Between 1905 and 1915, however, more and more modern interpretations of Indian verse by Austin, Sarett, Alice Corbin Henderson, and others, including Carl Sandburg, began to appear in literary magazines such as *McClure's, The Forum, Scribner's, The Delineator, Everybody's, Sunset, Others,* and *Poetry, A Magazine of Verse. Poetry,* the most influential poetry journal of the day, brought this activity to a head with a February 1917 number, a special "aboriginal poetry issue."

*Poetry's* aboriginal issue included interpretations of Indian verse by Austin, Henderson, Skinner, Frank S. Gordon, and Edward Eastaway. All but Eastaway, a British soldier who had never been to America, had had direct contact with Indian peoples. The collection was fairly representative of the various types of poetry and interpretive modes with which American poets were experimenting. These ranged from Gordon's imitations of chants and dance songs to Austin's explanatory reworkings of a Navajo ceremonial text; from Skinner's dramatic monologues attributed to individual Native Americans to Henderson's elaborate imagist re-creations of some cryptic magical charms, based on Frances Densmore's translations from Chippewa. More important, however, than its selection of individual poems was *Poetry's* implicit and explicit linking of Indian poetry with the concerns and practices of poetic modernism. Sandburg, who briefly ran along the fringes of this literary movement, made this linkage explicit in his extremely favorable review of Densmore's *Chippewa Music,* then only available in *Bulletins* nos. 45 and 53 of the Bureau of American Ethnology, Smithsonian Institution. He emphasized the likeness between the Chippewa charms and the modern imagist poem. "Suspicion arises," Sandburg wrote with tongue in cheek, "that the red man and his children committed direct plagiarism on our modern imagists and vorticists." This review, along with editorial tribute to ethnologists Densmore, Voth, Matthews, Lyman, Simms, Grinnell, and Cushing, pointed to Indian poetry as a rich source for the modern poet and reader. Further, Harriet Monroe, the editor of *Poetry,* went so far as to cite Cushing's translation of the *Creation Myth of the Zunis* as "a masterpiece of primitive song which should rank, and undoubtedly will rank, among the great epics of the world."[12]

Monroe, though not a generator of new views of poetry, had a knack for attracting them and a willingness to pass them on to the public through her magazine. Her support for imagism, free verse, and, later, objectivism is well known. Less well publicized is her long-standing interest in Indian cultures, the result of trips she made in 1901 and 1915 to the desert Southwest. There she visited the Pueblo tribes, the Grand Canyon, and the ancient Hopi "sky city" of Walpi where she witnessed the famous Snake Dance later described by D. H. Lawrence in *Mornings in Mexico.* Like other poets of the period who were attracted to the Indian, Monroe associated the Native American's poetry and ceremonial life with the land and considered them expressions of a spirit of place hardly available to white Americans. In a 1915 editorial in *Poetry* she wondered, "what would be the effect upon our art of those great heights and depths and spaces, those clear skies and living waters, those colors incredible and magnificent? For in spite of a few pioneers," she continued, "we have not yet taken possession of our inheritance, entered into its kingdom."[13] Monroe's impe-

rialistic language should not blind us to the significant senti-
ment she expresses, echoing as it does Old and New Testament
references to the Promised Land and the new spiritual condi-
tion implied there. Coming to grips with America as a place
with a spirit and character all its own was an artistic preoccu-
pation of the period that, thoughout the century, has contin-
ued to be a central concern of poets attracted to the Indian.
The red man, in effect, comes with the territory. We can find
this concern for *place* in various arts between 1915 and 1930:
in the painting of Georgia O'Keeffe and in the painting and
writing of Marsden Hartley; in the magazine *Contact,* edited
by William Carlos Williams; in the prose of Hamlin Garland,
Waldo Frank, D. H. Lawrence, and the Sioux writer Luther
Standing Bear; and in the poetry of Vachel Lindsay, Carl Sand-
burg, Hart Crane, and many others. All these artists discovered
in Indian people and their cultures a rich potential source of
contact with a spirit of place that they sensed could lead to
personal and artistic renewal. Unlike expatriate Americans like
Pound, H. D., and Gertrude Stein, they sought modern alter-
natives, renewal, and roots by digging into America itself.

## The First Anthology

One year after the appearance of *Poetry's* aboriginal issue, *Path
on the Rainbow* (1918), edited by George W. Cronyn, appeared.
Labeled by Austin in her introduction as "the first authorita-
tive volume of aboriginal American verse," *Path* climaxed
much of the preceding activity by gathering together many
translations of Indian poems by both ethnologists and poets.
It represents the first attempt to anthologize Indian poetry on
its own, without an accompanying descriptive text; and though
many anthologies have followed in the sixty years since its
publication, *Path on the Rainbow,* still in print, remains one of
the richest and most comprehensive.[14] *Path* contained more
than 350 pages of translated poetry; the first and largest section
consisted of 189 pages of ethnological translations, most of
which had been previously published exclusively in scholarly
journals. They were arranged in subsections designated Eastern
Woodlands, Southeast, Great Plains, Southwest, California,
Northwest Coast, and Far North to represent what Cronyn and

Austin believed to be distinct regional stylistic characteristics as well as the geographical distribution of America's tribal groups. These ethnological workings were followed by 150 pages of interpretations of Indian verse by the poets Constance Lindsay Skinner, Mary Austin, Frank S. Gordon, Alice Corbin Henderson, and a popular Canadian poet of Mohawk descent, Pauline Johnson. A third, 90-page section contained "The Hako: A Pawnee Ceremony." Translated by Alice Cunningham Fletcher, this included interpretive commentaries by Tahirussawichi, who is described as a *kuruhus* or head priest.

"The Hako" is a ceremonial song cycle made up of ninety-five different songs. These are framed within eighteen rituals, each of which is described in brief commentaries accompanying the text. "The Hako" is a celebration of the life force and the universal power and harmony inherent in it. Its purpose, as described by Fletcher in her original study, is to bring to certain individuals the "promise of children, long life, and plenty" and to bring friendship and peace to all those participating in the ceremony as well as to others belonging to different family clans and tribes.[15] The inclusion of "The Hako" in *Path on the Rainbow* served to suggest the rich ceremonial context of Indian poetry in general and to present an example of an extended Native American form. It made explicit for American readers the holistic awareness implicit in much of the shorter work.

A final eighteen-page section of *Path,* titled "Songs from the North and South," contained a selection of Densmore's translations from various tribes. It represented a tribute to this dedicated ethnologist, whom Austin in her introduction to *Path* singled out for her "great scholarship and penetrating insight, which have given her first place among students of Indian life." The total effect of the material collected in *Path on the Rainbow* was to reveal a rich Native American poetic tradition characterized by a broad range of styles, forms, and themes, as well as by an immense depth of spirit.

Path on the Rainbow *as a Contribution to American Poetry*

*Path on the Rainbow* attempted more than the resurrection of Native American poetry in response to a general literary interest in things Indian. Following the line of thought introduced by *Poetry* (whose aboriginal poetry issue was credited by Cronyn as the inspiration for his anthology), *Path* presents in Austin's introduction the most forceful assertion to that date of Indian poetry's importance as a model and as a source for a new, uniquely American poetry. Austin wrote:

> Probably never before has it occurred that the intimate thought of a whole people should be known through its most personal medium to another people whose unavoidable destiny it is to carry that thought to fulfillment and make of that medium a characteristic literary vehicle.
>
> To those unaware until now of the very existence of such a body of aboriginal verse, this may seem a large claim. But unless the occasion has some such significance, this is no time to divert public attention to mere collections of literary curiosities. Arresting as single examples of it are, a greater interest still attaches to the relationship which seems about to develop between Indian verse and the ultimate literary destiny of America.

Austin did little to elaborate on this prophecy until *The American Rhythm* appeared five years later. She made clear, however, that her claim rested on the premise that all great national art developed its distinctive characteristic from the very land that nourished it; and that poetry was, as she wrote in the introduction to *Path,* "of all man's modes, the most responsive to natural environment, the most sensitive and truest record of his reactions to its skyey influences, its floods, forests, and morning colors." Indian poetry, she observed, give us the opportunity of "establishing some continuity with the earliest instances of such reaction." It provides us with a measure by which we can gauge whether or not the "American poetic genius has struck its native note."

Like American writers before and since, Austin noted a general psychological, spiritual, and literary alienation among her contempoaries from America itself, evident in an overdependence on forms and values that were not indigenous. At the same time, she sensed that "it becomes appropriate and important that this collection of American Indian verse should be brought to public notice at a time when the sole instinctive movement of the American people is for a deeper footing in their native soil." This tension between a feeling of fragmented

21

alienation, on the one hand, and a longing for unity with place and the consequent psychological and spiritual wholeness on the other, continues to be a moving force propelling readers and writers toward the Indian.

*Indian Poetry and Imagism*

Following Sandburg's lead, Austin, in her introduction to *Path on the Rainbow,* emphasized "the extraordinary likeness between much of this native product and the recent work of the Imagists, *vers librists,* and other literary fashionables." Such a proclamation was a way of bolstering her claim that Indian poetry had immediate relevance to the concerns and direction of modern American verse. These similarities are, in fact, superficial at best and more apparent than real. Austin was one of the first to write insightfully on the difficulties of translating material that, being from an oral tradition, differed fundamentally from what was then standard American poetry. The Indian languages themselves were often extremely different in structure and conceptual ways from English, and their images and symbols were culture-bound to a very great extent, as Austin well knew. Her emphasis reflects her promotional acumen more than her literary insight.

We can affirm these radical differences. However, when the translators used imagist concepts and techniques to produce their English translations, the results were bound to bear a striking resemblance to imagist forms. Two of Densmore's translations published in *Path on the Rainbow* can serve as examples:

"The Water Bug and the Shadows"

The water bug
  is drawing
  the shadows of the evening
  toward him on the water.

"The Deer and the Flower"

The deer
looks at the flower.

These poems, one from the Yuman and the other from the Yaqui of the Colorado River Valley, brought out of their original context into English and set in imagist lineation on the page, certainly seem to work in the way many imagist or haiku poems do. Both these poems express their perceptions through a direct relation of images. They have no explanatory or abstract verbiage. The effect of the stark juxtapositions has been heightened by the translator's careful use of line breaks, which separate and isolate each image. These accent the sense of movement from image to image as well as the suggestive power of each image as a thing in itself.[16] The continuity or wholeness is gained very simply: each poem is a simple sentence, and each image is a grammatical constituent of its sentence, isolated as a separate line in the poem, so the reader is made to focus successively and sharply on each aspect of the overall statement that is the poem-sentence. Further, the poem's meanings are not conveyed rationally; they are impressionistic and holistic—dependent on the evocative interaction of the individual, relational, and total images. In print these poems reflect strategies that are basic to the modern imagist and traditional haiku poems, but they are silent strategies, developed for the page, directed at the mind.

The originals on which these poems are based are not written. They are sounded, not silent. Their dimensions of music, movement, and relation are more complex, more physical, for they are literally embodied in their singers. The translation, because it shifts the ground of the poem from the media of the singer's body and voice to the medium of the page, can only provide, at best, the roughest equivalent of the original.

Further, the more we know about the Indian culture that is a given poem's source, the more likely we are to discover levels of meaning that are uniquely Native American. This can be illustrated by another Densmore translation that can be read as an imagist poem, the Winnebago "Healing Song," found in *Path on the Rainbow*:

> They are in close consultation
> with their heads together
> Wenabojo
> and his grandfather.

The translation's title might direct the Western reader to interpret this as a poem in which the healing of presumed differences is achieved by a meeting of minds, a reasoning together, between the opposing generation represented by Wenabojo and his grandfather. Such a reading, however, brings Western cultural assumptions to the poem, as *Path on the Rainbow's* lack of contextual notes invites us to do. A minimal knowledge of Winnebago culture, however, suggests that, in the original, the poem's metaphorical meanings are relatively minor. In its original context, "Healing Song" was not an aesthetic object; it literally was used to heal. Its power in this regard is partially derived from untranslated cultural associations attached to Wenabojo and his grandfather. To the Winnebago, these two are not mere men of opposing generations. They are supernatural beings, high among a pantheon of such figures, who are in this instance called upon to contribute their considerable energies to the medical/spiritual task at hand.

Besides these culture-specific figures, another vital source of power and meaning in "Healing Song" resides in its oral performance. It is chanted with monotonous repetition over a patient by a medicine man of the sacred Midewiwin Society, a person believed to have great personal power. He may wear a "false face" mask having spiritual connotations, make significant gestures with his hands, blow on his patient with his breath, or employ other devices and techniques. His use of repetition in chanting eventually subordinates the referential aspects of the words to their musical and rhythmic properties. The song's musical sound and movement, its hypnotizing repetitions, its accompanying acts and devices, cannot of course be easily and effectively represented in the translation. Nor can the translation convey the most important relational aspect of the poem, which is not that between Wenabojo and his grandfather but that between singer and patient. To the Indian, thus, the verbal content of the poem is only one part of its meaning.

As Austin writes in *Path's* introduction, "It is not the words which are potent, but the state of mind evoked by the singing." Indian poetry seeks to be effective, not merely affective. Most of the early interpreters, whether they were ethnologists or poets, recognized that the Indian poem's situational, referential, and cultural complexities were inseparable from the verbal content, that, in fact, these complexities were crucial to the song's being more than just words—to its being supermeaningful, so to speak—and the literary translators sought to bring as much as possible of such riches over into English. They were severely limited, however, by the printed page, the English language, and the very different associations and contexts of American culture. Austin's emphasis on their superficial similarities to imagism and free verse obscures the fact that there is usually more to these little Native American imagistic poems than, in bare translation, can possibly meet the Western eye.

## Early Approaches to Interpretations by American Poets

American poets used various approaches to convey their sense of the elusive essence of Indian poetry to the reader of English. Alice Corbin Henderson, a close associate of Harriet Monroe, who coedited *Poetry* and the 1917 anthology *The New Poetry,* was one of the most widely published of these interpreters. She considered herself an imagist poet, and almost all of her Indian interpretations were reworkings of Densmore's translations. Her usual method was to begin with a phrase from the presumably literal Densmore version—an "Indian keynote" as Henderson called it—and expand from it with varying degrees of loyalty to the original.[17] Often the resulting poem bears little resemblance to the explicit or hidden meanings of the original.

For instance, a Densmore translation of a Chippewa song she calls "They Are Playing a Game" reads thus:

> The noise of passing feet
> on the prairie
> They are playing a game as they come
> Those men

In her accompanying commentary, Densmore provided the information that this was, in effect, a personal power song, occasioned during the return home of a Chippewa war party when one of its members sank exhausted to the ground. His companions remained nearby to protect him from wandering enemies, and even though, as Densmore's informant reports, "it seemed impossible that he should rise, he used his medicine, and after a time sprung to his feet singing this song which he composed at the time. The war party resumed its journey and he accompanied them, still singing his new song."[18] Henderson, however, ignored all of this information as well as Densmore's note that "playing a game" was probably a reference to lacrosse. Henderson's "translation" reads:

> The noise of passing feet
> On the prairie—
> Is it men or gods
> Who come out of the silence?

Henderson used the imagistic "keynote" as a springboard for creating a completely new and different poem. The new poem seeks to enter the Indian world from the outside, not by presenting or elaborating the specific incident that prompted the highly understated and referential original, but by attempting to evoke the more general aura of the magical and supernatural world that the red man assumes as a given. Her "echoes" are not of the Chippewa original, but of Keats's "Ode on a Grecian Urn"—a classical allusion characteristic of the Georgian poetry being practiced from 1910 to 1920.

While this interpretation strays far afield, in others Henderson attempted to use available background information to elaborate and explain Densmore's cryptic originals. For instance, a Chippewa war dance titled "On the Bank of a Stream," translated by Densmore, reads in its entirety:

> Across the river
> They speak of me as being.

Densmore's commentary reveals that the song honors the warriors in a celebrated battle along a river bank with the Sioux. Her informant mentions the mournful wails of the Sioux women on the other side of the river.[19] Henderson retitled the poem, "Where the Fight Was"; she used the "keynote" phrase "across the river" along with the available information to build a new poem that imaginatively re-creates the story:

26

> In the place where the fight was
>     Across the river,
> In the place where the fight was
>     Across the river:
> A heavy load for a woman
> To lift in her blanket,
> A heavy load for a woman
> To carry on her shoulder.
> In the place where the fight was
>     Across the river,
> In the place where the fight was
>     Across the river:
> The women go wailing
> To gather the wounded
> The women go wailing
> To pick up the dead.

The new version shifts the focus from the Chippewa man's grim exultation to the Sioux women's lamentation. It uses a form heavily dependent on parallelisms and repetitions that, though characteristic of much Indian poetry, is radically different from the form of the original poem in this case. What results is a more moving poem in English, but it is a poem about Indians and not an Indian poem.

Oftentimes, however, interpreters' attempts to expand and explain Indian originals do not result in the desired improvement in English. Austin, for instance, reworked a Washoe song given to her by an informant known as Washoe Sam into a poem she called "Glyph":

> A girl wearing a green ribbon—
> as if it had been my girl.
> —The green ribbon I gave her for a remembrance—
> Knowing all the time it was not my girl,
> Such was the magic of that ribbon,
> Suddenly,
> My girl existed inside me.

Actually, Sam's version in his own English, which he less pretentiously called "The Magic Ribbon," is considerably more concise and effective:

The Green ribbon,
When I saw a girl wearing it,
My girl existed inside me.[20]

In this form, the poem illustrates what Ezra Pound described as the imagist poem's attempt "to record the precise instant when a thing outward and objective becomes inward and subjective."[21] Austin's version simply belabors the point and slows down the poem's perceptions while adding nothing essential to its meaning.

Interpreters tried similar clarifying and elaborating techniques on less obviously imagistic Indian works. Austin, for instance, reworked some of the incantatory mountain chants of the Navajo translated by Washington Matthews. Both versions of one, translated by Matthews as "Invocation to Dsilye N'eyeani" and by Austin as "Prayer to the Mountain Spirit," are found in *Path on the Rainbow*. Matthews's original reads:

Reared within the mountains
Lord of the Mountains!
Young Man!
Chieftain!
I have made your sacrifice.
I have prepared a smoke for you.
My feet restore thou for me.
My legs restore thou for me.
My mind restore thou for me.
My voice restore thou for me.
Restore all for me in beauty.
Make beautiful all that is before me.
Make beautiful all that is behind me.
It is done in beauty.
It is done in beauty.
It is done in beauty.
It is done in beauty.

In Matthews's version, the poem's content implicitly suggests its original ceremonial context as a healing chant. Specific ceremonial preparations are described and specific parts of the body to be restored to health are named. The importance to the Navajo of the concept "beauty" is evident by its prominence and repetition in the poem. The song is one of many songs within one of many cycles in what the Navajo call the "Beauty Way." Its purpose is to correct illness by addressing what are perceived as its root causes: a lack of inner harmony and a lack of harmony with the surrounding universe. The chants and their accompanying ritual and medical activities attempt to restore the patient to the essential harmony of life, the "Beauty Way." Austin, in trying to make the song more understandable to the white reader as a prayer, deleted and diluted much of this meaning:

> Lord of the Mountain.
> Reared within the Mountain.
> Young Man, Chieftain,
> Hear a young man's prayer!
>
> Hear a prayer for cleanness.
> Keeper of the strong rain.
> Drumming on the mountain,
> Lord of the small rain
> That restores the earth in newness,
> Keeper of the clean rain,
> Hear a prayer for wholeness.
>
> Young Man, Chieftain,
> Hear a prayer for fleetness.
> Keeper of the deer's way,
> Reared among the eagles,
> Clear my feet of slothness.
> Keeper of the paths of men,
> Hear a prayer for straightness.
>
> Hear a prayer for braveness.
> Lord of the thin peaks,
> Reared amid the thunders,
> Keeper of the headlands
> That uphold the earth in harvest,
> Keeper of the strong rocks,
> Hear a prayer for staunchness.
>
> Young Man, Chieftain!
> Spirit of the Mountain!

Stylistically, Austin's version dilutes the urgency of the original's repetitions. They become more deliberate parallelisms, resulting in a distinct reduction of energy and a shift of tone. She omitted the precise namings of physical parts to be healed, substituting for their specific supplications more abstract descriptive terms like "cleanness," "staunchness," and "wholeness." These choices deemphasize the poem's ceremonial quality; they involve the loss of the process of centering and locating the patient in a universe restored to harmony and balance ("Make beautiful all that is before me / Make beautiful all that is behind me") as well as the loss of the ritual repetitions of the refrain "It is done in beauty" the sacred four times.

Austin interpreted the chant as a prayer in the Western sense. But in so doing she lost its original senses of immediacy and sympathetic magic that Matthews's original, more literal translation conveys. Her version is not all bad. It adds information, for instance, about the attributes of the spirit who is being invoked and some lines in the second stanza that convey the vital importance of rain to the Navajo; this passage also suggests the fine distinctions that their language can make about its various types. All in all, however, though her more abstract and deliberate version may be more conceptually understandable to the white reader, much of the original's intellectual and spiritual content has been sacrificed. The poem's form has been altered, its energy and specificity reduced, its most important philosophical term, "Beauty," deleted. It is a very different work from the one on which it is based.

These differences between the translations and interpretations illustrate some of the special difficulties associated with bringing Native American oral poetry to the Western printed page. As William Bevis has written:

> The degree to which a text should be liberated by poetic license depends a good deal on the use to be made of the result. Does the translator seek, at one extreme, to compose excellent poems in English, or at the other, to document some aspect of a foreign art form? A single translation of strange material seldom suits both purposes. Indian poetry translations fall all along this scale of intentions, and a single translation often evolves through different stages of use.[22]

Though it is arguable whether the early free interpreters of Indian poetry succeeded in producing excellent poems in

English, that was their intent. They were seeking ways of enriching American poetry by allowing it to enter the Indian world that, it should be emphasized, meant to most of them gaining fuller access to the world of America itself. In translating, they were inevitably faced with the unenviable choice of sacrificing the content in favor of preserving the form, or of sacrificing the original form to bring out the hidden content. Austin chose the latter course, admitting, "In my own interpretations I have been feeling rather for a full expression of Indian thought, than for lyric quality."[23] The problem is that in the Indian world the two are not easily separated—a fact that may be true of most poetries but is especially so with works composed within an oral tradition.

Other interpreters whose work is included in *Path on the Rainbow* displayed different approaches to entering the Indian's poetic world. In his poems, Frank S. Gordon sought to represent the very lyric energy of southwestern tribal chants that Austin sacrificed. His poems retain the insistent repetitions and include exclamatory interjections and occasional Indian words to heighten the reader's sense of the originals' Indian-ness, so that these poems tend to come across as more foreign and exotic than the works of other interpreters. Constance Lindsay Skinner wrote imaginative dramatic monologues from an Indian viewpoint. Her poems are based largely on childhood experience; she had frequently accompanied her father, a Canadian government official, on his visits to tribes of the Pacific Northwest. These translations tend to describe typically Indian domestic activities, but they are not at all Indian in lyric quality or form. The interpretations of the popular Canadian poet Pauline Johnson, the one interpreter of Native American ancestry (she was known as "the Mohawk warbler") are, ironically, the most traditionally Western and the least Indian in both content and form. Poems such as "The Lost Lagoon" and "Song My Paddle Sings" might have provided an appropriate lyrical score for Nelson Eddy and Jeannette MacDonald in the film *Indian Love Song,* for like the movie they are excessively romantic and have little to do with actual Native American modes of life and expression. They are justifiably ridiculed by critic Louis Untermeyer as "rhymed sweetmeats" and "sentimental jinglings." *Path's* editor, Cronyn, publicly blamed his publisher for insisting on Johnson's inclusion to boost the book's commercial appeal. Cronyn lamented that Johnson's poems "show how far the Indian poet strays from her own primitive tribal songs, when attempting the White Man's mode."[24]

## Characteristics of Indian Poetry

*Path on the Rainbow,* with its broad selection of ethnological and interpretive translations, illustrated many of the characteristic types of Native American occasional songs: the healing song, war song, ceremonial song cycle, love charm, dance song, hunting song, and so on. Austin's introduction pointed to the magical applications of these songs. The collection also illustrated the most prominent characteristics of style and motive of the Indian poem. Critical discussions of these characteristics began with Austin's introduction to *Path on the Rainbow* and have continued to evolve in commentaries found mostly in the steady trickle of anthologies that have appeared throughout the century. The most prominent of such sources are Austin's *The American Rhythm* (1923, reissued in expanded form in 1930); Nellie Barnes's "American Indian Verse: Characteristics of Style" (1921), and her *American Indian Love Lyrics and Other Verse* (1925); Eda Lou Walton and T. T. Waterman's "American Indian Poetry" *(American Anthropologist,* 1925); Herbert Joseph Spinden's *Songs of the Tewa* (1933); Ruth Underhill's *Singing for Power: The Song Magic of the Papago Indians of Southern Arizona* (1938); Margot Astrov's *The Winged Serpent: An Anthology of American Indian Prose and Poetry* (1946); A. Grove Day's *The Sky Clears: Poetry of the American Indians* (1951); and a spate of collections beginning in the late sixties, including Jerome Rothenberg's *Technicians of the Sacred* (1969) and *Shaking the Pumpkin* (1972); William Brandon's *The Magic World* (1971); Dennis Tedlock's *Finding the Center: Narrative Poetry of the Zuni Indians* (1972); John Bierhorst's *Four Masterworks of American Indian Literature* (1974); Abraham Chapman's anthology (including critical commentaries) *Literature of the American Indians: Views and Interpretations* (1975); and Geary Hobson's *The Remembered Earth: An Anthology of Contemporary Native American Literature* (1979). Taken together, these and other similar works comprise a body of criticism supporting Austin's assertion in *Path on the Rainbow* that Indian poetry has important contributions for America's literary and spiritual life. "I know of no task," Austin had written, "so salutary to the poet who would, first of all, put himself in touch with the resident genius of his own land."

What are the characteristics of the poetry of this "resident genius"? Barnes, in her pioneering 1921 study, *American Indian Verse,* defined the most important shaping force of Indian poetry as "the cosmic motive." This represents the Native American's "spirit of constant aspiration" to penetrate and become harmonious with the mysteries of the universe. The sense of harmony sought and often established in ceremony and song give the Indian and his poetry, Barnes wrote, a "consciousness of personal worth in the great scheme of life." Unlike much English verse, traditional Indian poetry is rarely tragic or sad. Instead, as Barnes observed, it is characterized by affirmation. Even the songs of the Ghost Dance religion of the late nineteenth century, composed in response to an unbearable situation—the destruction of Plains culture by military defeat, and eradication of the buffalo, and reservation life's subsequent dependency on the American government—are visionary charms that attempt to restore harmony and coherence to a broken world by affirmative poetic assertion. Such affirmation, Barnes wrote, "was the basis of achievement and cure among many scattered tribes."[25] Related ideas about the basic cultural role of Native American poetry are developed further in the eloquent and oft-anthologized essay by Paula Gunn Allen (herself part Laguna), "The Sacred Hoop," published most recently in *The Remembered Earth.* Allen suggested some of the central differences between the assumptions of the aspiring and affirmative Indian poetry and poetry in the Western tradition:

> The purpose of Native American literature is never one of pure self-expression. The "private soul at any public wall" is a concept that is so alien to native thought as to constitute an absurdity. The tribes do not celebrate an individual's ability to feel emotion, for it is assumed that all people are able to do so, making expression of this basic ability arrogant, presumptuous, and gratuitous. Besides, one's emotions are one's own: to suggest that

another should imitate them is an imposition on the personal integrity of others. The tribes seek, through song, ceremony, legend, sacred stories (myths), and tales to embody, articulate, and share reality . . . to verbalize the sense of the majesty and reverent mystery of all things, and to actualize, in language, those truths of being and experience that give to humanity its greatest significance and dignity. The artistry of the tribes is married to the essence of language itself, for in language we seek to share in the communal awareness of the tribe. In this art the greater self and all-that-is are blended into a harmonious whole, and in this way the concept of being that is the fundamental and sacred spring of life is given voice and being for all. The Indian does not content himself with simple preachments of this truth, but through the sacred power of utterance he seeks to shape and mold, to direct and determine the forces that surround and govern our lives and that of all things.[26]

The fundamental intention of most Indian poetry, to make and shape the world through the power and magic of the word, creates its style. What commentators have pointed to as its most pronounced stylistic characteristics—repetition, brevity based on imagistic and symbolic usages, and special rather than ordinary diction—all have strong magical associations. Virtually all commentators concur with Barnes's early observation that repetition is the most striking feature of Indian style. In *Path on the Rainbow* one finds both repetitions and partial repetition of individual words, lines, passages, and entire songs. We have already briefly discussed the magical repetitive chanting in the Winnebago "Healing Song." Essentially, repetition in Indian cultures, as Allen wrote,

> has an entrancing effect. Its regular recurrence creates a state of consciousness best described as "oceanic." It is hypnotic. . . . The individual's attention must become diffused. The distractions of ordinary life must be put to rest, so that the larger awareness can come into full consciousness and functioning. In this way the person becomes literally "one with the Universe," for the individual loses consciousness of mere individuality and shares the quality of consciousness that characterizes most orders of being.[27]

By establishing such a consciousness of oneness, repetition creates holistic awareness. The effects are, of course, more pronounced within the context of ceremony and ceremonial dance, where repetitive movements and rhythms become reinforcing factors to the verbal repetition. Repetition, as we have said, is basic to the very brief charm, which Northrop Frye described as "the hypnotic incantation that, through its pulsing dance rhythms, appeals to involuntary physical response, and is hence not far from the sense of magic or physically compelling power."[28] Repetition is also fundamental in longer magical incantations like those of the Navajo Beauty Way song cycles. Further, Astrov observed that repetition is the dominant mode of expression not only in poetry but also in Indian storytelling and dance, as well as in domestic arts like pottery, basketry, and textile design. "Repetition, verbal and otherwise," she wrote, "means accumulation of power."[29] To the Native American, repetition is an a priori principle of the universe, evident everywhere in familiar patterns of nature and time. It is a power that man, as an intelligent part of the universe, can harness and use.

A second prominent stylistic characteristic of Indian poetry, often cited by commentators, is its characteristic brevity. Given the current literary interest in imagism, Austin and others made much of its apparent resemblance to much Indian poetry. Although an effective way to promote the newly anthologized Native American translations and interpretations, this comparison tended to obscure the essentially linguistic and magical sources of the symbolic images and phrasings largely responsible for the conciseness of the Indian expression. Curtis had called attention to these in *The Indians' Book*:

> One word may be the symbol of a complete idea that, in English, would need a whole sentence for its expression. Even those who know the language may not understand the songs unless they know what meaning lies behind the symbolic words . . . where songs belong to sacred ceremonies or secret societies, the meaning is purposely hidden—a holy mystery enshrined—that only the initiated may hear and understand.[30]

Barnes, in her prioneering study, enumerated many of the most prominent pan-tribal symbolic images along with their magical associations: Lightning and snakes, for instance, are associated with regeneration, the morning star and the eagle with divine wisdom and intelligence, the whirlwind with a transforming cosmic energy, and so on. Such magical symbols are everywhere in Indian life because all things are seen as intelligent and related, and as physically and spiritually alive. As the twentieth-century Sioux medicine man, Lame Deer (John Fire), put it:

> We Sioux spend a lot of time thinking about everyday things, which in our minds are mixed up with the spiritual. We see in the world around us many symbols which teach us the meaning of life. . . . We Indians live in a world where the spiritual and the commonplace are one.[31]

The Indian use of symbols is complex, for it is not purely referential or emotive. Symbolic usages, to the Native American, have a level of meaning that is quite tangible and real. Coyote is both the crafty scavenger in the bush and the super-but-all-too-human trickster figure, creator, or demiurge of Native American tribal myth. Allen wrote that "symbols in Native American tribal myth are not symbolic in the usual sense of the term. The words articulate reality—not 'psychological' . . . reality, not emotive reality captured metaphorically in an attempt to fuse thought and feeling but that reality where thought and feeling are one, . . . where speaker and listener are one, where sound and sense are one."[32] Symbolic usages in Native American poetry thus help to enact the magic that is already perceived as ever-present in the world. They fuse the personal consciousness with the communal one, shaping communion and the integrative process at the heart of Indian ceremonialism.

A third stylistic quality cited by Barnes and other commentators is the poetic language often found in Indian poetry. This language differs markedly from that of ordinary speech. It can involve archaic words whose meaning is known, archaic words whose precise meaning is not known but whose sound is believed to retain the original magical power, and distortions of common words that, along with vocables, or meaningless sound syllables, are employed for their emotive effects and to fill out a rhythmic measure. Barnes's phrase "poetic language" is misleading, for such usages do not represent heightened language in a purely literary or aesthetic sense. As R. F. Fortune wrote, much tribal song is characterized by "a secret esoteric language, a language of power." Anthropologists like Fortune and Bronislaw Malinowski regard devices like archaisms, vocables, and word distortions in a tribal context as elements of magic language, which, as Malinowski wrote, is "primeval langauge, and naturally it is different from the language of everyday speech; it is 'true speech,' distinct from the way we talk."[33]

The characteristics found in Indian poetry are not unique to the literature of Native American cultures. Repetition, imagism, dense symbolism, and special linguistic modes are basic to the poetries of both the preliterate and literate worlds. Their magical usages in Indian cultures are, of course, alien to us today, though we are beginning to understand how our own poetry is rooted in such "primitive" practices.[34] Indian poetry's association with integration of the self and with personal and even group communion is, however, becoming less alien to contemporary uses of poetry.

In the twentieth century, poets have turned increasingly to nonlinear, incantatory modes. Allen Ginsberg's *Howl* and *Kaddish,* for instance, two of the most widely read English-language poems of the past quarter-century, are structured on the very repetitive patterns central to tribal poetry. Imagism, dadaism, surrealism, symbolist poetry, projective verse, and performance poetry are all twentieth-century approaches that have moved modern poetry out of predictable linear patterns into more spatial, incantatory, imagistic, or holistic ones. Some of the poets practicing these techniques recognize, acknowledge, and draw on tribal sources while many, caught up in the avant-garde aspects of modernism, do not. Such adaptations of ancient practices are hardly limited to poetry. One has only to explore the impact of African and Oceanic art on Picasso and other painters at the turn of the century, or of tribal dance on Isadora Duncan, to realize that the renewing influence of the primitive has extended beyond poetry and has affected many facets of twentieth-century art.

This discussion is not primarily intended as an evaluation of the work of the earliest interpreters of Indian poetry.

Rather, I have mainly tried to demonstrate the characteristics and the appeal of Indian poetry and to record that several poets and editors understood their interest in Indian poetry not as antiquarianism, but as a vital concern with the development of a new American poetry that could speak in ways that would serve the literary and spiritual needs of modern America. None of them understood or articulated this better than Mary Austin.

*Austin's "The American Rhythm"*

In 1923 Austin published *The American Rhythm,* a collection of her reexpressions of the poetry of various Indian tribes. In a long introductory essay of the same title that outlined her views on the significance of Indian poetry for modern American verse, Austin followed the lead of Louise Pound and other contemporaries by tracing the origins of poetry back to the tribal dance, where rhythm, movement, and sound were combined to pursue the impulse toward "a reconciliation with the allness through group communion." Indian ceremonialism and its poetry are thus likened to early Greek dance, the acknowledged root of Western poetry and drama.

Austin's central premise is that "all verse forms that are found worthy of the use of great poets are aboriginal, in the sense that they are developed from the native soil that produced them." The prophecy that follows from this is "that American poetry must inevitably take, at some period of its history, the mold of Amerind verse, which is the mold of American experience shaped by the American environment."[35]

Austin provides a broad overview of the English poetic tradition that America inherited. Her analysis holds that English poetry lost much of its own aboriginal energy at an early point in its history owing to corruption of its original communal function by priestly, aristocratic, and military castes. Poetry became the property of these groups; the common people were left with the folk ballad. Subsequently, English poetry hardened into fixed metrical forms that incorporated nonindigenous influences from Greek, Roman, and Hebrew verse, making it more accessible to educated classes than to commoners. In Austin's analysis, America's democratic social structure protected it against the unfolding of a similar pattern. She asserted that Native American poetry represented a useful model and source for American poetry in several ways. First, it was "a form as lacking in tradition as the American experiment itself." By this Austin did not mean that Indian poetry lacked tradition, but that it was not rigidly locked into the past and, like democracy, was open to individual innovation and self-renewing change. Second, it was, in her view, "democratic in the sense that it was within the capacity of the democratically bred. Anybody could use it." Third, Indian poetry represented to her "a statement of life as . . . life presented itself on the western continent, in terms of things lived rather than observed or studied." Indian poetry was a model that encouraged poets to "represent the rhythm of men attempting to move concertedly from their own base, rather than to be waved forward by the batons of kings and academies."

Austin likened American Indian poetry to the modern free-verse movement just coming into its own. She claimed "never to have met an Indian with the slightest disposition to force words into a predetermined mold."[36] This view differed radically from the observations of students of Indian song like Densmore, who believed that preexisting melodic patterns often dictated the shape of accompanying poetic langauge Nevertheless, it was the kind of half-truth that, like Austin's comments on imagism and Indian poetry, represented good promotion—an attempt to call attention to the immediate literary relevance of the rich Native American poetic heritage.

Austin analyzed the rhythmic sources of Indian poetry and used her analysis to establish what she felt should be the basis of the modern American free-verse poem. She recognized that the sources of poetic rhythm were necessarily complex. Essentially, she felt that Indian poetry was the expression of free individuals living in harmonious relationship with their own environment, physicality, labor, and heritage. Intimacy with the surrounding American landscape was central to her conception of both the old and new American poetry. She named this poetry the "landscape line," calling attention to the "streams of rhythmic sights and sounds" of a natural environment, which she believed contributed importantly to regional styles among American tribes. Austin had first been struck by the importance of this environmental influence when an Indian friend pointed out how the rising and falling patterns of the wind were expressed in the movements, rhythms, and fluctuating vocal intensity of the participants in a ceremonial dance they were observing. Later she claimed to be able to identify the regional sources of Indian songs in unfamiliar languages simply by listening to them on phonograph recordings and analyzing their rhythmic patterns.

Austin believed that environmental rhythmic patterns became ingrained in the physiology of the person who was attuned to them:

> the rhythmic forms to which the environment gives rise seem to pass through the autonomic system, into and out of the subconscious without our having once become intellectually aware of them. Rhythm, then, in so far as it affects our poetic mode, has nothing to do with the intellectual life.[37]

Dissociating poetic rhythm from predetermined forms imposed by the mind and by convention was central to Austin's theory. By calling attention to the importance of the environment or "landscape" in the development of an indigenous American poetry, she made an association that other poets have developed. Though few, if any, have talked as explicitly as Austin does of landscape as a source of rhythm, the theme of intimacy with the local environment as a basis of American identity and poetry is prominent in the works of a long line of modern poets, including Vachel Lindsay, Carl Sandburg, Hart Crane, William Carlos Williams, Allen Ginsberg, Gary Snyder, and Charles Olson.

A second nonintellectual, "natural" source of poetic rhythm stressed by Austin was the body itself. She defined the landscape line as "the line shaped by its own inner necessity." That definition sought to call attention to a complex of factors: the landscape, the relationships between words and rhythms in the internal life of the poem itself, and the rhythms inside the poet out of which the poem arises. A poem essentially, Austin asserted, emerges and is shaped by the bodily rhythms of the individual man or woman—from "the breath, the *lub*-dub, *lub*-dub of the heart," the various imperceptible rhythms of the central nervous system—where the psychic and emotional life of the individual are registered.

Related to the physical and environmental sources are what Austin called the "characteristic motor responses." This phrase refers to common work or dance rhythms that, through repetition, are ingrained in the body. She cited Lincoln's Gettysburg Address as an expression of American poetic genius for its success in capturing the rhythms of the rail splitter, a "characteristic motor response" of Lincoln's own life and region.

A final influence on poetic rhythm suggested by Austin is human heredity itself. Specific rhythmic patterns and preferences, she speculated, may be passed on genetically. Poetic composition is thus holistic, the result of a complex of rhythmic forces. Austin described it as "the orchestration of organic rhythms under the influence of associated motor and emotional responses recapitulated from generation to generation."[38] The key term in this description is *organic*. American poetry, she said, must not be based on forms preestablished and imposed by the mind alone; it must grow out of the natural, organic rhythms surrounding and within the individual at the time of composition. Like Indian ceremonialism it must strive for "the binding up of the body and the self in its expressiveness." Such a poetry requires poets who are sensitive to their inner lives and to their environment, who are living not just in their minds, but holistically, where they are, in the world.

"The American Rhythm" prophesied that the poet's relationship to the American environment and to his or her own physicality would become important shaping forces of the modern American poem. Indications that such a process was already beginning, Austin observed, were evident in the works of contemporaries. She saw Vachel Lindsay's work as sometimes drawing on popular song and dance rhythms and at other times as expressing "points of simultaneity with the rhythms of all deep forested river bottom lands in which the Mississippi and Congo have place and kinship."[39] In Carl Sandburg's poems in *Smoke and Steel* (1922) she heard the rhythms of modern industry native to his city of Chicago. In Sherwood Anderson's poems she detected "characteristic cornland movements" strikingly similar to corn-dance rhythms of southwestern Indian tribes.

Austin also predicted that American poetry would develop forms suitable to restoring the communal experience she observed in Native American cultures and believed to be at the heart of the poetic impulse. This process of restoration, like the use of landscape and physical rhythms, she sensed had already begun:

> Although we have not yet achieved the communality into which the Amerind has entered by easy evolution, there is evident striving for it in the work of such men as Masters, Frost, and Sandburg; all our recent poetic literature is touched with a profound nostalgia for these happy states of reconciliation with the Allness, which is the business of poetry to promote.[40]

Austin understood that American Indian culture and poetry offered more than literary models to the modern American poet. Her own experience had taught her that entering the Indian world through Native American poetry could lead to an expanded awareness, a more fulfilled sense of self through a holistic understanding of life. "The Indian sees no better than the white man," Austin wrote, "but he sees more, registers with every sense, some of which have atrophied in us, infinitely more."[41] Austin suggests that knowledge of the Indian can help Americans restore themselves to psychic and perceptual wholeness. "The American Rhythm" called attention to Native American cultures as sources of expanded human awareness, of poetry that reflected unity of body and mind and a sense of the unity of the inner and outer realities. Austin introduced important themes—intimacy with the American environment, open-form poetry based on the organic rhythms of the body, communality, and holistic awareness—that other poets interested in the Indian and concerned with issues of American poetry and identity were to develop.

*Critical Responses*

*Path on the Rainbow* and *The American Rhythm* drew mixed critical responses. The fact that these works represented the culmination of literary activity that had been enthusiastically supported by *Poetry,* the most influential and modern of American poetry journals, lent weight to Austin's claim in both books that Indian poetry was of crucial importance to American mainstream literature and insured that there would be a critical response. Most critics were politely positive in a general way toward the poetry but were neutral or skeptical toward Austin's grandiose claims for its place in a wider literary tradition. Lewis Mumford wrote in *The New Republic* that "Mrs. Austin's work is as important as it is vigorous and wise," but he qualified his praise with the comment that "it is easier to accept Mrs. Austin's general thesis than it is to follow her particular illustrations.[42] R. M. Allen similarly damned with faint praise, observing in *The Literary Review*, "There may be more in Mrs. Austin's theories than she has taken the time to make clear."[43] Comments like these reflect on Austin's curious prose style in "The American Rhythm," a style that she herself acknowledged was afflicted with "a habit of doubling an idea back into its verbal envelope so that only the two ends of it stick out."[44] Earlier critics seized on the more obvious defects of *Path on the Rainbow:* Pauline Johnson's poems; the mislabeling of Carl Sandburg's poem "Early Moon" as a translation; Austin's apparent obliviousness to the fact that "The Marriage Song of Tikaens," which she described as a masterpiece of Indian literature, was a notorious forgery that had been exposed as a hoax by Daniel G. Brinton thirty years earlier. The most negative reviews came from Louis Untermeyer and Carl Van Doren, critics who were not fully comfortable with the inroads made by imagism and free verse and who were even less comfortable with Austin's claims for these as forms of an indigenous American classicism. Austin's promotion of Indian poetry as a model for a new American poetry rooted in place, body, and communality represented a threat to the rationalism, intellectualism, and elitism of the Western tradition that these critics represented and defended. Untermeyer attacked "the arbitrary arrangement of words and a pretentious typography that is foreign to our nature—though it is native to Ezra Pound, H. D., and Richard Aldington." Such imagist-like poems, he concluded, only proved that "the harsh aborigine can commit poetry as trite and banal as many an overcivilized paleface."[45]

Untermeyer's response prompted an acrimonious debate carried on for six months on the letters page of *The Dial*. Austin and Cronyn defended their position that, as Austin wrote, *"vers libre* and Imagism are in truth primitive forms, and both of them generically American forms, forms instinctively created by people living in America and freed of outside influences." Untermeyer expanded his attack, pointing to the need for footnotes to clarify contexts and meanings of Indian translations, a criticism that Austin conceded had some validity but claimed was impractical to implement for commercial reasons.[46] Untermeyer responded to a crude personal attack by Cronyn[47] with a tasteless racist remark, ridiculing what he characterized as Austin's and Cronyn's proposition that "a good Indian . . . is not so much a dead Indian as a singing Indian." But despite his antipathy to the idea of the Indian as poet and to the implications of Austin's large claims for the red man's poetry, Untermeyer conceded that as "an ethnic document this anthology is of indubitable value; as a contribution to creative Americana it may grow to have importance."[48] A decade later, in *American Poetry from the Beginning to Whitman* (1931), Untermeyer had come round to Austin's view to the extent of including a review of the history and style of Indian poetry in a discussion of the origins of American poetry.

Regarding Untermeyer's comments on *Path on the Rainbow,* Austin complained, "If Mr. Untermeyer could get his mind off the Indian anthology as a thing of type and paper, he might have gotten more out of it."[49] The comment unwittingly points to the paradoxical problem of translating, and in the process transforming, oral poetry to "a thing of type and paper." Untermeyer, a self-described "mere man of letters," could take the poetry no other way. Austin never fully came to grips with the need to find a way to bring poetry off the page, to meet the underlying challenge posed by Indian poetics, that of integrating that poetry and the emerging American poetry more totally into the wider culture. Nor did she fully come to grips with the quasi-ritual attempts to combine poetry and music in public readings by her contemporaries Lindsay, Sandburg, and Sarett. Though Austin recognized a general spirit of communality in their work, she never specified the importance of performance poetry in serving this end.

The most enthusiastic response to Austin's and Cronyn's work came in *The Nation,* from Hartley Burr Alexander, himself a student of Indian cultures and their literature.[50] Unlike Untermeyer, Alexander recognized that "Cronyn's anthology must be appreciated in the fullness of the imagination and with unrestrained sensibility. The Indian," he continued, "makes no concession [to] the audience; it is either with him totally or not at all. But being with him, it will surely discover its reward in the directness and intensity of the imaginative experience."[51]

The two poles of response to Indian poetry and the claims made for it by Austin were sensitive to its radical implications for American poetry and identity. The conservative, defensive view was represented by Untermeyer; by John Gould Fletcher, who criticized Austin's "lack [of] a sense of proportion";[52] and by Carl Van Doren, who wrote, somewhat hysterically, that Austin "is ready to sacrifice all that we have for the sake of something we might have if we saw poetry and America the way she sees them . . . she is ruthless and would destroy a great deal of value."[53] The opposite view was expressed by Alexander: "we are coming to see that the lore of the Indian contains much that is a treasure for our inner life."[54] Later poets and critics were often to take sides, lining up behind one or the other of these aesthetic positions, both of which were concerned with establishing the roots of American identity. The conservatives linked American identity to a historical relationship with Europe and the Western tradition, a linear, chronological relationship resting on the axis of time. The radicals saw the meaning of America as being dependent on its break from Europe. For them, American identity was most importantly related to experiencing and creating "the New World." Toward this end, the Native American was regarded as a resource and a relative. Identity for the radicals thus rested no longer primarily on linear time but on space. We could only understand who we are, they sensed, by knowing fully where we are.

# ◆ 2 The Indian as a Symbol: Vachel Lindsay, Hart Crane, and William Carlos Williams ◆

I do believe the average American to be an Indian, but an Indian robbed of his world—unless we call machines a forest of themselves.

William Carlos Williams, *In the American Grain*

Early twentieth-century poets were not only interested in the Native American for his poetry, rooted in the rhythms and images of place. The red man himself served as a symbol of both the American continent and a new American identity based on a harmonious relationship—a mystical participation—with the land. Three poets writing in the 1920s best illustrate this power of the Indian as a symbol: Vachel Lindsay, Hart Crane, and William Carlos Williams. To each, the Indian was a being at one with the land and so was a powerful symbol in the battle against alienation that was so painfully widespread in America of the 1920s. Like D. H. Lawrence in *Studies in Classic American Literature* (1923), these writers viewed alienation from place as one of the central problems of American history and of the American psyche. Lawrence wrote:

> There is always a certain slightly devilish resistance in the American landscape, and a certain slight resistance in the white man's heart. . . . The American landscape has never been at one with the white man. Never. [1]

*Vachel Lindsay*

Lindsay sought to resolve this problem by poetic fiat. In several of his poems he proposes, or imposes, a genealogical linkage to the Indian as a way of rooting and legitimizing American experience on the continent. "Our Mother Pocahontas," for instance, employs Pocahontas as a symbol for the indigenousness historically and psychologically missing from the American experience. One could say that Lindsay tried to crawl back into the land through an Indian mother. "Our Mother Pocahontas" attempts to bridge the gap between individual and place by blunt assertion:

> John Rolfe is not our ancestor.
> We rise from out of the soul of her
> Held in native wonderland,
> While the sun's rays kissed her hand,
> In the springtime,
> In Virginia,
> Our Mother, Pocahontas.

In making Pocahontas "Our Mother," Lindsay twists the historically malleable Indian-princess myth to his own purposes.

Leslie Fiedler, in *The Return of the Vanishing American* (1968), provides a cogent analysis of this myth. He traces its origin in sixteenth-century conventional cartographic images of America as a dancing Amazonian woman—an "Indian queen"—bearing a war club, with a severed male head at her feet. Fiedler describes how John Smith's Pocahontas story tempered this image of a terrifying and dangerous female figure to a younger, more loving, and more accepting one who would save the neck of the European rather than sever it; and how, following the spread of Smith's Pocahontas tale, mapmakers began changing the cartographic images of America to that of a warmer Indian princess. The severed head at the feet of the Indian queen was conventionally replaced by a hogshead of tobacco, thus inviting the commercial exploitation of the New World by seventeenth-century Europe.[2]

Pocahontas or the "Indian princess" has traditionally been, as Fiedler put it, a symbol of "reconciliation with the wilderness." Lindsay uses her in this way. But in making Pocahontas "Our Mother," and in associating her with Americans' renunciation of their European heritage, Lindsay deviates sharply from tradition.

Smith's Pocahontas is a powerful image for the sixteenth, seventeenth, eighteenth, and nineteenth centuries precisely because she accepts European ways. She travels to England, dresses in an elaborate gown like an English lady, and meets the queen. For Lindsay (the transplanted European as twentieth-century poet), however, Pocahontas is antagonistic to European monarchies. She represents the American earth itself, in which a new American man can be rooted and regenerated:

> Because gray Europe's rags august
> She tramples in the dust,
> Because we are her fields of corn;
> Because our fires are all reborn
> From her bosom's deathless embers.

The poem concludes with hope for the American future embodied in a new breed of citizens harmoniously linked to the spirit and body of Pocahontas and the American earth:

We here renounce our Saxon blood,
Tomorrow's hopes, and April flood
Come roaring in. The newest race
Is born of her resilient grace. . . .
She sings of lilacs, maples, wheat,
Her own soil sings beneath her feet,
Of springtime,
Of Virginia,
Our Mother, Pocahontas.

In picturing a new breed of Americans born out of close harmonious contact with the Indian, "Our Mother Pocahontas" projects a familiar New World myth whose major literary source is James Fenimore Cooper's Leatherstocking Tales.[3] Like Cooper's Indians, Lindsay's Pocahontas and the Indians that appear in some of his other poems are purely symbols. One hundred years after Cooper, however, the kind of simplistic wish-fulfillment fantasy we find in "Our Mother Pocahontas" seems problematically naive and glib in the face of available information on the actual history of white-Indian relationships. "Our Mother Pocahontas," like virtually all of Lindsay's major Indian poems, expresses the need for a unity of some sort with the Indian and the land and for a subsequent new consciousness, but it fails to confront the psychological, spiritual, or historical reasons why this need exists. The unity and kinship it expresses seem to gloss over or be ignorant of historical realities, and its optimism is thus somewhat hollow.[4]

Lindsay was not, in fact, ignorant of history. In two minor poems omitted from his *Collected Works,* "The Hunting Dogs" and "The Babbitt Jamboree," he briefly alludes to the outrageous injustice of the Indian wars and land appropriations and expresses his sympathy for the red man. Still, in his more ambitious and widely read poems in which the Indian figures, Lindsay exhibited a remarkable insensitivity to the Native American as a human being and an inability to confront the disturbing psychological and historical issues for Americans that are implicit in him as a subject. Lindsay comes closest to suggesting this traumatic quality in "The Ghost of the Buffaloes." There he describes a terrifying dream in which the city he lives in has suddenly disappeared and been reduced to a single hut by a stream. An angry band of Indian ghosts appears:

> With bodies like bronze, and terrible eyes
> Came the rank and file, with catamount cries,
> Gibbering, yipping, with hollow-skull clacks,
> Riding white broncos with skeleton backs,
> Scalp-hunters, beaded and spangled and bad,
> Naked and lustful and foaming and mad,
> Flashing primeval demoniac scorn
> Bloodthirst and pomp amid darkness reborn.

They disappear, burning out "like meteors" in the sky, and are followed by a herd of rampaging buffalo that likewise rage, snort, and vanish. The poem's tone of terror, however, is incongruously compromised by the childish delight of the refrain:

> A-la-la, a-la-la
> A red god show
> A red god show

The psychological guilt or historical tragedy implicit in the images are obscured by this tone of un-self-conscious popcorn pleasure, which leads to the comfortable acceptance of the poem's concluding lines:

> Life is west-going dream-storm's breath,
> Life is a dream, the sigh of the skies.

Such half-baked Eastern mysticism ultimately denies the poem's psychic reality and undercuts its potential power.

In "Doctor Mohawk" Lindsay once again fantasizes an Indian "ancestral protector," this time modeled after his own father, a physician. This paternal medicine man, we are told, "breathed Mohawk fire through me." Jolly Indians, pictured as happy-go-lucky jokers, "singing and swimming their pranks and their notions," Lindsay writes, "will stand by me, and save and deliver, / With the pearl near my heart they will love me forever. . . ." The pearl in the poem is described as "the Soul of the U.S.A." It is also described as "without flaw." The Indian is represented as having cheerfully passed on the soul of the land to the white man, whom he subsequently loves.[5] The poem marches on, replete with unfurling star-spangled banners, to its conclusion. Its message is that the white man will be healed in his moments of spiritual distress by the loving Indian, that somehow a reconciliation has been reached with the red "other." As in "Our Mother Pocahontas," America's manifest destiny is affirmed and fortified by the miraculous acquisition of the Indian's bloodline and spirit.

This acquisition, or should we say appropriation, of the Indian's blessing, blood, and spirit is an obsession with Lindsay. It reaches its most unintentionally comic and absurd fruition in "In Praise of Johnny Appleseed." Lindsay could personally identify with John Chapman, the Johnny Appleseed of American myth. He had analogously stumped the country, spreading his seeds by hawking poems and broadsides on the streets of New York and his native Springfield, Illinois, and by embarking on a long walking tours of Kansas and New Mexico preaching "The Gospel of Beauty" and exchanging poems for bread and lodging. The Indian plays a central role in the Johnny Appleseed poem, but Lindsay fails to acknowledge and was probably ignorant of a Native American mythic parallel: Kokopilau or Kokopelli, the hump-backed flute player, a culture hero of the Pueblo tribes, who spread seeds from the pouch on his back as his people emerged into the new world.[6] Nevertheless, Lindsay's Indians recognize Appleseed as a kindred spirit:

> Painted beings in the midst of a clearing
> Heard him asking his friends the eagles
> To guard each planted seed and seedling.
> Then he was a god to the red man's dreaming.

Lindsay's Indians worship Johnny as a great white nature god—an incongruous concept—and help him to sate his more earthly lusts with wine, women, and song. Finally, Johnny must move on to his colonial mission, the civilizing of the wild American landscape with apple trees. He takes off, having acquired the Indians' love and "medicine":

> he left their wigwams and their love.
> By the hour of dawn he was proud and stark;
> Kissed the Indian babes with a sigh,
> Went forth to live on roots and bark,
> Sleep in the trees, while the years howled by.

The godlike Johnny's descent upon the earthly Native Americans, his lovemaking with the "Indian babes," and his gestation period in the hollows of trees before moving on to his task represent an initiation and rebirth sequence. Johnny becomes one with the Indian, the possessor of the spirit of the continent, and is reborn out of the earth itself. He becomes a white-Indian—literally, for Lindsay, "Johnny Appleseed—Medicine Man." His apple trees have no biblical connotation of original sin but, because of his initiation and rebirth, are miraculously Native American. Their apples provide more than mere physical sustenance; they contain the vision of a great American civilization. By infusing Johnny with the Indians' love, spirit, and medicine (and subsequently dropping the Native American from the poem), Lindsay makes Johnny the red man's descendant. The Indians bless Johnny and his activities and, through him, the American dream:

> a ballot box in each apple
> A state capital in each apple
> Great high schools, great colleges
> All America in each apple.

The implications of this poem are, of course, absurd in the light of historical realities. But Lindsay's obsession with the theme of Indian ancestry expresses a very real cultural need for intimacy with the land and for absolution by the wronged Indian, the custodian of the land's spirit.

Linday's confident resolutions of these problems are too easy. They fail to confront the complex underlying historical, psychological, and spiritual issues involved in actual white-Indian relations. This is especially disappointing given the fact of the literature available to him;[7] and the fact of his apparently genuine sympathy for and affinity with the Native American shown by his personal predilection, by his sensitivity to the need for a "new localism," and by his pioneering of performance poetry.

Lindsay's Indian poems exhibit weaknesses characteristic of much of his verse, especially those poems that explored American subjects with mythic content. As Nils Erik Enkvist wrote of Lindsay's folk heroes, "There is consistently more emotion than fact, and the most popular qualities get the loudest praise."[8] Lindsay's poem "The Statue of Andrew Jackson," for instance, puffs the popular image of Jackson as a fierce warrior and democrat while completely ignoring his political excesses and his bloody, brutal, and inhumane Indian policy. Lindsay ultimately failed in his ambition to become a beloved American poet-mythmaker. His poems tended to be superficial; to seek easy, happy resolutions; to curry popularity by telling their audience what it already knew or wanted to hear. His Indian poems never achieved the status of genuine myth because they shied away from acknowledging or exploring the deeply rooted, dark, historical, and psychological truths from which they sprung.

## Hart Crane's "The Bridge"

Like Lindsay, Hart Crane employed the Indian as a symbol associated with the land and with a new American identity, an expanded consciousness based on a mystical participation in the land's spirit. In "The Bridge," as Crane wrote in a July 4, 1927, letter, "the reader is led back in time to the pure savage world." Unlike Lindsay, however, Crane recognized that to "unlatch the door to the pure Indian world . . . is a very complicated thing to do."[9]

The symbols and meanings of "The Bridge" are much more complex and multilayered than anything found in Lindsay's poetry. The poem lacks a conventionally linear beginning, middle, and end and instead works by juxtapositions and interpenetrations of levels of language and historic, mythic, and personal images. Generally, the poem can be said to be concerned with restoring to modern consciousness a mythic sensibility that is equated with an Indian sensibility. As R. W. B. Lewis wrote:

> Between the poem's wave-like start and its elusive finish, there occurs the long movement of consciousness away from the mechanical and urban and toward a mythic interpretation of nature and human experience; followed by a serial exploration of various centers and corners of contemporary life, carried out by reference to the vision and especially to the visionary language acquired in "The Dance."[10]

"The Dance," in section II of "The Bridge" (significantly titled "Powhattan's Daughter"), is the visionary center of the poem. It is where the elusive, heightened awareness that Crane sought is approached and briefly achieved. It is the piece most fully focused on the Indian world, where the poem's speaker momentarily becomes one with the Native American. In "The Dance," the mysterious female figure with whom the speaker seeks oneness and understanding, and whose identity shifts throughout "The Bridge," materializes as Pocahontas. As Crane wrote in the later "Cape Hatteras" section, Pocahontas's "eternal flesh" is "our native clay" with "its depths of red." She is, as he wrote his friend Otto Kahn, "the mythological nature-symbol chosen to represent the physical body of the continent or the soil."[11] Pocahontas's eyes are described as "wide" and "undoubtful" in contrast to the narrow, individual, unseeing, "bright window eyes" of "Cyclopean towers across Manhattan waters," images of the spiritual dissociation of the modern world. As Lewis put it, "It is, by submitting in erotic reverence to the reality of the American earth that the poet can, so he hopes, find his own eyes opened and his doubts removed."[12]

But such submission is not so easy. Modern man's ability to subordinate himself in quasi-religious eroticism, as well as his ability to perceive, let alone contact, the spirit of the American earth, is inhibited by historical, spiritual, and psychological forces beyond his control. These forces comprise the emotional tensions with which "The Bridge" is built. Pocahontas herself is painfully elusive:

> Mythical brows we saw retiring—loth,
> Disturbed and destined, into denser green.
> Greeting they sped us, on the arrow's oath;
> Now lie incorrigibly, what years between. . . .
>
> There was a bed of leaves, and broken play;
> There was a veil upon you, Pocahontas, bride—
> O Princess whose brown lap was virgin May;
> And bridal flanks and eyes hid tawny pride.

Ultimately, Pocahontas is unknowable—"virgin to the last of men"—yet, Crane suggests, there are special moments when contact can be made. In "The River," the piece that precedes

"The Dance" in section II, there is reference to one such moment:

> Papooses crying on the wind's long mane
> Screamed redskin dynasties that fled the brain,
> . . . Dead echoes! But I knew her body there,
> Time like a serpent down her shoulder, dark,
> And space, an eaglet's wing, laid on her hair.

The language of this passage suggests both a physical and a mystical experience, a union with and thereby a transcendence of time and space. The images of serpent and eagle's wing recall an early symbol for the emerging American nation but also evoke their Indian associations with regeneration and illumination. In "The Dance," Crane leads us to one such mystical, visionary experience. The poem's speaker roams the continent, exploring its mysteries and searching for Pocahontas, its elusive spirit. He discovers this Indian spirit and in the process discovers himself:

> Over how many bluff, tarns, streams I sped!
> —And knew myself within some boding shade:—
> Grey tepees tufting the blue knolls ahead,
> Smoke swirling through the yellow chestnut glade. . . .
>
> A distant cloud, a thunder-bud—it grew,
> That blanket of the skies: The padded foot
> Within,—I heard it; till its rhythms drew,
> —Siphoned the black pool from the heart's hot root!

The Indian spirit that Crane's speaker discovers is within himself. It is freed by the padded feet of the ecstatic dance that "siphons" the "black pool," the oily film of industrialism—dehumanizing modern consciousness—inhibiting the human engine, the heart.

The poem suddenly shifts at this point to a vision of the Indian prince, Maquokeeta, as he is being consumed at the stake in sacrificial death. In the midst of the conflagration, Maquokeeta continues to dance exultantly as, around the pyre, not only other Indians but also all of nature dances:

> A birch kneels. All her whistling fingers fly,
> The oak grove circles in a crash of leaves.

This passage, depicting a union with the red man and with nature, climaxes in images of rebirth and regeneration amid destruction as the speaker identifies so closely that he momentarily becomes one with the dancing figure:

> Dance, Maquokeeta! snake that lives before,
> That casts his pelt, and lives beyond! Spirit, horn!
> Spark, tooth! Medicine-man, relent, restore—
> Lie to us,—dance us back the tribal morn!
>
> Spears and assemblies: black drums thrusting on—
> O yelling battlements,—I, too, was liege
> To rainbows currying each puissant bone:
> Surpassed the circumstance, danced out the siege!

The regenerative thrust of this passage is underscored in the passages that follow, as "The Dance" moves more serenely to its conclusion, culminating in images of Pocahontas as the land moving from her "speechless dream of snow" into the renewed bloom of spring.

The ecstatic vision of "The Dance," however, is not without its undercurrent of despair. The medicine man, who, as the merging indentities in the passage suggest, could be also seen as the modern poet, can renew our energies and our consciousness but only, the poem tells us, at the ultimate cost to himself. Further, to restore "the tribal morn," he must "lie to us"—the disturbing implication being that his ecstatic dance provides only an illusion, that in actuality we are beyond the point of no return, that our day-to-day cultural awareness is forever clouded and limited by the industrial sludge and competitive materialism of the modern world.

Nevertheless, the vision achieved in "The Dance" represents the heights of awareness and perception achieved in "The Bridge." As with Lindsay's Indian symbolism, Crane associated the Native American with the spirit of the land itself and with a revitalized and expanded American awareness and identity. Unlike Lindsay, however, Crane was much more cognizant of historical and contemporary factors that mitigate against the ultimate achievement of this vision. "The Dance" provides "The Bridge" with a momentary peak that enables us to gauge the depths to which we have, in actuality, sunk. As Lewis wrote, "After 'The Dance,' the poet has something by reference to which the contemporary actuality appears as parodic and debased." The most blatant example of this is the piece called "National Winter Garden" in which the description of a striptease dancer parallels, in a mocking way, those of Pocahontas.[13] Unlike the facile optimism of Lindsay's poetry, Crane's "The Bridge" is ultimately a dark, disturbing poem. Its symbolic Indians are simultaneously images of our own unfulfilled human potential and of our alienation from the land and from our own inner resources.

## William Carlos Williams

The need for American poetry and consciousness to reflect a more intimate and harmonious relationship with the American landscape and its elusive spirit—implicit in the work of the first translators of Indian poetry, explicit in Austin's prophetic utterances, and reflected in the imagery of Lindsay and Crane—dominates the literary efforts of William Carlos Williams from 1918 to 1930 and establishes an aesthetic foundation for his later work. In his essay "The American Background" (1947), Williams asserted that this relationship with "place" was the basis of culture itself, which he described as

> The realization of the qualities of a place in relationship to the life which occupies it; embracing everything involved, climate, relative size, history, other cultures—as well as the character of its sands, flowers, minerals and the condition of knowledge within its borders. It is the act of lifting these things into an ordered and utilized whole.[14]

In 1920 Williams founded and edited the magazine *Contact* "to emphasize the local phase of the game of writing." *Contact,* through Williams's manifesto-like editorials, encouraged writers to "take . . . the land at your feet and use it." This meant the "achievement of a locus," a rootedness in the actual physical, historical, and spiritual conditions of America. As Williams wrote: "If Americans are to be blessed with important work it will be through intelligent, informed contact with the locality which alone can infuse it with reality."[15]

With *Contact,* Williams posited an alternative to the expatriatism of his friend Pound and his archenemy Eliot. Williams's aesthetic of *contact* urged American writers to dig in rather than move away. "We're not putting the rose, the single rose, in the little glass vase in the window," Williams wrote, "we're digging a hole for the tree—and as we dig we have disappeared in it."[16]

*Contact* reflected an impulse similar to the one that impelled poets to translate Indian songs. It pointed to the need for an intimate relationship with place and for a revitalized American cultural identity based on that intimacy. Williams was less influenced during this period by writers, however, than he was by the artists and photographers associated with Alfred Stieglitz's Gallery 291 in New York City. Though this group, which included Stieglitz, Georgia O'Keeffe, Stuart Davis, Charles Scheeler, Marsden Hartley, Arthur Dove, and John Marin, never developed a uniform aesthetic philosophy, all of these artists were opposed to a classical approach to art. Most were literalists, interested in the evocative power of the particulars of the American rural and urban landscapes. Williams's evolving sense of the poetic image and his poetic credo, "No ideas but in things," no doubt were influenced by exchanges with his friends in the visual arts.[11]

One of these friends, Marsden Hartley, had made several trips to the American Southwest, where his own sense of an emerging American aesthetic had been importantly influenced by his observations of Native American ceremonialism and culture. He wrote about his reactions in two essays that Williams probably read: "Tribal Aesthetics" (1918), and "The Red Man" (1921). Hartley was impressed by the mythic depth of Indian ceremony and culture, which seemed to him a reflection of the Native American's close relationship to the physical and spiritual reality of the land itself. He admired the harmony that he sensed within the people:

> You feel that at last here is a people in accord with the universe, wanting little or nothing from a world of invented subterfuge, being the equal of the very dawn and of the going down of the sun, vastly superior to all the hosts of vulgarities with which we, who belong to the newer civilization, befool ourselves.[18]

Similar interpretations appear, a few years later, at the heart of Williams's major prose work, *In the American Grain* (1925).

Like other poets and artists of the period who were concerned with the issue of American cultural identity and the related issue of our relationship to the land, Williams ultimately discovered the Indian. *In the American Grain* represents his attempt to redefine American history by reassessing the implicit values and the relationship to the New World embodied in its central figures. Toward this end, men like Hernando Cortez, Cotton Mather, Benjamin Franklin, George Washington, and Alexander Hamilton are critically downgraded, while others, like Thomas Morton, Père Sebastian Rasles, Daniel Boone, Sam Houston, and Edgar Allan Poe are elevated to a more prominent position than they traditionally inhabit and are proposed as truer heroic models for a new American identity. The criterion employed by Williams in his reevaluation is each figure's openness to influence by the conditions and spirit of the New World, the spirit of nature surrounding and within. The Indian serves as a model for Williams's notion of the heroic, for the red man, in his view, had accepted and reacted directly and creatively to the conditions of "the local," building truly indigenous cultures out of his responses. As Alan Holder observed, *In the American Grain* amounts to "a celebration of the Indian, linking him to the spirit of the American earth."[19] In contrast, most of our history's heroic figures, Williams suggested, resisted the New World's new spirit. Instead of seeking creative contact with it, they sought to control it, often by imposing alien, Old World systems.

As with *Contact, In the American Grain* can be seen as a manifestation of a similar impulse to that which impelled poets to translate Indian poetry or to employ symbolic Indians in their poems. It was affected by the impact of such things as the closing off of the American continental frontier, the available factual information about Indians, increased mechanization and its effects on the individual, and the disturbing disillusionment following World War I. As James Breslin notes, it resembled other prose works of the period that reexamined American history, literature, and values and also reflected the influence of the new social science of psychology:

Williams' book in many respects resembles such radical reassessments of American literature as Van Wyck Brooks' *America's Coming of Age* (1915), Waldo Frank's *Our America* (1919), D. H. Lawrence's *Studies in Classic American Literature* (1923), and Lewis Mumford's *The Golden Day* (1926). A major tendency in these polemical works is to see American history as developing out of a Freudian conflict between repression and liberation, between will and body. They often stress the need for a biological adjustment to places. Accordingly, the Indian emerges as the buried hero of American history, while the Puritan, sternly imposing an alien ideology on the primitive continent, becomes a kind of demonic figure.[20]

All of the historical figures whose value Williams discounted do, in fact, embody this puritanism in one way or another. In *In the American Grain,* Williams, for instance, stressed how Cortez imposed the "alien ideologies" of Christianity and greed for gold while remaining blind to the highly cultivated and sophisticated achievements of the Aztecs. The conquistadors, Williams wrote, failed to contact "the earthward thrust of their logic" or "the realization of their primal and continuous identity with the ground itself, where everything is fixed in darkness."[21] In another version of this theme, Williams quoted extensively from the writings of Cotton Mather to reveal how this spokesman for puritanism never saw the actuality of the New World at all. The biblical ideology that Mather imposed on the New World saw the woods as "desarts" and the Indians as "devils." Williams devoted an entire chapter to Mather's contemporary (and foil), Thomas Morton. Morton embodied for Williams the attempt to meet and share experience and consciousness with the red man. Morton trades with the Indians and joins them in ceremony with the liberating dance around Merrymount's Maypole. Morton thus contacts the spirit of place symbolized by the Indian, celebrating the primitive sexual energies that the Puritans repress.

Benjamin Franklin represented, for Williams, still another type of puritan. He is described as a "voluptuary," who obsessively channels his sexual energy into mundane projects. He is the practical man, compulsively imposing his will on everything to control it and himself: "Do something, anything, to keep the fingers busy—not to realize—the lightning." Franklin, Williams wrote, "was the dike keeper, keeping the wilderness out with his wits. Fear drove his curiosity." He embodies our forefathers' inability to be "inspired by the new QUALITY about them, to yield to loveliness in a fresh spirit."[22] The repression of self implicit in Franklin becomes explicit in George Washington as Williams portrayed him. He cited the emphasis in Washington's writings and speeches on self-control as setting a tone for an American consciousness that has never flowered into new identity: "resist, be prudent, be calm—with a mad hell inside that might rise, might one day do something brilliant, perhaps joyously abandoned—but not to be thought of." [23] The converse of this self-repression and control is found in the literary exploration of the "hell inside" of Edgar Allan Poe, which Williams called attention to in a separate chapter as a uniquely American response to the conditions of the New World.

Williams suggested that the impulse, derived from the Puritans, to repress, control, and impose is evident in our physical treatment of the land. His chapter on Alexander Hamilton portrays him as the first major corporate exploiter of the land, scheming to harness the Passaic River and to get rich quick from the industrialization of Williams's home city of Paterson, New Jersey. As with Franklin, Hamilton's "industrious" view of the land precludes contact with its spirit.

Williams's opposition to the pervasive puritanism he saw as dominating American attitudes and blinding us to where we are and, ultimately, to who we are, becomes at times shrill and obsessive:

> This stress of the spirit against the flesh has produced a race incapable of flower. Upon that part of the earth they occupied true spirit dies because of the Puritans, except through vigorous revolt. They are the bane, not the staff. Their religious zeal, mistaken for a thrust up toward the sun, was a stroke in, in, in—not toward germination but the confinements of a tomb. . . . And it is still today the Puritan who keeps his frightened grip upon the throat of the world lest it should prove him—empty.[24]

Opposed to this destructive puritanism is the Native American. "Nowhere the free, open assertion," William writes, "save in the Indian."

Throughout *In the American Grain* Williams, like Lindsay and Crane, employs symbolic images of an Indian woman, marriage, and birth to suggest the possibility of a new relationship to the American spirit of place. In the chapter titled "DeSoto and the New World," the land speaks as the voice of a dark, savage, seductive Indian "She," luring the explorer "down" as he explores the rivers of her lush interior and finally devouring him. Another Indian woman figure, the powerful Abnaki sachem, Jacataqua, is posed by Williams as a new role model for "the American girl, who must be protected in some other way so she is frightened." Jacataqua's challenge to American troops, "You hunt with me? I win," both mocks and frightens them. Only Aaron Burr can respond openly and positively to what, for Williams, represents the attractive yet terrifying promise of personal liberation—expansion through a marriage to the spirit of place embodied in the Indian. Burr's open response is linked by Williams to his independent and expansive spirit and to his ability to resist "schemers" like Hamilton. Similar symbolic marriages to the New World spirit are portrayed in Williams's chapters on Sam Houston and Père Sebastian Rasles. Williams cites Houston's significance as lying not in his political exploits but in his running away to join the Cherokee as a child and in his later marriage to an Indian woman. Likewise, Rasles, a crippled Catholic priest, marries himself to a tribe. He spends more than thirty years among the Abnaki in Maine, learning their language, adopting many of their customs and values, and functioning as a doctor—sharing, in effect, his medicine with theirs. Ultimately, he supports the Abnaki in their warfare against the English and the French. This gesture of rejection of the old European cultures represents for Williams the depth of Rasles's immersion in the new. Williams describes him in terms of symbolic rebirth: "In Rasles one feels the Indian emerging from within the pod of his isolation from eastern understanding, he is released AN INDIAN."[25]

Perhaps the most powerfully rendered of Williams's heroic models is Daniel Boone. Like Franklin, Boone is described as a "voluptuary," but, unlike Franklin, Boone is not compulsive and self-cancelling. Boone is Williams's prime example of the man who does not fearfully repress his instinctual desire for new experience. He is consequently successful in merging with the spirit of the New World as few Americans ever are:

> because of a descent to the ground of his desire was Boone's life important and does it remain still loaded with power . . . among all the colonists, like an Indian, the ecstasy of complete possession of the new country was his alone.[26]

Williams portrayed Boone as giving himself openly to the Indian and the wilderness. Instead of losing himself, like DeSoto, Boone discovers himself anew, like Houston, Burr, and Rasles. He learns to perceive the animal life around him in an Indian way, learns to hunt expertly, yet with respect. Even when his eldest son is killed by Indians, "he never wavered in his conception of the Indian as a natural part of a beloved condition, the New World."[27] Boone's vision of the New World approaches an ecological one in which all creatures are related to one another through their common relationship to the earth. His life epitomizes the "new wedding" to the spirit of place that can produce the new man and the new consciousness for which, Williams suggested the New World was destined:

> There must be a new wedding. But [Boone] saw and only he saw the prototype of it all, the native savage. To Boone the Indian was the greatest master. Not for himself surely to be an Indian, though they eagerly sought to adopt him into their tribes, but the reverse: to be *himself* in a new world, Indian-like. If the land were to be possessed it must be as the Indian possessed it.[28]

Williams makes it clear in this passage that he is not suggesting that Americans imitate or become Indians. Rather, he is saying that, like Indians, we should truly become Americans— that is, we should live fully where we are, responsive to the nature around and within us. Only by becoming Indian-like in our knowledge of where we are, Williams suggests, can we ever hope really to know who we are.

*In the American Grain* represents Williams's fullest statement of these themes. Periodically, however, they crop up in his poetry as well. The dark woman, for instance, can be found woven throughout the poems in *Spring & All* (1921). An example is the following short, untitled poem:

> Black-eyed susan
> rich orange
> round the purple core
>
> the white daisy
> is not
> enough
>
> Crowds are white
> as farmers
> who live poorly
>
> But you
> are rich
> in savagery
>
> Arab
> Indian
> dark woman

Here we see the dark woman as a black-eyed susan, a plant indigenous to North America. She is associated with Arabs or Indians, native peoples whose savagery enables them to live lives that are rich. In contrast, the white daisy, defined in *The American Heritage Dictionary* as "a low-growing European plant," is described as "not enough" and is associated with the "crowds who live poorly." The white daisy can be read as representing white European consciousness and the poem as an early expression by Williams of the need for white people to contact the dark, savage spirit of place developed in *In the American Grain*.

Also in *Spring & All*, in the famous poem beginning "The pure products of America go crazy," we encounter another dark woman, Elsie, who represents a different type of spirit of place. Elsie, we are told, is "thrown up" by a marriage with "a dash of Indian blood." She is "addressed to cheap / jewelry and rich young men with fine eyes / as if the earth under our feet / were / an excrement of some sky"; and thus she expresses "with broken / brain the truth about us." Elsie is the spirit of modern America, and her truth reveals the tawdriness of the age, the lack of deeply rooted values, the sexual and emotional repression ("succumbing without / emotion / save numbed terror"); as well as a dumb longing for something we "cannot express," something associated with the landscape ("we degraded prisoners / destined / to hunger until we eat filth / while the imagination strains / after deer / going by fields of goldenrod in / the stifling heat of September").

The Indian appears in several of Williams's later poems as well, most notably two of his masterpieces: *Paterson* and "The Desert Music." In *Paterson* the Indian is a fleeting presence, darting periodically in and out of the main action of the poem in sudden fragmentary flashes. Glimpses of the ghostly Indian are usually disruptive and disturbing to the narrator. "Forget it!, for God's sake, Cut / out that stuff," he interjects,[29] breaking off a description of an Indian raiding party dragging away captives and returning to the interrupted description of modern couples lying on a beach, exchanging "pitiful thoughts." Paterson's declared theme of divorce is the converse of *In the American Grain's* theme of contact. The Indian's barely glimpsed, elusive, disruptive presence symbolizes the divorce theme, suggesting Americans' divorce from the landscape, its spirit, its history.

"The Desert Music" is a poem also, in a sense, about divorce—divorce from the self. It describes Williams's own identity crisis, his sense of inadequacy as a poet. In recounting through the poem the experiences in the border town of Juárez, Mexico, which triggered the crisis of self-doubt, Williams confronted and resolved the issues that troubled him, and the poem concludes as a stirring affirmation of his own aesthetic and his own identity as a poet. Significantly, the image in the poem that inspires its sense of self-renewal and affirmation is that of an Indian fast asleep, wrapped in a blanket as he lies on the bridge over the Río Grande so that tourists like Williams must step over him. When he first encounters the sleeping figure, Williams views him as worthless, just as he views himself: "They probably inspect the place / and will cart it away later. / Heave it into the river. / A good thing."[30] Later, however, at the poem's conclusion, after recounting the dis-

jointed thoughts, images, and chatter of an unenjoyable eve-
ning consisting of dinner among strangers groping to make
conversation with "the poet" and a later visit to a cheap night-
club in the squalid town, William again encounters the sleep-
ing figure as he crosses the bridge back into America. This
time, while deeply immersed in the process of making poetry,
despite himself, out of the banality of his experience, Williams
sees the "egg-shaped" Indian anew:

> There it sat
> in the projecting angle of the bridge flange
> as I stood aghast and looked at it—
> in the half-light: shapeless or rather returned
> to its original shape, armless, legless,
> headless, packed like the pit of a fruit into
> that obscene corner—or
> a fish to swim against the stream—or
> a child in the womb prepared to imitate life,
> warding its life against
> a birth of awful promise.

The sleeping Indian becomes a symbol for life itself. And si-
multaneously it represents the incipient material of poetry, pro-
tected and drawn into life by the music, which is associated in
the poem, as in Austin's "American Rhythm," with inner and
outer nature.:

> to place myself (in
> my nature) beside nature
>
> —to imitate
> nature (for to copy nature would be a
> shameful thing)

Poetry, identity, and the sense of the life force animating both
fuse in the close examination of the sleeping Indian. The image
leads Williams to reassert his shaken sense of self:

> I *am* a poet! I
> am. I am. I am a poet, I reaffirmed, ashamed.

Here, as in earlier works by Williams, Crane, and Lindsay,
the Indian, though not associated with the land per se, is a
symbol for a renewed sense of identity based on contact with
one's inner life and with the actualities of one's surroundings.

Lindsay's, Crane's, and Williams's symbolic Indians reveal that the need for intimacy with the American landscape as a means to American identity, which Austin had predicted would become a prime concern for modern poets, was indeed felt by others. As Williams exhorted in *In the American Grain:*

> The land! don't you feel it? Doesn't it make you want to lift dead Indians tenderly from their graves, to steal for them—as if it must be clinging to their corpses—some authenticity?[31]

Grave robbing might not be the most desirable means to the desired end of authenticity, though at times, particularly in the works of Lindsay, it might be an apt metaphor for the poet's efforts. Actually, Lindsay, Crane, and Williams all lacked firsthand contact with living Indians and all based their writing on an imaginative and symbolic revival of peoples who were alive for them primarily in spirit. But more important, these poets shared the intuition that intimacy with the land and its spirit was central to a new, expanded American consciousness and identity and that the Indian was somehow the key to this needed contact and consciousness. D. H. Lawrence, in his essay "Fenimore Cooper's Leatherstocking Novels," in effect summarized the implications of the issues of spirit and consciousness that Lindsay, Crane, and Williams attempted to address:

> The spirit can change. The white man's spirit can never become as the red man's spirit. It doesn't want to. But it can cease to be the opposite and the negative of the red man's spirit. It can open out a new great area of consciousness, in which there is room for the red spirit too.
>
> To open out a new wide area of consciousness means to slough the old consciousness. The old consciousness has become a tight-fitting prison to us, in which we are going rotten.[32]

Other writers of the period, such as Lew Sarett and John G. Neihardt, sought to cut through prevailing stereotypes by bringing forward relatively literal examples of this Native American consciousness based on an actual contact with the Indian that Lindsay, Crane, and William lacked.

# ♦ 3 Translating Indian Consciousness: Lew Sarett and John G. Neihardt ♦

You might say, if these men were so intelligent, why didn't they progress as we do? The answer would be that they did not have the concept of progress that we have: bigger and better all the time. Their desire was to make a perfect adaptation to their environment and to the Great Spirit. I would call it the "Higher Piety." They wanted to live in harmony with all other living things. They even called the buffalo their relatives—all living things were relatives. . . . This is the idea: the holy spirit that the good grass gives to animals, and the animals to men—(men eat animals) and give back into the grass again . . . it's a cycle of life going around and it's holy.

John G. Neihardt, *Epic America* lecture, 1963

William Carlos Williams, Hart Crane, Vachel Lindsay, and D. H. Lawrence tuned their individual imaginations to interpret the Indian as a symbol of a renewed American consciousness and identity based on a harmonious relationship with the land. Their work closely followed the first wave of translations of Indian literature by American poets, but there is little evidence that it was directly influenced by those translations. Their work was, after all, a different kind of translation, more responsive to each writer's sense of the disturbed condition of the contemporary American psyche than to actual knowledge of Indian literature and cultures. These writers' work did, however, dovetail with Mary Austin's prophecy that modern American poets must somehow strive for a relationship with the spirit of place so elusive in the literature of our past. Meanwhile, during this same period of the 1920s, other poets who were less self-conscious about their psychological motivations than Williams, Crane, Lindsay, and Lawrence were befriending Indian people and drawing on their firsthand knowledge to portray "Native American consciousness" directly in their work. This work paralleled that of the first wave of translators, for it depended on intimate knowledge of living Indians. It extended the emphasis, implicit or explicit in the work of all the writers discussed thus far, on Indian consciousness as an important alternative model for modern Americans, by portraying that consciousness in its living human and historical contexts and thereby further defining it. It is thus discussed here as still another mode of interpreting the Indian.

## Lew Sarett

Two of the more popular poets at work in this fashion in the twenties were Lew Sarett and John G. Neihardt. Sarett's many Indian-related poems were published widely in the leading literary journals of the day, including *Poetry, A Magazine of Verse,* beginning around 1915, and later were collected in the volumes *Many, Many Moons* (1920), *The Box of God* (1922), and *Slow Smoke* (1925). Some of the poems, especially those found in the "Red Gods" section of *The Box of God,* are closely related to the work of the translators in that they attempt to portray Indian ceremonialism. Sarett's attempts to bring this ceremonialism across to readers of English were even freer and less literal than those of his predecessors. He wrote that,

> Obviously, a literal translation or a transcription of an Indian song or ceremony is inadequate. Few words may be uttered in the course of a medicine-dance lasting an hour; nevertheless, the event will be highly significant to those who comprehend the philosophy, the religion, and the psychology of the Indian, the spirit of the music of his symbols, of his pantomime and his dancing.[1]

Sarett paid little attention to the literal verbal content of the ceremonies he worked with, writing impressionistic original poems rather than translations. In these he tried

> to capture and to communicate something of the poetic beauty and the spiritual significance of Indian ceremonies . . . as they are revealed to one whose experience of Indian life in its setting of mountains and forest make him particularly sensitive to Indian thought and feeling.

Despite his confidence in his own particular sensitivity, these demands proved more than Sarett could master. The necessity to simplify and synthesize the complexities of an Indian ceremony into an English poem, especially without the Indian verbal poetry to use as a starting point, too often resulted in Sarett's falling back on a simplistic, cliché-ridden image of the Indian, which defeated his intent. In the "Thunderdrums" section of *The Box of God,* for instance, in which Sarett tried in a series of six poems to portray several "dance pantomime" solos in a war dance, we are given little sense of each dance's poetic imagery, visual spectacle, or spiritual depth. Instead we are given, with strikingly few visual images to stimulate our imaginations, the supposed consciousness of the Indian dancer. Unfortunately, each poem's "voice" is unconvincing. In "Iron Wind Dances," quoted below, for instance, the voice is that of a cardboard "bloodthirsty savage," more consistent with "the metaphysics of Indian hating" satirized by Herman Melville than the Winnebago metaphysics of warfare:

Over and under
The shaking sky,
The war-drums thunder
When I dance by!—
Ho! a warrior proud,
I dance on a cloud,
For my axe shall feel
The enemy reel;
My heart shall thrill
To a bloody kill,—
Ten Sioux dead
Split open of head! (p.57)

The bad poetry of the cliché image is compounded by the straining rhymes and jerky rhythms. The inverted syntax and contorted English used to force rhymes and the deadening predictability of the rhymes Sarett forced are appalling, coming as they do after Pound, Williams, Lawrence, and Eliot had fought against such papier-mâché statuary for a decade and more. It's as if by straining to fit the Indian into the old poetic mold of rhymed regularity, Sarett had distorted him into the oldest, tritest image of himself. Poems like these may have worked slightly better on the performance circuit, where Sarett regularly toured with Carl Sandburg, accompanying himself on a tomtom, but they are woefully inadequate and transparent on the printed page. "Thunderdrums" fails to explore two potentially interesting avenues with which Sarett was, in all likelihood, familiar: the Indian dancer's human individuality, and his irony-laden historical situation as a twentieth-century Indian trying to reclaim something of his own past. These perspectives, curiously absent from Sarett's attempts at poems "translating" Indian ceremonialism, are what give a few of his other Indian poems their unique authority.

While the ceremonial poems too often reinforce existing stereotypes, Sarett intended his Indian poetry to have the opposite effect. Toward this end of ultimate accuracy, he often wrote poems based on actual examples of council oratory with which he was familiar. In these, he saw himself as correcting an American literary tradition that tended to distort true Indian speech patterns with the result that "the few examples of

Indian oratory in the English language are more white than Indian." He complained that

> The Indian has been made too completely ideal and romantic; the poetry of his speech, its naivete and simplicity, its humor both broad and subtle, and its crude wild beauty— these have been smothered and lost in rhetorical elegance. (p. 84)

Sarett's distrust of the literate and literary translations of Indian speeches was based not on any knowledge of Native American language, but on his experience listening to "the broken pidgin-English dialect that a not-too-civilized mixed-blood interpreter would use." Following on his premise that "poetic beauty, sometimes simple and stark but very real, enfolds all the modes of [Indian] expression" (p. 85), he sought to translate the "crude wild beauty" of this dialect. As the following passage from "Medals and Holes" reveals, these poems did avoid "the smooth and rhetorically precise language of the white man." From a contemporary perspective, however, their dialect tends to reinforce unfortunate stereotypes by inadvertently anticipating the speech patterns of the countless Hollywood Indians who began to appear a decade later in the films of the thirties:

> Me—Yellow Otter,
> I'm going to mak'um big talk, 'Spector Jone' . . .
> Clothes no good! Got-um holes in legs—plenty big holes
> Wit' much clot' around; and too much buttons off,
> Gov'ment clothes she's coming every two year—
> Long tam between, too much—wit too much holes. (p. 63)

Despite the unfortunate associations of the dialect, the poem moves in a distinctly different direction from the symbolic interpretations of the Indian attempted by Lindsay, Crane, and Williams: toward the humanization of the "noble savage." We sense Yellow Otter more as a particular person in a particular situation than as a literary and historical abstraction. Though his English is crude, he is capable of rhetorical sophistication of a sort, exploiting an ironic tension between the golden medal awarded him in Washington and the broken promises symbolized by the holes in his clothing. He advises the inspector to deliver this message to the President:

Tell-um holes in pants now big, plenty big—
Bigger than golden medal on chest! (p.65)

Beneath the speaker's obvious humor, we can sense his pride, pathos, and bitterness. He comes off as a relatively complex, unidealized human being. Unlike the Indians created by many American poets, Sarett's are often portrayed as existing within a contemporary reality and comprise many types. They can be admirable wise men, devoted mothers, clowns, beggars, drunkards, or fools. Usually, despite being unlettered, they are keenly aware of the tragic and demeaning position in which history has placed them. Nevertheless, in his best poems, they reveal an inspiring humanity and a nobility through their expression of emotion, be it a deeply felt pain, a bittersweet laughter, or a mixture of both.

Sarett's best-known and most admired poem was the title poem of *The Box of God*. It is a long narrative, written from the point of view of a white man, recalling the conversion and subsequent death of an Indian friend. The poem is a moving attack on the missionary activity of the Christian clergy among Indian peoples, which Sarett portrays as a method of taming, controlling, and ultimately killing the red man and the spiritual principles he has traditionally lived by:

O high-flying eagle
Whose soul, wheeling among the sinuous winds,
Has known the molten glory of the sun,
The utter calm of dusk, and in the evening
The lullabies of moonlit mountain waters!—
The black priests locked you in their House of God,
Behind great gates swung tight against the frightened
Quivering aspens, whispering perturbed in council,
And muttering as they tapped with timid fists
Upon the doors and strove to follow you
And hold you; tight against the uneasy winds
Wailing among the balsams, fumbling upon
The latch with fretful fingers; tight against
The crowding stars who pressed their troubled faces
Against the windows. In honest faith and zeal,
The black robes put you in a box of God,
To swell the broken chorus of amens
And hallelujahs; to flutter against the door,
Crippled of pinion, bruised of head; to beat

With futile flying against the gilded bars;
To drop, to dream a little, and to die. (p.8)

The poem reveals, often by indirection, important aspects of
Indian consciousness. The Native American identification with
nature is suggested both by the image of the caged eagle (the
eagle being, as Barnes had discovered, a pan-tribal symbol of
communication with the Great-Spirit) and by what Sarett im-
plies is the locking-out of nature from the church, though na-
ture tries to enter in the person of the "frightened quivering
aspens," "uneasy winds," and the "troubled faces" of the stars
pressing against the windows. Inside, we are shown the sti-
fled spirituality of the Indian, forced "to swell the broken cho-
rus of amens and hallelujahs" of the white man's faith, while
being locked in and unable to know the potentially revelatory,
surrounding elements of nature.

The "box of God" itself is one of Sarett's best images. It
speaks to us on a literal, architectural level describing a physical
church. But, simultaneously, "box" is the accurate and apt
term for the spiritual jail the church represents to the impris-
oned Indian. More indirectly, it suggests something alien to
the Indian, something unnatural and antinatural; its rectangu-
larity may make us sense the Native American's affinity for
its opposite, the circle, a more organic form reflected in the
cyclical processes of nature and time.[2]

Sarett's attempts at rendering particular details of Indian
thought, speech, and values are at least a step toward a creative
celebration of Indian consciousness in the early twentieth
century. While his work is uneven in quality and is at best
mediocre, Sarett is one of the first twentieth-century poets to
try setting the Indian in the context of his contemporary reality
and thereby bringing him back down to earth, placing the
Native American consciousness idealized by many back in
human perspective. Sarett's work fails to achieve lasting sig-
nificance as poetry, however, because, among other reasons,
Sarett failed to find an appropriate poetic form to contain and
convey his often rich perceptions. Other poets in the century
discovered that bringing Indian consciousness effectively into
poetry required a new poetic style. Sarett chose to use the dead
poetic idiom and syntax that Pound had already dissected. He

took the popular route, which required old forms so much better used by Service and Kipling. He failed to realize that working with a new area of understanding required a new poetic style. The old bottles would hold only stale wine or would turn the new wine stale.

## John G. Neihardt

In a December 28, 1928, letter, Sarett wrote to John G. Neihardt, "You and I are working in the same field, America, her wild earth, her primitive people, her heroic story."[3] Though Sarett's work never approached the epic sweep to which this comment shows us he aspired, the two men did have much in common. Both were midwesterners whose writing reflected a love for their region. Both spent a great deal of time among Indian people, whose history, consciousness, and concerns dominated their work. Both avoided the Cooperesque *idea* of the Indian and instead portrayed particular human beings in particular human circumstances. As Neihardt wrote to his friend and biographer, Julian T. House:

> I am not interested in *Indians* as *Indians*—only as people in a particular situation. Human nature in the grip of fate— not Indian nature as curiosity—interests me. And their poetry interests me because it is human and poetry.[4]

Despite these general similarities between him and Sarett, Neihardt is by far the more important writer. His work has a greater historical breadth and spiritual depth than Sarett's. His masterpiece, *Black Elk Speaks* (1932), which has been called "the only religious classic of the twentieth century,"[5] is still one of the best presentations of Indian life, history, and consciousness available in our literature.

Neihardt's first contact with Indian peoples occurred in 1900, when his family moved to Bancroft, Nebraska, on the edge of the Omaha reservation, and he went to work for a local merchant who did most of his trade with the Indians. Government policy of the time had released heirship lands on the reservation for sale to the highest bidder and, as Neihardt recalled it, "a rank money smell was abroad in the land, and the money-hungry white sons of civilization flocked about the reservation like buzzards around a rotting carcass."[6] The depressing quality of reservation life coupled with the get-rich-quick atmosphere surrounding it served to provide an introduction to Native Americans that would upset any idealistic notions. Neihardt observed

> that my first acquaintance with the Omaha gave me a conception of that mythical abstraction, the "American Indian," very different from the "noble red man" of the romantic sentimentalist. Reservation Indians, as I first saw them with no historical perspective and out of cultural context, seemed as little noble as they were red. It was two or three years before I came to know and respect the Omaha as an ancient people with a rich culture that was dying out with the old, unreconstructed longhairs to be remembered only as a matter of curious interest.[7]

Following his own "curious interest," Neihardt befriended many of his Omaha neighbors, including some of the old "longhairs." Gradually they took Neihardt under their wing, shared ancient stories with him, and eventually honored him by giving him the Omaha name *Tae-Nuga-Zhinga* ("Little Bull Buffalo") because of his compact, muscular physique. Many of the tales Neihardt heard during his years among the Omaha he rewrote as short stories that he began to publish in national magazines. Eventually these stories were collected in *The Lonesome Trail* (1907) and *Indian Tales and Others* (1926).

Doubtless Neihardt's intimacy with the Omaha as a young man had a profound effect on his career and outlook. Looking back on his long life as a writer in his autobiography, *Patterns and Coincidences* (1978), Neihardt cited praise lavished upon his stories by the brilliant Susan LaFlesche Picotte, the first American Indian woman to earn an M.D. degree, as the most meaningful of the many honors bestowed on his work. Picotte told him that his "were the only Indians in literature from Cooper to Remington that had not been offensive to her, adding that she could not understand how a white man could represent the Indian idiom so perfectly in the English language.[8] Neihardt's skill in these areas was striking. It reached even higher levels of achievement in later work such as *Black Elk Speaks* and in the Indian books of his epic poem, *The Cycle of the West* (*The Song of the Indian Wars*, 1925; and *The Song of the Messiah*, 1935).

Among the awards that Neihardt received during his long career was the poet laureateship of Nebraska in 1921, the first such honor given an American poet by a state. Ironically, the legislators awarded the laureateship on the basis of the first two "Mountain Men" books of *The Cycle of the West* and the avowed patriotic intent of the entire project. Neihardt did initiate the epic with the intent of celebrating the indomitable human qualities that facilitated the settling of the West and, more broadly, of celebrating this settlement as the culmination of a long historical process involving the persistent westward movement of the white race. As Neihardt's research deepened, however, and he began work on the Indian books, his outlook changed. The *Cycle* in its complete form comprised five books written over thirty years and was more a celebration of Native American spirituality and values than of white indomitability. The first turnings in this shift toward alternative values are evident even in the early Mountain Men books. There we see the courage and resourcefulness of the protagonists being overshadowed by the disturbing passions of jealousy, violence, and greed that move them to destroy each other and themselves. Neihardt took advantage of the occasion of the laureateship award ceremony to deliver a stinging address condemning American individualism and materialism as destructive of the important lessons of democracy, which he took to be essentially cooperative and spiritual.

Neihardt's affinity with Indian peoples and their values was based on two essentially intertwined qualities: a personal mysticism derived from his own visionary experiences, and an intimate love of the land. Like Austin, he had had a spiritual experience as a young child that stayed vividly with him throughout his life. At the age of six he stood on a bluff overlooking the Missouri River during flood stage and found himself profoundly moved by his "first wee glimpse into the infinite."[9] Throughout his life, Neihardt mystically identified with his "Titan brother," the Missouri, and his life's work can be seen as a poetic history of the region it traverses. He had many similar mystical flashes throughout his life, leading him to the belief that such experiences represented *the* central fact of life, uniting all humanity and spurring human development. He observed that the capacity for mystical experience is common to the human species. I believe that it is because that is true that man has become as human as he is. . . . all our higher values grow out of mystical experience.

Neihardt also believed that the knowledge found at the heart of the mystical experience was universal:

> The hallmark of the genuine mystical experience is evident in its applicability to normal human experience. Although what you bring back from the mystical experience depends on what you are, there are certain universal constraints. You should be more kind, more loving, and you should be able to see all things as part of a universal being.[10]

In Black Elk, Neihardt found a man who had had the experience and was living the teaching.

When he met Black Elk in 1930, Neihardt was a writer of mystical temperament who had for thirty of his forty-nine years been on intimate terms with Indians through personal friendships, scholarly investigation, and attempts to interpret their history, stories, and thought in his writing. What I now offer is a close examination of the collaboration between the two men, based largely on a study of the transcript of their conversations in the spring of 1931 from which *Black Elk Speaks* was adapted. I try particularly to see how Neihardt succeeded where Sarett and others had failed—that is, how he provided a successful translation and interpretation of Indian consciousness into English. Who Neihardt was and what he had done prior to their meeting were certainly important factors, and so also were the initiative and direction given by Black Elk from the very beginning, as well as the spiritual affinity that quickly developed between the two men. Much was contributed also by Black Elk in conversations, quite apart from the formal interviews for the book. These contributions, often made simply through the old man's "mood and manner" or through his personal familial kindness toward Neihardt and his children, as well as through formal ceremonies in which they were included, importantly influenced, I believe, the decisions that the poet made in editing the raw transcriptions into the finished *Black Elk Speaks*. They are therefore crucial to Neihardt's interpretation of the message at the heart of Black Elk's complex vision. I attempt to reveal the nature of these decisions through a description of Neihardt's meetings with Black Elk in 1930 and 1931, based on the poet's subsequent testimony and on the testimony of the transcripts. What I offer here is essentially a comparison of key passages as they appear first in Neihardt's original interview-transcript and then as they appear in the printed text of Black Elk Speaks.

Ironically, *Black Elk Speaks* is a book that Neihardt did not anticipate writing. He met Black Elk in the summer of 1930 while researching *The Song of the Messiah,* the book of *The Cycle of the West* that was to deal with the Ghost Dance religious movement among the Plains Indians in the late nineteenth century. He was looking for Indians willing and able to give him a firsthand account of what took place during this turbulent period. An Indian agent on the Pine Ridge reservation who was a friend of Neihardt steered him to Black Elk, then a nearly blind old man living by himself in a shack near the tiny town of Manderson, South Dakota. Black Elk was regarded as an eccentric and as "something of a preacher," but it was said that he had been active among the Oglala Sioux as a *wicasha wakan* or holy man during the time of the Ghost Dance movement.

Neihardt went to see Black Elk, bringing along with him his son Sigurd, a Sioux interpreter named Flying Hawk, and a pocketful of cigarettes to offer as gifts. Although Black Elk had refused to speak with a woman reporter the week before, he greeted these visitors so cordially that all three had the strong impression that the old man had been expecting them. Nevertheless, Black Elk was unresponsive to Neihardt's attempts to get him to talk about the good old days on the plains or about the Ghost Dance. Instead, he broke the long silences in which the men sat smoking and sizing one another up with oblique and intriguing references to a sacred vision he had had years before. After a particularly long silence, Black Elk suddenly gestured toward Neihardt and announced:

> As I sit here I can feel in this man beside me a strong desire to know things of the Other World. He has been sent to learn what I know, and I will teach him.[11]

Neihardt was stunned. He felt as though Black Elk had seen right through him. "He was right," he observed. "I certainly was interested in learning the secrets of the Other World."[12] Black Elk said little more at this first meeting about his visions and teaching, for such sacred material could be passed on only after proper spiritual preparations had been made. But initial affinity had been established between the two men, and Black Elk proceeded to reinforce it. He presented Neihardt with a rawhide-thong necklace on which a star, an eagle feather, and a piece of buffalo wool were suspended. The morning star, Black Elk explained, represented wisdom: "Who sees the Morning Star shall see more, for he shall be wise." The eagle feather represented the protection of the Great Spirit, and the hide, from the animal that had provided the Sioux with food, clothing, and shelter, represented all the good things of the world. Through these gifts Black Elk was drawing Neihardt closer to him and to his way of seeing the world.

Black Elk went on to tell Neihardt: "I am just a common man, but I have a gift of vision which has been hereditary in my family, and I must tell you of my people before I tell you of my life so that you may trust me." He then proceeded to recount his family lineage—"much as an old Homeric hero used to do," as Neihardt wrote to his friend and biographer, Julius T. House. Neihardt reported the eerie sensation that, "Very often it seemed as though I, myself, were telling the things he told me, but I got something from him I cannot describe." Toward the end of the five-hour visit, arrangements were made for Neihardt to return the following spring to receive Black Elk's sacred teachings. Soon after, he wrote House enthusiastically of his plans to interrupt his work on *The Cycle of the West* "to write the complete life of Black Elk, for it would be a revelation of the Indian consciousness from the depths."[13]

Thus began the collaboration between the Oglala Sioux holy man Black Elk and the poet John G. Neihardt that resulted in *Black Elk Speaks*. The project was agreed upon by both men, and in a very real sense it had been initiated by Black Elk himself when he proposed to teach Neihardt, whom he knew to be a writer, "the secrets of the Other World." The resulting book covers an important period in Black Elk's life and the collective life of his people, the Sioux. It begins at the time of Black Elk's Great Vision, which came to him as a young child while he lay unconscious and deathly ill, sometime in the 1860s. The story takes us through the 1870s—a period dominated by warfare with the whites—including the exhilarating victory over Custer at Little Big Horn in 1876 and the tribe's ultimate defeat by the end of the decade—and on through the 1880s, a depressing period for the Sioux. It describes the sudden dependency and confinement of reservation life with its resulting self-doubt and soul-searching. We are told how Black Elk and others toured with Buffalo_Bill's Wild West Show to try to discover the secret of the white man's mysterious power. We are shown the sudden resurgence of spiritual energy and cultural unity that accompanied the rise of the Ghost Dance movement and then the final crushing defeat at Wounded Knee in 1890. In short, this thirty-five-year span takes us over the heights and depths of Sioux history as lived by Black Elk while he struggled with the special burden and responsibility vested in him by his vision.

The vision itself can be said to be the real subject of the book. For Black Elk, it is all that gives his life importance. The vision does not compel him to renounce a real world; in his vision the spiritual and material worlds are inseparable. Black Elk's vision prophetically projects the world events that follow it, flashing onto the page the story of Sioux cultural unity and strength declining gradually into disunity and weakness. In his vision Black Elk is given special powers, in the form of gifts from the six grandfathers, with the implied responsibility for using these to stave off the impending tragedy he is shown, and the implied hope that somehow he will be able to restore "the broken hoop" and "flowering tree." Black Elk's struggle to understand this spiritual obligation parallels and intertwines with his people's struggle to walk the dark road from the Little Big Horn to Wounded Knee.

Despite the apocalyptic grandeur of this sacred vision, despite speaking for the holy man at the center of this book's events, Neihardt's triumphant achievement lies in keeping *Black Elk Speaks* on a movingly human level. We get to know Black Elk initially through what seem convincingly to be his own words. Neihardt did, in fact, follow closely the English translation of Black Elk's narrative, as recorded in a transcript prepared from the original interviews by his daughter Enid. Interestingly, however, a textual analysis by Sally McCluskey that compares the story of White Buffalo Woman as told by Black Elk in *Black Elk Speaks* and in *The Sacred Pipe* (1953), Joseph Epes Brown's narrative also drawn from conversations with Black Elk, finds the sentences in Neihardt's book to be more rhythmic, more dramatic, more concrete, simpler in syntax, and yet more apt to be so constructed as to rise to a climax.[14] If nothing else, this stylistic heightening represents a further tribute to Neihardt's ear for Indian idiom, even if it meant that, for the most part, he had the good sense to leave well enough alone.

We further sense Black Elk's full humanity in *Black Elk Speaks* by following him from childhood to manhood to old age, through periods of laughter and tears, joy and despair, anguish and anger, confusion and power. We see the shaman and healer as a complex individual, sharing our own feelings and weaknesses, overwhelmed and bewildered at times by the special burdens imposed by his power in the midst of historical and spiritual forces that are beyond him. *Black Elk Speaks,* a book of prose, is, ironically, Neihardt's greatest poetic achievement. It may prove to be, equally ironically, Black Elk's greatest healing ceremony. As literature, it is tragedy in the greatest sense—a moving human story of declining fortune and ultimate fall from power, but one with a transcendent vision that inspires and uplifts all those who read it with understanding.

The story of how Neihardt managed to write this book is interesting and instructive, for no white writer before or since has so effectively managed to reveal Native American consciousness and spirituality in such a moving and human way. Neihardt's previous experience with the Omaha, his writings, his historical research, his spiritual attitudes and experiences all prepared him to write *Black Elk Speaks*. Similarly, the spiritual affinity quickly established between the two men helped in the book's making, as did Black Elk's active and enthusiastic guidance and collaboration. But it was the nature of his collaboration—his being so clearly the holy man and teacher fitted to the task of teaching the vision imposed—that had the most immediate and profound effect.

The transcript of the interviews on which *Black Elk Speaks* is based reveals that the book is not, as is often assumed, simply a literal recording of Black Elk's story. Much is, apparently, drawn verbatim from the original translation of Black Elk's account, but Neihardt exercised important editorial choices in shaping the final book. As he related in a 1971 interview with Sally McCluskey:

> *Black Elk Speaks* is a work of art with two collaborators, the chief one being Black Elk. My function was both creative and editorial. I think he knew the kind of person I was when I came to see him—I am referring to the mystical strain in me and all my work. He said, "You have been sent so that I may teach you, and you recieve what I know. It was given to me for men and it is true and it is beautiful and soon I will be under the grass." And I think he knew I was the tool—no, the medium—he needed for what he wanted to get said. And my attitude to what he said to me is one of religious obligation.
>
> But it is absurd to suppose that the use of the first person singular is not a literary device, by which I mean that Black Elk did not sit and tell me in chronological order. At times considerable editing was necessary. The beginning and ending are mine; they are what he would have said had he been able. At times I changed a word, a sentence, sometimes created a paragraph. And the translation—or rather the transformation—of what was given me was expressed so that it could be understood by the whole world.[15]

Effectively to transform what Black Elk related "so that it could be understood by the whole world" required that Neihardt himself have a clear sense of what precisely needed to be understood—what, essentially, Black Elk's message actually was. As Neihardt wrote, "it was not the facts that mattered most"; rather, it was the transcendent teaching to be found in those facts of Black Elk's life, in the complex sequence of images that made up his vision, in "the mood and manner of the old man's narrative," and in the verbal and nonverbal ways in which Black Elk related to Neihardt and his two daughters during the spring of 1931 when the interviews were conducted.

When Neihardt and his daughters Enid and Hilda arrived

in April, they found that special preparations had been made for their visit. A tepee with sacred symbols painted on the outside had been set up for the Neihardts to live in and a circle of small pine trees had been transplanted to ring Black Elk's tiny cabin. A sacred environment had been created for the passing on of the sacred teachings. Black Elk was thoughtful of worldly comforts as well. He had bought a big brass bed so that on cold nights, when it was necessary to sleep in the shack, Neihardt's daughters would not have to join the men on the floor. In order for Neihardt and his daughters to receive the sacred teachings, not normally intended for profane ears, it was necessary for Black Elk to adopt them formally. A ceremony and feast were conducted for this purpose during the course of which Black Elk gave Neihardt the large, shield-like symbol of the sacred hoop of the world and a sacred pipe that had been passed down from father to son for several generations within his family. This gift symbolized Black Elk's adoption of Neihardt as a spiritual son. Neihardt received an Oglala name that he prized for the rest of his life: *Peyta-Wigimou-Ge* ("Flaming Rainbow"), after one of the most vivid images in Black Elk's vision.

The conversations began the next day and lasted for several weeks. Their dynamics tended to unite the two families further. His natural son, Ben Black Elk, interpreted Black Elk's narrative and Neihardt's questions, while Enid Neihardt took stenographic notes. After the final interview had been completed, Black Elk performed a ceremony in which he lined up with Ben on his right to represent his own people and their succeeding generations and with Neihardt and his daughters on his left to represent the succeeding generations of whites and then offered a long prayer requesting success for the book and its ultimate goal of restoring the sacred hoop to the world. By this time, Black Elk saw the proposed book as the reason that Neihardt had been sent to him by the spirits. He recognized, as he had not decades earlier, that his vision might have been intended not just for his people, but for all people. He told Neihardt:

> The more I talk about these things the more I think of
> old times and it makes me sad, but I hope that we can

make the tree bloom for your children and for mine. We know each other now, and from now on we will be like relatives, and we have been that so far, but we will think of that deeply and set that remembrance down deep in our hearts; not just thinly but deeply in our hearts it should be marked. From here we can see the Black Hills and the high peaks to which I was taken to see the whole world and the good things; and when I think of that, it was hopeless, it seems, before I saw you, but here you came. Somehow the spirits made you come to revive that tree that never bloomed.[16]

Black Elk's mood, manner, ceremonies, and remarks all underscored for Neihardt that the central messsage implicit in his story was "the brotherhood of man and the unity and holiness of all life."[17]

The editorial decisions that Neihardt made were primarily intended, in a spirit of "religious obligation," to reinforce that main theme. Neihardt created several key passages and deleted several powerful but distracting sections of the vision to focus better this teaching of what Black Elk called "the great circle of relatedness which is the power of the world." The most significant of Neihardt's created additions is found in the "Great Vision" chapter and represents one of the most frequently quoted passages in the book. It occurs toward the end of the visionary sequence, after the fourth and final ascent in which Black Elk sees himself restoring his fractured and fragmented nation to health with the aid of a sacred healing herb of power. Following this vision, Black Elk flies on horseback to the top of a great mountain:

I looked ahead and saw the mountains there with rocks and forests on them, and from the mountains flashed all colors upward to the heavens. Then I was on the highest mountain of them all, and round about beneath me was the whole hoop of the world. And while I stood there I saw more than I can tell and understood more than I saw; for I was seeing in a sacred manner the shapes of all things in the spirit, and the shapes of all shapes as they must live together as one being. And I saw that the sacred hoop of my people was one of many hoops that made one circle, wide as daylight and as starlight, and in the center grew one mighty flowering tree to shelter all the children of one mother and one father. And I saw that it was holy.[18]

Prior to this point in the Great Vision account, Neihardt had followed Black Elk's original description, as recorded by Enid, almost verbatim. But the transcribed speech that corresponds to this passage is much more prosaic:

As [I] looked [I] could see the great mountains with rocks and forests on them. I could see all colors of light flashing out of the mountains toward the four quarters. Then [the grandfathers] took me on top of a high mountain where I could see all over the earth.[19]

Neihardt evidently created this vision of "one of many hoops that made one circle" himself. Probably he did so for both poetic and thematic reasons. Neihardt chose this climactic moment in the account of the Great Vision to expand and develop Black Elk's recurrent imagery of the sacred hoop or circle in order to crystalize for the reader the universal significance of the book's central teaching.[20]

Literarily, this creation by Neihardt proves a brilliant stroke, but Neihardt did not exactly pluck this vision out of the air. Black Elk had looked "all over the earth," and in an aside during the initial interviews he had told Neihardt, "the sacred hoop means the continents of the world and the people shall stand as one."[21] The passage illustrates the kind of poetic license that Neihardt occasionally employed. When he made changes, Neihardt almost always used or developed Black Elk's imagery or thought rather then creating something totally new. The beginning and ending passages that Neihardt added, for instance, largely serve the literary need for an overview, and these likewise depend on the pervasive tree-and-hoop imagery and on comments attributed to Black Elk elsewhere in the transcript. Unlike most other poets who took liberties in translating Indian materials, Neihardt's changes tend to read like extensions of his informant's consciousness, reflecting less the white writer's independent and impressionistic judgment than a hard-earned mutual understanding and trust. Often, Neihardt relates, reaching this understanding proved "a grueling and difficult task requiring much patient effort and careful questioning of the interpreter."[22] The degree of mutual commitment to the project and the spiritual affinity that quickly developed between the two men appear to be the main sources of the unique personal rapport that determined the ultimate success of the translation.

Just as he created, Neihardt likewise deleted several powerful sequences of Black Elk's vision. These omissions from *Black Elk Speaks,* never before discussed in the literary, anthropological, or psychological literature touching on the book, change the overall pattern and tone of the vision significantly—a fact that may shock religious, anthropological, or ethical purists. They are justifiable, however, if we accept the premise that is supported, I believe, in comments quoted earlier and attributed to both Neihardt and Black Elk in the transcript, that the book's purpose was to reveal not the original vision but the teaching of the Black Elk of 1930. Essentially, Neihardt's deletions tone down the militaristic and violent content of the vision, thereby enhancing the pacific message of unity.

The first change is small but significant. Neihardt described thus the fifth grandfather encountered by Black Elk during his Great Vision:

> He stretched his arms and turned into a spotted eagle hovering. "Behold, he said, "all the wings of the air shall come to you, and they and the wind and the stars shall be like relatives. You shall go across the earth with my power." Then the eagle soared above my head and fluttered there; and suddenly the sky was full of friendly wings, all coming toward me.[23]

The implication left here is that the power of this grandfather is associated with the unity between man and the beings of the sky, and in Black Elk's original account, he does say in less ornate style that "things in the sky shall be like relatives." The original description continued, however, defining this grandfather's power quite differently:

> They shall take you across the earth with my power. Your grandfather shall attack an enemy and be unable to de-

stroy him, but you will have the power to destroy. You shall go with courage. That is all.[24]

In Black Elk's original account the vision of unity, which Neihardt used, is linked with the warlike power to destroy, which he omits.

The second deletion is even more important, for it occurs during the fourth ascent, prior to another vision of the unity and holiness of life included by Neihardt. In Neihardt's version, Black Elk is shown his entire nation starving and suffering and fighting continually. He is given a song of power and a sacred herb that he uses to heal his scrawny, starving horse. A vision of horses follows and then a vision of four virgins. The virgins, carrying the sacred gifts of the wooden cup of water, the white wing, the pipe, and the sacred hoop dance amid beautiful, healthy horses:

> The virgins danced, and all the circled horses. The leaves on the tree, the grasses on the hills and in the valleys, the waters in the creeks and in the rivers, and the lakes, the four-legged and the two-legged and the wings of the air— all danced together to the music of the stallion's song.[25]

A more concise version of this vision of the unity and holiness of living things is found in Black Elk's original account. It is preceded there, however, by a long description of a vision that Black Elk has of himself attacking and defeating an enemy:

> The horse's tail was lightning and the flames were coming out of his horse's nose. As I went I could see nothing but I could only hear the thunder and lightning and of course I could see the flames. All the rest of the troops went around this enemy. A spirit said: "Eagle Wing Stretches, take courage, your turn has come." We got ready and started down on the cloud on our bay horses. One Side and I were coming down together. I could see the lightning coming off my arrows as I descended. Just as we were about to hit the earth, I struck something. I could hear thunder rolling and everyone cheered for me, saying: "Unhee!" (Kill!). . . . I made a swoop again on the west side of the enemy, whatever it was, and when I

killed it, I looked at it and it was a dog, which had a very funny color. One side of him was white and the other side was black. Each one of them struck the dog (couped), meaning all had a hand in killing it. (This meant that when you go to war you should kill your enemy like a dog.)[26]

As in the account of the fifth grandfather, Neihardt retained the vision of unity and holiness while dropping the militaristic vision linked to it.

The third and most striking omission occurs after the fourth ascent and the mountaintop vision that climaxes the "Great Vision" chapter. Neihardt's account follows Black Elk from the mountaintop to "the center of the world" where the grandfathers give him the daybreak-star herb, symbolic of his power to heal as a medicine man. In Black Elk's original account, however, he describes being given not one, but two gifts: the healing daybreak-star and a terrifying, destructive, "war herb":

> I looked down upon the earth and saw a flame which looked to be a man and I couldn't make it out quite. I heard all around voices of moaning and woe. It was sad on earth. I felt uneasy and I trembled. We went on the north side of this flaming man. I saw that the flame really was a man now. They showed me the bad in the form of a man who was all in black and lightning flashes going all over his body when he moved. He had horns. All around the animals and everything were dying and they were all crying. . . . They said: "Behold him. Someday you shall depend upon him. There will be a dispute all over the universe." As they said this the man transformed into a gopher and it stood up on its hind legs and turned around. Then this gopher transformed into a herb. This was the most powerful herb of all that I had gotten. It could be used in war and could destroy a nation.[27]

The grandfathers give this "most powerful herb of all" to Black Elk, prophesying that "there will come a time of dispute of nations when you will defend your nation with this herb." The devastating destructive power of this war herb terrifies Black Elk. He does not want the awesome responsibility of having to use it, going on at some length in his original account to Neihardt about the power of this herb and his fear of it. Even in 1931, the memory of this herb seems vivid to him, its terror immediate. It reminds the modern reader of a nuclear weapon, so awesome does it seem to Black Elk.[28] To Black Elk, the "soldier weed" is an ever-present force of evil for which he feels somehow responsible:

> If you touch this herb it will kill you at once. Nothing grows near it because it is killed immediately if it does. . . . This herb is in the Black Hills. Every animal that near it dies. Around where it grows there are many skeletons always. This medicine belongs only to me—no one else knows what this herb looks like—and it looks like a little tree with crinkly leaves, reddish in color.[29]

At one place in his original account Black Elk says that he was not old enough when the time came to use this herb. Later, he seems to contradict himself, saying that he was intended to use it when he was thirty-seven years old, but that he worried so much over the harm it would do to innocent women and children that he forsook ever using it and instead joined the Catholic church. Neihardt, unfortunately, apparently never sought a clarification. In any case, the war herb is the only part of the vision that Black Elk himself seems to reject. "It was too terrible to use," he tells Neihardt, "and I am glad I did not use it." Later he indicates that he is at peace with himself about this decision: "Perhaps I would have been a chief if I had obeyed [and used the herb], but I am satisfied that I didn't become a chief."[30]

The deletion of the war-herb passage underscores the fact that Neihardt was more interested in the teachings of the man, Black Elk, who had had a Great Vision than in the literal content of the vision itself. He did not approach the writing of *Black Elk Speaks* with an anthropologist's absolute dedication to factual accuracy. Instead, he approached the collaboration as a poet, interested in images and in essences. He succeeded in telling, through the development of memorable imagery true to its original source, a moving human story that remains essentially Black Elk's. Neihardt's editorial decisions tended to reduce ambiguity and enhance the clarity and power of what he interpreted as Black Elk's essential teaching: "the brotherhood of man and the unity and holiness of all life."

Any controversy surrounding the poetic license employed by Neihardt in *Black Elk Speaks* is best put into perspective by these comments of the contemporary Sioux essayist Vine Deloria:

> Present debates center on the question of Neihardt's literary intrusions into Black Elk's system of beliefs and some scholars have said that the book reflects more of Neihardt than it does of Black Elk. It is, admittedly, difficult to discover if we are talking with Black Elk or John Neihardt, whether the vision is to be interpreted differently, and whether or not the positive emphasis which the book projects is not the optimism of two poets lost in the modern world and transforming drabness into an idealized world. Can it matter? The very nature of great religious teachings is that they encompass everyone who understands them and personalities become indistinguishable from the transcendent truth that is expressed. So let it be with *Black Elk Speaks*. That it speaks to us with simple and compelling language about an aspect of human experience and encourages us to emphasize the best that dwells within us is significant. Black Elk and John Neihardt would probably nod affirmatively to that statement and continue their conversation. It is good. It is enough.[31]

The transcendent truth that Deloria speaks of is attested by the national and international popularity of *Black Elk Speaks*.[32] Significantly, the book is highly regarded by contemporary Native Americans, including the Sioux. Deloria reports that for the contemporary generation of young Indians, *Black Elk Speaks* "has become a North American bible of all tribes. They look to it for spiritual guidance, for sociological identity, for political insight, and for affirmation of the continuing substance of tribal life."

*Black Elk Speaks* paints a movingly human picture of Indian consciousness. It goes far toward pinning down the Native American's holistic awareness that is implied and suggested by other American poets. Black Elk's humane values are posed implicitly by Neihardt as a challenging alternative to whites.

In the book we see Black Elk's magnanimity and sense of unity opposed to the selfish and competitive individualism he encounters in his associations with whites. We see underscored, through Black Elk's eyes, how the white society confines—confining the individual within himself, misfits in jails, Indians on reservations. Black Elk on the other hand, embodies the more open gesture of giving—the giving of food to the needy within the tribe, the giving of personal power to the people through ceremonialism and healing, the giving of the vision and its teaching to the world through *Black Elk Speaks*.[33] In other works, Neihardt also drew Native American characters who were not idealized but "real-ized," so to speak. The rival chiefs, counselors, and holy men we encounter in *Song of the Indian Wars* and *Song of the Messiah* are, for instance, capable of personal ambition, jealousy, excessive pride, and hatred; but inevitably even these characters subordinate their often selfish individual interests and passions to what is perceived as the collective interest of the tribe. The value of relatedness is an ever-present given of the Native American consciousness that Neihardt depicts.

Published in 1932, *Black Elk Speaks* was remaindered shortly after its appearance at the height of the depression. It was not until its publication in 1971 as a mass-market paperback, following the ninety-year-old Neihardt's appearance on Dick Cavett's television show, that the book began to achieve its remarkable popularity. It had been revived somewhat earlier in scholarly editions largely because of the interest of European anthropologists and psychologists, most notably Carl Jung. The book thus spans the two major twentieth-century periods of cycles of interest in Native American literature, appearing at the end of the flowering of the 1900–1920s and then again at the height of the Vietnam War–protest era. Its popularity has influenced the publication and republication of a spate of books dealing with white attempts to expand consciousness through contact with Native American shamans. These include Antonin Artaud's *The Peyote Dance* (1936), Allen Ginsberg and William Burroughs's *The Yage Letters* (1963), Carlos Castaneda's *The Teachings of Don Juan: A Yaqui Way of Knowledge* (1968) and its sequels, and Richard Erdoes's *Lame*

*Deer: Seeker of Visions* (1972). The prevalence and pervasive influence of such works reflect the commercial success of *Black Elk Speaks;* more important, they suggest that something is amiss and uneasy in the contemporary American psyche. These works and the general interest in Indian consciousness address, in Jerome Rothenberg's phrase, "the quest for unity in our time."[34]

# ◆ 4 Toward a New Poetry and a New Man: Charles Olson's Projective Verse ◆

Maximus, March 1961—2

> by the way into the woods

> Indian      otter
> "Lake"      ponds     orient

> show me     (exhibit
> myself)

Charles Olson, *Maximus Poems,* IV, V, VI

At this point, we make a chronological leap of sorts. We move from poets like Mary Austin, Vachel Lindsay, Hart Crane, John G. Neihardt, and William Carlos Williams—writers whose formative development took place at the turn of the century or shortly thereafter—to poets of the succeeding post–World War II generation—Charles Olson, Jerome Rothenberg, and Gary Snyder. For these poets, the main link to the preceding generation was Williams, whose experiments with imagism and organic, open-form poetry, as well as his preoccupation with "place" and with the development of a uniquely American language and literature, represented a starting point for their work. Olson, Rothenberg, and Snyder, in turn, represent the main links to the counterculture poets of the seventies.

In the first three chapters of this book, I have traced the first great wave of interest in the American Indians by twentieth-century poets, showing how it crested in the 1920s with the appearance of the earliest poetry anthologies and first major work of Native American critical theory, Austin's "The American Rhythm," which initially brought together the poetics of the Indian shaman and modern American poet; with Lindsay's, Crane's, and Williams's development of the Indian as a symbol for a new American identity based on a new relationship to place; and with more literal attempts to depict Indian consciousness by Sarett and Neihardt. I have indicated that these developments were related to a complex of cultural and historical factors, including the end of the Indian wars and the closing off of the frontier, the growing information available about Native Americans, the active search for a new American poetics, the widespread disillusionment with contemporary values following the end of World War I, and the rapid shift to an increasingly mechanized and urbanized American society. Such an atmosphere encouraged and nurtured the search for new values and roots.

The postwar period begins the second great literary surge of interest in the Indian, gathering its energy slowly in the wake of the war and the atom bomb until it exploded in the seventies as another war wound down in Southeast Asia. The work of the post–World War II poets discussed here embodies a revival and a further development of the concerns of their

101

predecessors for a new American poetry, a new relationship to place and nature, and new values and identity. Olson, Rothenberg, and Snyder each studied Indian cultures as a source of poetic renewal. They opposed to the white man's historical way of "regeneration through violence" the beginnings of a reorienting renewal through poetry and teaching—the Word, as it were—drawing on Native American among other sources for their inspiration. Two postwar anthologies—Margot Astrov's *The Winged Serpent* (1946) and A. Grove Day's *The Sky Clears* (1950)—helped turn these and other poets to the Indian.

Olson, Rothenberg, and Synder were among different groups of American poets in the fifties and sixties who were disillusioned with establishment concepts of literary and societal values. Olson as the chief force of the Black Mountain School, Snyder as the most prominent West Coast Beat, and Rothenberg at the center of the Deep Image poets in New York City all sought alternatives to the sedate and smug poetry of irony and disillusionment upheld by what they perceived as a rapidly aging New Criticism entrenched in the academies. At the same time they shared a cultural radicalism based on the sense that in the new nuclear age the American Dream had degenerated into a nightmare, that individualism and competition inevitably led to war, that mechanized and dehumanized modern man had so removed himself from nature that his own psychological, spiritual, and physical survival was imperiled, and that alternative ways of being and seeing must be found.

*Olson's "The Kingfishers" and the Backgrounds of Projective Verse*

Olson based his poetics on this postwar vision, and he studied Indian cultures as one possible source for alternatives. Not only did his projective verse aim to revolutionize American poetry, but, ultimately, it aimed to produce a new man. In his essay, "Projective Verse," which first appeared in the magazine *Poetry New York* in 1950, Olson articulated a technical and philosophical aesthetic for a "New American Poetry"[1]—an organic, free-verse poetry that drew heavily on the actual practice of predecessors like Pound, Williams, Cummings, Crane, and

Lawrence. "Projective Verse" proposed an open-form poetry with plenty of room for spontaneous expression rising out of the poet's intuitive faculties. Borrowing Williams's concept of "composition by field" (and its implied association with modern physics) and acknowledging the influence of E. E. Cummings's work, Olson emphasized the importance of *relationships* of sound, sense, and the visual typographic markers on the spatial field of the page. But more important, in "Projective Verse" Olson called for a new relationship between subject and object and between man and the nature around and within him.

Like Austin's "landscape line . . . formed by its own inner necessities," "Projective Verse" demanded a poetry intimately related to man's physical nature, an organic poetry not just of the mind but of the entire body. Lawrence and Williams had said much the same thing earlier. In 1920, Lawrence had called for "a poetry of the immediate present" based on "the sheer appreciation of the present moment, life surging into utterance at its very wellhead."[2] In 1936, Williams wrote that poetry must involve "the deeper, not 'lower' (in the usual silly sense) portions of the personality speaking, the middle brain, the nerves, the glands, the very muscles and bones of the body itself . . . the mysterious ebb and flow of the life process."[3] Olson developed these basic premises of organicism further than Lawrence and Williams by exploring both their practical applications in the poem and their implications for modern consciousness. Williams subsequently paid Olson the ultimate tribute in his *Autobiography* (1951) by titling one of its chapters "Projective Verse" and by including a lengthy section of Olson's original essay.[4]

Significantly, Olson was immersed in the study of American Indian cultures while he was writing "Projective Verse." From 1945 to 1954 he planned, researched, and wrote grant proposals for an epic poem to be called "Red, White, and Black."[5] Its strategy was to juxtapose stories, legends, and historical accounts to reflect the experience of the three races as they encountered the physical and spiritual reality of the American continent. For this project Olson studied Aztec, Pueblo, Plains, and Woodland cultures; explored linguistic research on Indian languages by Edward Sapir and Benjamin

Lee Whorf; examined the California gold rush and its effect on Indians;[6] the Cabeza de Vaca expedition; the experience of mixed bloods such as Jim Beckwith; and the geographical writings of Carl O. Sauer. In 1951 he spent six months living in Yucatán, Mexico, an experience that proved to be one of the most important of his life, as his close friend Robert Creeley recalled,[7] and as is evident in Olson's correspondence with Creeley published in *The Mayan Letters* (1953). Though "Red, White, and Black" was never completed, Olson's immersion in Indian studies had an important influence on his developing poetics and on his view of its implications for human consciousness as is reflected in "Projective Verse" and subsequent writings.

The earliest strong indication of Olson's sense of the importance of the Indian for American consciousness is found in one of his best poems, "The Kingfishers" (1949). "The Kingfishers" has been called by Guy Davenport "the most modern of American poems, the most energetically influential text of the last thirty-five years."[8] While this evaluation may be somewhat extravagant, the poem does forcefully announce an important theme for Olson and for a generation of later poets: the rejection of a dying Western civilization and the possibility for personal and cultural rebirth out of its ashes in a new form as kin of non-European peoples. This new form is embodied in "The Kingfishers" in the "new people" of the revolution in contemporary China and in images and echoes from the Native American past.

As Carol Kyle has pointed out, the essentially positive outlook of "The Kingfishers" reverses in theme and name the hopeless, desperate exhaustion pervading another poem about the decline of the West, T. S. Eliot's "The Waste Land" with its central image of a "fisher king." The kingfisher is a symbol, or, as Davenport called it, a "totem," running through Olson's long poem. As such, it functions in a traditionally Native American way. Among South American tribes, the kingfisher, which nests in the dead of winter during the period of the winter solstice and the turn of the new year, is, as Kyle wrote, "mythologically and ornithologically a symbol of regeneration." She observed that "The kingfisher tale is chanted . . .

to facilitate the entrance of the ancestors into the bodies of the dancers."[9] Olson's poem functions in an analogous fashion, calling American "poets to come" to partake of the ancestral spirits of their own place. Olson employed the kingfisher's underground "nest of excrement and decayed fish bones," out of which the young are born, as an apt image for his theme of renewal amid the "slime" of a decaying and dying culture.

"The Kingfishers" is a poetic meditation on the theme of change. Davenport wrote:

> the theme states that when our attentions change our culture changes. [Olson] uses the firm example of Mayan cultures, overgrown with jungles. The Mayan shift in attention was culturally determined: every fifty-two years they abandoned whole cities in which the temples were oriented toward the planet Venus, which edges its rising and setting around the ecliptic. The new city was literally a new way to look at a star (this is one meaning of "polis is eyes").[10]

The Mayan image runs throughout the poem as Olson juxtaposes example upon example reflecting various types of change—political, attitudinal, natural—building to a climactic passage in which he urges his readers to consider their own need to change by reconsidering their "whiteness":

> in the west, despite the apparent darkness (the whiteness
> which covers all) if you look, if you can bear, if you can
>                     long enough . . .
>
> and, considering the dryness of the place
>     the long absence of an adequate race
>
>     (of the two who first came, each a conquistador,
>                     one healed, the other
>     tore the eastern idols down, toppled
>     the temple walls, which, says the excuser
>     were black with human gore
>
> hear
> hear, where the dry blood talks
>     where the old appetite walks[11]

The passage demands that we "hear" the ancient voices of the continent. It suggests that we reexamine two conquistadors: the famous Cortez, who comes heroically down to us as the destroyer of the barbarous Aztec's temples; and, less acclaimed but more remarkable in the light of our present needs, Cabeza de Vaca, who, shipwrecked in the early sixteenth century among the Indians of the Gulf Coast, adapted to their customs and beliefs and discovered healing powers and other inner resources he had not known he possessed. Olson urges us to look beyond "the whiteness which covers all" to the spirit of the former Native American cultures and, like Cabeza de Vaca, to contact the primitiveness within ourselves.

In the poem's final section, its message becomes explicit: "I am no Greek," Olson announces, "And of course, no Roman." In place of blood link to the European tradition he proposes, in lines whose language recalls Pound,[12] the basing of kinship on kindship and choice:

> But I have my kin, if for no other reason than
> (as he said, next of kin) I commit myself, and
> given my freedom, I'd be a cad
> if I didn't . . . (p. 173)

Olson points himself and the reader—this time with phrasing echoing Rimbaud,[13] a poet who, unlike Pound, abandoned civilization for the primitiveness of jungle and desert—to the Native American past on the continent:

> if I have any taste
> it is only because I have interested myself
> in what was slain in the sun. (p. 173)

The poem ends by urging the reader to join Olson in searching for meaning and "next of kin" in the ruins of the continent beneath his feet, to "hunt among the stones." Life was to imitate art two years later when Olson journeyed to Yucatán to poke around in the Mayan ruins. Twenty years later, the prophetic nature of Olson's interest would seem even more projective as thousands of young, longhaired, headbanded, and beaded Americans assembled in Golden Gate Park in San

Francisco, California, for a "Human Be-In" billed as "a gathering of North American tribes."

## "Projective Verse" and "Postmodern" Man

The essay "Projective Verse," published a year after "The Kingfishers," appears on the surface to have little to do with Olson's Indian studies. Yet there are important connections. A cursory or unsympathetic reader of the text, however, might agree with James Dickey's critical indictment that its central idea of organic poetic form is commonplace, and that Olson's theory "is simply to provide creative irresponsibility with the semblance of a rationale which may be defended in heated and cloudy terms by its supposed practitioners."[14] But such a reading misses the point. Olson's main intent was not, as Dickey supposed, simply to provide the technical rationales for open forms by proposing the typewriter's uniformities as an instrument of spatial measure, or by using breath and the spoken voice as the basis of rhythmic units. Rather, "Projective Verse" is as much a work of philosophy as of literary criticism. In theory, it is used to explore "composition by field" as a means for pointing man back to "his dynamic," to his life force, and to a proper relationship to the nature within him and outside him. It is here, in its view of people and their "stance toward reality," that "Projective Verse" and its sequels, "Human Universe" (1953) and "Letter to Elaine Feinstein" (1959), make their main contribution; and it is here that Olson draws meaningfully on his knowledge of Native American cultures.

Breath is central to "Projective Verse." But it is not solely important as a means of ordering and measuring the poetic line. The projective poet must, Olson wrote, draw "down through the workings of his own throat to that place where breath comes from, where breath has its beginnings, where drama comes from, where, the coincidence is, all act springs." Breath is the animating spirit of life. It is a source of projective, or larger than human, power. As such, it is the link to both the natural and the supernatural. Olson's concept of breath as creative power is analogous to that of Benjamin Lee Whorf, whom he read avidly. In his study of Hopi language and culture, Whorf reported that the Hopi relate the "spirit of breath" to both the human heart and "the very heart of the Cosmos."[15] Breath, for Olson as for the Hopi, represented the key to harmony with the self and with the universe.

Olson believed that Western men, particularly Western literary men, had lost touch with their physical nature, and that the poet could, through breath, begin to reconnect with his own physical center and, on a deeper level, with the animating principle of the material and spiritual worlds. Fifteen years later Olson published "Proprioception" (1965) to demonstrate the proposition "that one's life is informed from and by one's own literal body" and to assert that by drawing down into the depths of the body one reaches beyond the "ego position" and contacts what is commonly called "soul," which, like William Blake, he felt was one with true bodily existence.[16]

Olson adopted Whorf's principle that "a change in language can change our appreciation of the cosmos."[17] "Projective Verse" represented a prescription for revolutionizing modern consciousness. He hoped to "shift the mode of discourse" to facilitate "the getting rid of the lyrical interference of the individual as ego, of 'the subject and his soul,' that peculiar assumption by which Western man has interposed himself between what he is as a creature of nature (with certain instructions to carry out) and those other creatures of nature."[18] Breath as the basis of the poem served this purpose of restoring a proper relation to nature, or at least of beginning the process, by returning the poet to "live in his body."[19] Only thus, Olson wrote, could man dwell in his total "human universe." Projective verse was intended to provide the modern poet with a practice, akin to the Eastern meditation techniques later pursued by Beat and other poets, that would help him to avoid falling into what Olson took to be the "Western box" of relying too heavily on the intellectual, rational mind and its tendency to abstract and stand back from experience and thereby become habitually removed from nature.

Olson saw this abstracting tendency as the bane of Western man. In his lectures during the sixties, he liked to quote Heraclitus's dictum, "Man is estranged from that with which he is most familiar." He traced this abstracting tendency in

"Human Universe" back to habits of language and thought established by the Greek philosophers: Socrates' "universe of discourse," Plato's "world of ideas," and Aristotle's emphasis on logic and classification. Olson saw these habits as culminating in the alienation and "spectatorism" of the twentieth century. In "Projective Verse," Olson proposed new habits of thought and discourse. These implied a new "stance toward reality" for modern man, which he called "objectism." Objectism would revise, Olson wrote, "how [man] conceives his relation to nature, that force to which he owes his somewhat small existence."[20] The habits of expression he sought were to be less descriptive and more reflective of the actual process that made up the reality of life. Olson wanted a discourse that was part of and not apart from process, language that was "the act of the instant" and not "the act of thought about the instant."[21]

The discourse capable of enacting rather than describing process would, in theory, be animated by the natural and supernatural energies of breath. But Olson drew on Sapir's and Whorf's studies of Indian cultures in other ways in developing his poetics. "Projective Verse" emphasized the need for speed in the presentation of poetic perceptions and placed a new emphasis on the verb rather than on the noun or on descriptive markers like adjectives or adverbs. In his "Letter to Elaine Feinstein" Olson suggested that Hopi and other tribal grammars might provide useful syntactical models that would better reflect the flux of process. Whorf's study of Hopi language, "An American Indian Model of the Universe," suggested that its model of the world is dominated by verbs. Such an emphasis tended to reflect better a constantly shifting process. "Hopi does not in any way formalize as such the contrast between completion and incompletion of action," Whorf wrote. "It can have verbs without subjects, and this gives to the language system power as a logical system for understanding certain aspects of the cosmos." The Hopi language presents time with a similar attention to process, in concrete rather than abstract terms, for "the element of time is not separated from whatever element of space enters into the operations."[22] Ultimately, Hopi expresses a world view in which hardly anything is perceived as fixed and separate, and in which ever-evolving relationships on a spatial field dominate consciousness. Further, the Hopi do not usually make a clear linguistic separation between themselves and what is outside themselves. Their language guides them to what the anthropologist Levy-Bruhl, studying African tribes, called *participation mystique* ("mystical participation")—a sense of oneness with the surrounding world. This sense of relatedness to all life, shared by many tribal peoples, was what Olson sought through projective verse. Olson believed that the habits of abstraction we inherited from the Greeks had removed us from such a natural involvement with the world. His poetics sought to reengage modern man with the actual process of the "human universe." In a late *Maximus* poem (in *Maximus Poems III*) entitled "to get the rituals straight," Olson makes this explicit, praising "poets whose mental position does permit them to know order—Allen Ginsberg, John Wieners, Ed Dorn, and Robert Creeley," because they are all "for participation mystique."

In Yucatán in 1951, a year after publishing "Projective Verse," Olson discovered in the flesh and in the ruins evidence of the very human qualities that he had somewhat hopefully and hypothetically proposed with objectism. As Creeley wrote of that experience:

> The alternative to a generalizing humanism was locked, quite literally, in the people around him, and the conception, that there had been and could be a civilization anterior to that which he had come from was no longer conjecture, it was fact. He wrote me, then, I have no doubt . . . that the American will more and more repossess himself of the Indian past. [23]

Olson wrote Creeley that he was impressed by how, even among the contemporary Maya, whom he acknowledged were "a culture in arrestment,"

> the individual peering out from that flesh is precisely himself, is, a curious wandering animal (it is so beautiful, how animal the eyes are, when the flesh is not worn so close it chokes, how human and individuated the look comes out. [24]

He was struck by a people who lived comfortably and humanly within their own bodies, who did not pull back, as Americans did, from a chance touch on a rocking bus. The Maya seemed to Olson to be living in harmony with their inner nature and within nature itself. He noted how, during the period of a solar eclipse, the ancient myths of the sun and moon were still vital for them, how the heavenly bodies were not perceived as scientific abstractions but as living relatives.

Olson studied Mayan glyphs and saw them as vividly embodying the qualities of the poetic art he sought and the type of attention it demanded:

> there was a concept at work which kept the attention so poised that . . . men were able to stay so interested in the expression and gestures of all creatures including at least three planets in addition to the human face, eyes, and hands, that they invented a system of written record, now called hieroglyphs, which on its very face is verse, the signs were so clearly and densely chosen that, cut in stone, they retain the power of the objects of which they are the images.[25]

Olson sought an art with similar power. In contrast to what he perceived as the emphasis on abstract and referential meaning in Western thought and expression, he proposed that "that which exists through itself is what is called meaning."[26] He hoped that a poetry in touch with the animating force of breath, and one that "enacted" rather than described, would have such directness and would contribute to the creation of new ways of being and seeing for Americans. In "Human Universe," an important sequel to "Projective Verse" in that it develops the stance toward reality introduced there as objectism, Olson lifted important passages from his "Mayan Letters," like those quoted earlier, to illustrate the model of human consciousness his postmodern poetics implied. Olson's rediscovery of Mayan culture in 1951 thus made tangible and real for him the abstract implications of his poetics. The experience had the effect of revitalizing his own energies, propelling him into a very active and creative period of spreading his aesthetic—which he came to realize was both literary and spiritual—through teaching, correspondence, poems, essays, and lectures.

111

"Projective Verse," Olson wrote Elaine Feinstein in a frequently published letter, meant "the replacement of the Classical representational by the *primitive abstract.*"[27] The German critic Ekbert Faas equated this aesthetic with the definition of tribal art as "the establishment of nature's animating forces which turns art into an 'expression of intrinsic vitality.' "[28] Like Lawrence, Olson wanted to restore the life force to art and consciousness. Depite their affinity with primitive consciousness, however, Olson did not see projective verse and objectism as representing a backward gesture for modern man. "Primitive" to him meant "primary, as how one finds anything, pick it up as one does new—fresh, first."[29] Like Austin, Lawrence, and Williams, Olson understood expansion into primitive consciousness as a recovery of something lost and as a necessary step forward for an evolving humanity. In fact, he understood the evidence of Native American tribal cultures and language to be part of a fabric of modern sources of knowledge pointing Western man away from his egotism, isolation, and alienation and toward a fuller and a more harmonious relation with the universe around and within. Other indications of this emerging postmodern consciousness, for Olson, included Einstein's relativity theory and related discoveries by Heisenberg and others in subatomic physics; Sauer's geographical writings on the relationship between land and life; Keats's "negative capability," which pointed man away from the false knowledge associated with the "irritable reaching after fact and reason"; Whitehead's philosophy in *Process and Reality,* which Olson summarized as "Process *is* reality"; and Melville's merger of the material and spiritual worlds in his definition of "visible truth" as "the absolute condition of present things."

Like those of other poets who have learned from the Indian, Olson's arguments for a new poetics and a new consciousness implied a close relationship to the land. We see an early statement of this in "The Kingfishers," where Olson directs the reader to the material and spiritual essences of American earth and stone. His major poetic work, the open-ended or unfinished epic (in Pound's sense of "a poem including history") called *The Maximus Poems,* reflects this relationship

112

further in its attempt to create a voice that is both man and place. Olson tells us in "Letter 27" that,

> An American
> is a complex of occasions,
> themselves a geometry
> of spatial nature.

He must "have this sense / that I am one / with my skin. / Plus . . . / the geography / which leans in / on me." *(Maximus Poems,* IV, V, VI). Olson's American, in other words, must be one with both his body and his place, the total "geometry" of his "spatial nature." Olson perceived an analogous involvement in the human universe in our predecessor on the American continent, the Indian. "Projective Verse" and its outcome, the *Maximus Poems,* thus urge in theory and practice a new American poetry, conceived and begotten by way of the poet's relationship to nature and place. The idea and the idiom are Olson's own, but a major source and influence are in traditional Native American cultures.

The new American consciousness and identity that Olson proposed revive and renew for the postwar generation the efforts initiated by Austin and others earlier in the century. Olson's work brings together the ideas of a new organic poetics, a new ecological relationship to nature, and a new, more fully evolved human being. It points us positively toward a postmodern future and yet, simultaneously, points us back to the tribal past. Olson attempted a synthesis of the primitive and the modern and was the first since Austin to articulate the implications and scope of this effort. It involved for him poetic renewal on one level; on a deeper level, it meant spiritual renewal and, ultimately, human survival. His influence as a thinker on poets of his own and the current generation has been widespread. The poet Robert Duncan pictures his friend Olson, when a teacher at Black Mountain College, as shaman-like in his attempts to transform his students. "He saw education as spiritual attack," Duncan wrote. "Charles wanted to produce a new and redeemed man."[30]

# ♦ 5 Jerome Rothenberg: New Forms from Old ♦

The friendly and flowing savage. . . . Who is he?
Is he waiting for civilization or past it and mastering it?

. . . . . . . . . . . . . . . . . . . . . . . . . . . . . . . . .

Behaviour lawless as snow-flakes. . . . words simple as
    grass. . . . uncombed head and laughter and naivete;
Slowstepping feet and the common features, and the
    common modes and emanations,
They descend in new forms from the tips of his fingers
They are wafted from the odor of his body or breath. . . .
    they fly out of the glance of his eyes.

Walt Whitman, *Song of Myself*

Measure everything by the Titan rocket & the transistor radio, and the world is full of primitive peoples. But once change the unit of value to the poem or the dance-event or the dream . . . & it becomes apparent what all those people have been doing all those years with all that time on their hands.

Jerome Rothenberg, "Pre-Face" to
*Technicans of the Sacred*

## Convergence of the Primitive and the Modern

Jerome Rothenberg's two collections of tribal poetry—*Technicians of the Sacred: A Range of Poetries from Africa, Asia, America, and Oceania* (1969), and *Shaking the Pumpkin: Traditional Poetry of the Indian North Americas* (1972)—are the anthologies most responsible for drawing poets of the Vietnam War era to Indian materials. Rothenberg extended the work, begun by Austin and continued by Olson, of placing tribal poetries and the consciousness behind them within a modern literary and historical context. In addition, Rothenberg's concept of total translation draws on the inclination toward performance poetry in twentieth-century European and American avant-garde literary movements, including projective verse. It uses American Indian poetries as the basis for developing new, postmodern performance forms intended to extend America's sense of what a poem is and can be. Rothenberg explored further than any of his predecessors the formalistic implications of using Native American poetry as a model.

Rothenberg came to Indian poetry steeped in European and American modernist movements.[1] As an American poet in the 1950s, alienated from the dominant poetics of ironic noncommital based on the poetry of T. S. Eliot, W. H. Auden, Robert Lowell, and the New Criticism, Rothenberg discovered kinship with the contemporary Beat and projective-verse movements and their common roots in William Carlos Williams and Ezra Pound. Rothenberg had first discovered the magic, incantatory power of the word earlier, as a high-school student in the Bronx, New York, by immersing himself in the writings of Gertrude Stein. Her work led him to avant-garde movements, to dadaism, surrealism, and concrete poetry. What these European and American groups had in common that set them apart from the New Critical poetic practice was their antirationalism: the poem was conceived as an "intellectual and emotional complex in an instant of time" in Pound's phrase,[2] that came from and was addressed to more than just the linear-thinking conscious mind. Their holistic sense of the poem placed an emphasis on sound and image—on *melopoeia* and *phanopoeia*—rather than on referential meaning. This included primarily a reliance on incantatory rhythmic and rhetorical structures, especially repetition, and direct juxtaposition of images without explanatory linkages. In the more experimental work it included the visual images of concrete poetry and surrealist ventures into film, as well as the spectacle and music of dadist, projective, Beat, and other poets' experiments with mixed-media performances.

Rothenberg, along with other New York poets in the early sixties—Robert Kelly, Jackson MacLow, David Antin, and Rochelle Owens—sought to bring some of these influences together in the Deep Image movement. The sense of a poem among poets in this group was that it is "the record of movement from perception to vision," a view that represented a kind of hybrid crossing of imagist and surrealist precepts. Pound's emphasis on "image," Rimbaud's definition of the poet as "voyant"—a surrealist precept—led inevitably, Rothenberg and his cohorts would suggest, to the Indian on the mountaintop singing for a vision. Rothenberg edited the Deep Image group's magazine, *Poems from the Floating World,* in which he brought together the work of many of his American contemporaries with that of international poets outside the New Critical framework like Pablo Neruda, Paul Celan, Gunter Grass, Carl Alberti, and André Breton. He also published many avant-garde writers in a Hawks Well Press series of chapbooks, another outgrowth of Deep Image. In 1960 the American surrealist poet Philip Lamantia introduced Rothenberg to a collection by Roger Caillois and Jean Lambert, *Trésor de la poésie universelle,* an anthology containing many archaic and tribal works. Although he had a prior acquaintance with tribal poetry through the anthologies of Astrov and Day and the Bureau of American Ethnology reports, the timing of Rothenberg's reimmersion in the archaic in 1960 had an important impact. He was struck by an affinity between many of the ancient tribal works in the anthology and what he sensed was being sought after in the various experimental and avant-garde approaches. *Floating World* began publishing translations of archaic poetry alongside contemporary poems. Soon afterward, Rothenberg began to explore this compatibility further by experimenting with it off the page. Along with other Deep Imagists, some of whom, like MacLow, were already deeply committed to performance poetry, Rothenberg participated in a series of public readings at the Poets Hardware Theater in New York City. These readings were, in fact, "happenings" in which both contemporary and tribal poems were performed, often with accompanying ritual, musical, and dramatic activity. These efforts evolved over several years, culminating in a Folkways recording of tribal poems, *From a Shaman's Notebook* (1968), and in the large anthology, *Technicians of the Sacred* (1969).[3]

*Technicians of the Sacred* represents a great effort of synthesis. It attempts to present tribal poetry within a modernist perspective and to suggest basic affinities, convergences, and analogies between primitive and modern poetry systems and patterns of thought. Rothenberg discusses these parallels in the book's nearly two hundred pages of commentaries, illustrating them with statements on their craft by tribal shamans and with modern poems that bear resemblances to the primitive and tribal ones.

In his "Pre-Face," Rothenberg sketches six basic areas of analogy between experimental or avant-garde modern poetries and those of tribal peoples. First, he cites as a fundamental compatibility the "preliterate" tribal context in which the poem is vocalized, chanted, or sung and the rapidly evolving twentieth-century cultural context of non-print-oriented communications systems—radio, film, television, phonograph records, video systems, audio tapes—described by both Marshall McLuhan and Charles Olson as "post-literate." To underscore the translated tribal poems' oral/aural dimension, that is, their relationship to the spoken word, Rothenberg often transcribes them, according to the precepts of projective verse, in breath units.

Second, Rothenberg points to the dominance in tribal poetry, of "concrete or non-causal thought in contrast to the simplifications of Aristotelian logic."[4] He compares this dominance to a similar antirational tendency in a variety of modern European and American sources, including Blake, Rimbaud, imagism, *symbolisme,* deep image, and chance and concrete poetries. The archaic and tribal works in the anthology that he uses to illustrate this compatibility include single-image poems drawn from African and Native American cultures, the illogical juxtapositions of African "Bantu Combinations," image "Correspondences" drawn from the Chinese *Book of Changes,* and the highly imagistic and often illogically self-contradictory Aztec definitions. Like Austin, Rothenberg cites a similarity between modern imagistic practices and tribal poetry. Like Olson, he holds up as a useful model tribal man's transcendence of logical thought.

Third, Rothenberg suggests that in European and American poetry of the postlogical type we find participatory demands analogous to the ceremonial contexts of Indian song. This is, he tells us, a "minimal art of maximum participation." Such art elicits an active and creative rather than a passive response, he suggests, for the gaps in meaning which the reader must somehow fill in make intense demands on "the 'spectator' as [ritual] participant."[5]

Fourth, Rothenberg suggests a basic analogy between the "intermedia situation" of tribal poetry, in which one "poem" may comprise words, music, dance, visual art, and ritual drama, and the increased experimentation with similar mixed-media practices by twentieth-century poets in dadist soirees, prose poems, picture poems, films by poets, and happenings.

Fifth, Rothenberg cites the "animal body rootedness" of primitive poetry. By this he means, on the one hand, the body as a physical energy source for the poem's form, a perception that we have seen was important to Austin, Lawrence, Williams, and Olson. On the other hand, "animal body rootedness" refers to the urges, functions, and excesses of the body as legitimate subject matter of the poem itself, as might be illustrated by the work of Walt Whitman or his descendants among the Beats. Rothenberg is the first anthologist to stress the prominence of body-related imagery in primitive poetry. Most early translators of Indian materials had ignored, often out of squeamishness or incomprehension, the sexual or physical explicitness that is frequently at the center of the verbal or ritual language of tribal poetry. Rothenberg's anthologies, of course, have the dual advantage in this regard of appearing at a time of relaxed literary and cultural attitudes toward the body and of being able to draw on pioneering scholarship like Paul Radin's *The Trickster* (1956), which revealed the pervasiveness of sexual and scatological imagery, usually of a comic nature, in Indian literature.

Such imagery was widespread on the American continent in trickster stories and in the ritual activities of sacred clowns.[6] In commentaries, Rothenberg makes the crucially important point that Native American cultures view physical and sexual urges without the taint of dirtiness that they acquire in the West. Instead, these aspects of the human condition are viewed in stories, songs, and ceremonies as part of a fabric of sacred mystery and power and are approached with a mixture of awe, consternation, and humor. In ceremonies, the sacred clown often interrupts the most solemn rite with an outrageously raunchy performance that violates every possible canon of normal propriety. Clowns in the Southwest, for instance, were reported to eat and drink their own excrement and to wear enormous artificial phalluses with which they would simulate copulation with women in the crowd.[7] The clown's purpose is not merely to provide comic relief, as is often assumed by Western observers, but also to break down conventional barriers and to open people up for essentially sacred ends. As Black Elk said of the *heyoka's* (sacred clown's) function among the Sioux: "It is planned that people shall be made to feel happy and jolly at first so that it may be easier for the power to come to them."[8] Trickster stories, with their outlandish and obsessive preoccupation with scatology and sex, serve a similar opening-up function, as Carl Jung suggested.[9] Rothenberg is the first anthologist to include translations of a broad range of poems that are blunt and often extreme in their bodily and sexual references, as suggested by titles like "Coyote borrows Farting Boy's asshole, tosses up his eyes, rapes old women, & tricks a young girl seeking power." Many reflect an explicitly comic yet implicitly apiritual attitude.

Rothenberg's sixth point of analogy between modern and tribal poetics is perhaps the most often cited yet most problematical: the correspondence between the poet and the shaman. Rothenberg suggests that the shared emphasis on vision in modern sources such as Blake, Rimbaud, Rilke, and Lorca; in dadaist, surrealist, and Beat poetry; and in psychedelic be-ins points to a shared movement toward a shamanistic stance. In a talk delivered at the first Ethnopoetics Conference held at the University of Wisconsin–Milwaukee in 1975, Rothenberg discussed some basic analogies between the archaic shaman and the modern performance poet:

> The poet, like the shaman, typically withdraws to solitude to find his poem or vision, then returns to sound it, give it life. He performs alone . . . because his presence is considered crucial and no other specialist has arisen to *act* in his place. He is also like the shaman in being at once an outsider, yet a person needed for the validation of a certain type of experience important to the group . . . like the shaman he will not only be allowed to act mad in public, but he will often be expected to do so. The act of the shaman—& his poetry—is like a public act of madness. It is like what the Senecas, in their great dream ceremony now obsolete, called "turning the mind upside down. . . ." It is the primal exercise of human freedom against/& for the tribe.[10]

Of course, Rothenberg's parallels only go so far; these similarities between poet and shaman are presented as analogies. Rothenberg himself acknowledged that these correspondences between the work of the shaman and modern poet are hardly exact:

> In all this the ties feel very close—not that "we" & "they" are identical, but that the systems of thought & the poetry they've achieved are, like what we're after, distinct from something in the "west," & we can now see & value them because of it. What's missing are the in-context factors . . . the sense of the poems as part of an integrated social & religious complex; the presence in each instance of specific myths and locales; the fullness of the living culture.[11]

These missing "in-context factors" mark an enormous qualification to any discussion of similarities between primitive and modern poetry. They point to the fact that, until our poetry becomes an integral part of the socio-spiritual fabric of our community, it will only pale as a unifying cultural force when compared to the work of the most primitive tribal shaman. Here we run up against the real challenge posed by tribal poetry, the real question left unanswered by modernism: how to reintegrate the poet into the culture. Austin's pointing the modern poet toward communalism, Olson's striving for a poetry of "act" that could restore the lost sense of the supernatural and change ingrained ways of seeing, and Rothenberg's enumeration of the common impulses to be found in an archaic shamanism and an evolving modernism represent bare beginnings toward this ideal. Despite the magnitude of this task, which includes the even larger proposition of reintegrating modern man into his full human potential, each of these writers detects a changing consciousness developing in the twentieth century that permits hope, if not unqualified optimism, about the uses to which knowledge of primitive poetry and consciousness can be applied. Rothenberg wrote in *Technicians of the Sacred,* for instance, that "Analogous aspects of primitive & modern poetry reveal that primitive poetry & thought are close to an impulse toward unity in our own time, of which the poets are the forerunners."[12] Rothenberg's chronological perspective and knowledge of experimental literary movements in America and Europe throughout the century allow him to synthesize, supplement, and extend Austin's and Olson's efforts to place tribal poetry in a meaningful modern context. Rothenberg's outline of six basic areas of convergence represents the first comprehensive attempt to map points of intersection and a common path for a new and renewed humanity.

Likewise, Rothenberg is the first anthologist to cite the importance for modern writing of statements made by tribal shamans on their art. These statements tend to remind us of the organicism emphasized by Austin and Olson, and several of them bear a striking resemblance to the principles articulated by Olson in "Projective Verse." A statement by the Eskimo songman Orpinkalik, for instance, recalls Olson's sense of the poem as a spontaneous language act rooted in breath. It also parallels Austin's intuitive connection of the poem to rhythmic forces in the local landscape:

> Songs are thoughts, sung out with the breath when people are moved by great forces & ordinary speech no longer suffices. Man is moved just like the ice floe sailing here & there in the current. His thoughts are driven by a flowing force when he feels joy, when he feels fear, when he feels sorrow. Thoughts can wash over him like a flood, making his breath come in gasps & his heart throb. Some-

thing like an abatement in the weather will keep him thawed up. And then it will happen that we, who always think we are small, will feel still smaller. And we will fear to use words. But it will happen that the words we need will come out of themselves. When the words we want shoot up of themselves—we get a new song.[13]

Similarly, a New Guinea shaman's statement shares this emphasis on the bodily source of the poem. It goes further, however, suggesting, as "Projective Verse" does, the supernatural power to be drawn from this essentially physical source:

> Songs are thoughts, sung out with the breath when people are moved by great forces and ordinary speech no longer suffices. The mind, *nonola,* by which term intelligence, power of discrimination, capacity for learning magic formulae, & all forms of non-manual skill are described, as well as moral qualities, resides somewhere in the larynx. . . . The memory, however, the store of formulae & traditions learned by the heart, resides deeper, in the belly. . . . The force of magic, crystalized in the magical formulae, is carried by men of the present generation in their bodies. . . . The force of magic does not reside in the things; it resides within man and can escape only through his voice.[14]

The New Guinea shaman's larynx and belly are the channels of the "force of magic," which seems very close to what Olson called "life force" or "breath." According to Rothenberg, one intention in providing statements from tribal shamans like those just quoted is "to get across a sense of these poets as individualized functioning human beings." Here his intent parallels that of Sarett and Neihardt discussed earlier. More obviously, such statements tend to reinforce the physical and organic sources of tribal poetics cited by Austin, Olson, and Rothenberg himself.

*Native American Forms and a New Modern Poem*

Like these earlier poets, Rothenberg was also interested in drawing on Native American language and poetry to develop new American forms. Toward this end, he was the first poet to draw directly on specific Native American performance and ritual practices as models for a new type of American poem. Such a movement into the oral and performance dimension was, of course, implied by Austin's emphasis on communalism and by Olson's emphasis on "act," as well as by his involvement in early mixed-media happenings at Black Mountain College. Rothenberg's interest in the European history of performance poetry beginning with the dada soiree and his collaboration in experimental "poet's theater" productions in the sixties prepared him well for his task. The most influential factor in moving Rothenberg in this direction, however, was the experience, following the completion of *Technicians of the Sacred,* of living in a community of Seneca Indians in upstate New York and studying their living poetry in the field.

Poet Gary Snyder and anthropologist Stanley Diamond had been instrumental in making the necessary contacts and arrangements for Rothenberg to pursue this project, which was ultimately supported by a grant from the Wenner Gren Foundation. Rothenberg worked directly with Seneca songmen and women who had a good knowledge of English, seeking to understand and, in some cases, to translate Seneca poetry. His work among the Seneca provided the central experience out of which grew the anthology of Indian poetry *Shaking the Pumpkin* and Rothenberg's idea of "total translation." Where *Technicians of the Sacred* had drawn its poems largely from the anthropological scholarship of the late nineteenth and early twentieth centuries, reworking many of the translations into more modern language and forms, *Shaking the Pumpkin* drew primarily on contemporary work with Native American people and their literary materials by anthropologists such as Stanley Diamond, David McAllester, Munro Edmonson, and Barbara and Dennis Tedlock and by Nathaniel Tarn, William S. Merwin, James Koller, Edward Field, Anselm Hollo, and other poets. Where *Technicians of the Sacred* sought to provide a geographic sampling of non-Western poetry and to isolate certain important characteristics of that poetry (for example, sound poems, naming poems, visions and spells, imagistic correspondences), *Shaking the Pumpkin* provided a less programmatically organized sampling of poems, which this time were chosen primarily for their vitality and usability in translation for contemporary Americans. Rothenberg described his principle of organization thus in the "Pre-Face" to *Shaking the Pumpkin:* "the poetry appears in four miscellaneous sections or services ('service' in the sense of a religious ritual), each one corresponding to an evening's public reading under those circumstances in which we commonly share poetry with one another." Rothenberg invited his readers to experience the poems communally in an oral and ritual context of their own making. The anthology itself is thus presented as a means to invite creative participation by its readers in the reconstruction of an old form.

Rothenberg defined *total translation* as "a term I use for translation (of oral poetry in particular) that takes into account any or all elements in the original beyond the words . . . in the light of the possibilities of poetry opening to us in this time and place."[15] The suggestion that readers, along with their friends, share the poems by sounding them aloud in "services" underscores the concern of total translation in renewing the communal functions of poetry. But Rothenberg's discussions of the actual techniques of total translation reveal a variety of approaches to conveying the "elements beyond the words" (that is, characteristic sound, tone, spectacle, use, or participatory nature), each dependent upon the particular nature of the original poem. In a "Seneca Women's Dance Song," for instance, Rothenberg sought an English-language equivalent for the meaningless vocables prominent in the original. He worked from a literal translation provided by his Seneca informants, Avery and Fidelia Jimeson, which read thus:

> hey heya yo oh ho
> nice nice nice-it-is
> when–they–dance–the–ladies–dance
> our-mothers
> gahnoweyah heya
> graceful-it-is
> nice nice nice-it-is
> when–they–dance–the–ladies–dance
> our mothers
> gahnoweyah heya (& repeat)

Rothenberg, in this case, arrived at a rather simple translator's solution. His reworking substitutes common English interjections like "hey," "yeah," and "oh" for the vocables:

hey, it's nice it's nice
to see them yeah to see
our mothers do the ladies dances
oh it's graceful & it's
nice it's nice it's very nice
to see them hey to see
our mothers do the ladies dances.[16]

The resultant poem sounds more fluid and natural than the literal translation. The "equivalent language" doesn't call attention to itself as ostentatiously as reproducing the original vocables does and thus helps to maintain a loose, playful tone akin to the original's. Not all solutions, however, are this simple.

In the case of the Navajo "Horse Songs" of Frank Mitchell (a twentieth-century Navajo medicine man), which are probably the most celebrated total translations, Rothenberg again confronted the problem of translating vocables. But in that case, conveying the elements beyond the words proved more complex, for he sensed that the original's music—the relationships of sounds set up largely by the vocables (some of which were in the form of word distortions)—were central to its meaning and emotive power. Rothenberg wrote:

> My decision with the Navajo horse-songs was to work with the sound as sound: a reflection in itself of the difference between Navajo and Seneca song structure. For Navajo is much fuller, much denser, twists words into new shapes or fills up the spaces between words by insertion of a wide range of "meaningless" vocables making it misleading to translate primarily for meaning or, finally, to think of *total* translation in any other terms than sound.[17]

Unlike Seneca songs, in which the vocables were indeed meaningless, conventional markers used to fill a melodic line or to prepare a listener for a transitional shift, in the Navajo horse songs Rothenberg discovered that the vocables had a clear sense of continuity and relationship with the verbal material. They were made meaningful through relationships of assonance, rhyme, and pun and thus represented a form of word play of considerable evocative power. Rather than delete the vocables, as earlier translators had, or reproduce them in their original form as David McAllester (his anthropological source) did, Rothenberg sought again to find equivalents, but this time he needed to find ones that would bear similar relationships to the translation's English words.

He worked from a literal translation, from a transcription of the original Navajo text provided by McAllester, and from a tape of Mitchell singing. Rothenberg studied the ways in which the vocables distorted and rhymed with the Navajo words and composed by *singing* the translation into a tape recorder while listening to Mitchell's performance of the original. During this process Rothenberg found himself making small changes in the literal translation and developing a melody in response to the pressures of the English words themselves as sounded. His attempts to replace Mitchell's vocables with sounds that functioned similarly in relation to the English at first took the form of English words:

> Go to her my son & one & go to her
> my son & one & one & none & gone. . . .[18]

As he continued to repeat the process, however, he found his voice sliding more and more over the vocable words he was providing until they were increasingly becoming pure sounds like "wnn," "nnn," and "gahn," sounds that still faintly echoed their punlike meanings as with Navajo vocables. "What I was doing," Rothenberg wrote, "was contributing and then obliterating my own level of meaning, while in another sense I was as much recapitulating the history of the vocables themselves, at least according to one of the standard explanations that sees them as remnants of archaic words which have been emptied of meaning."[19] Such a view is at odds with the more accepted notion of "sound poetry," which as articulated by C. M. Bowra and others views vocables as preverbal or "rockbottom poetics."[20] Rothenberg's view suggests that vocables, at least in the Navajo use of them, represent a more sophisticated stage of artistic development, that they are essentially abstractions of literal meaning analogous to certain approaches of modern art. "Primitive," he tells us, "means complex."

In a further effort toward the total translation of the

horse songs, Rothenberg published two versions as a phonograph-record insert in *Alcheringa: Ethnopoetics,* a magazine of primitive and modern poetry that he coedited with anthropologist Dennis Tedlock.[21] Prominent among *Alcheringa*'s stated purposes were to explore "the full range of man's poetics, [and] to enlarge our understanding of what a poem may be."[22] The regular record-insert feature sought to do just that. One of the recorded versions of the horse songs is done with two voices. Overdubbing and echo are employed to convey the supernatural aura of the original. The second, flip-side version is a four-track affair featuring echoes and multiple voices. It represents an attempt to capture the sound and indeterminacy of an actual performance in which the lead singer is accompanied by ritual participants whose vocalizations tend to be somewhat unsynchronized with his. This total translation, though it may go far in its faithfulness to the original, is, to the listener who exists outside of the actual performance, almost unbearable to listen to. It carries literal translation to painful extremes.

At the other extreme, total translation can involve the taking of extraordinary liberties with the Indian original. In translating Seneca Ido poems, for instance, Rothenberg sought an equivalent form that would suggest the underlying playfulness and participatory energy of the audience, which he observed was a very real, if unstated, part of these tiny, repetitive poems. An Ido whose total verbal content is simply the phrase "The animals are coming by—he—he—he—he," chanted deliberately and repeatedly until concluding with a loud, exhausted exhalation, gets translated in *Shaking the Pumpkin* thus:

|  |  |
|---|---|
| t | |
| h | |
| e | HEH E HHEH |
| | HEH E HHEH |
| the animals are coming by | HEHUHHEH |
| n | HEH E HHEH |
| i | HEH E HHEH |
| m | |
| a | |
| l | |
| s | |

The concrete poem is chosen as an equivalent form, Rothenberg said, to suggest "the semblance of Seneca verbal art to concrete & minimal poetry among us." The poetry of the Seneca, he observed,

> when it uses words at all, works in sets of short songs, minimal realizations colliding with each other in marvelous ways, a very light, very pointed play-of-the-mind, nearly always just a step away from the comic (even as their masks are), the words set out in clear relief against the ground of the ("meaningless") refrain.[23]

Rothenberg's version seeks to provide a vehicle that will suggest these unspoken poetic qualities in the alien print medium and will translate "the melody in particular into equivalent visual patterns that hold the page."[24] A poem that is oral and communal in its original form thus gets translated onto the page as an essentially visual poem. It retains, technically, the literal wording of the original, including the vocables and the final "HUH" buried in their center, though repetition of the main phrase is only vaguely suggested by the acrostic format. The translation is designed for the reader to respond to in a playful, participatory, creative way, which Rothenberg took to be analogous to the poem's original spirit. He was encouraged in this adventurous approach to translating the Idos by his Seneca collaborator, Richard Johnny John, who urged him to "play around" with the originals and "to add a little something" of his own.[25]

Such a free approach, admittedly, has severe limitations. These Idos, for instance, are healing songs to the Seneca, the property of the Society of Mystic Animals. As such, despite their playfulness, they also possess a dimension of high seriousness that does not come through in Rothenberg's printed version. As Rarihokwats, former editor of the Native American national newspaper, *Akwesasne Notes,* has written:

> while an American may read the sacred curing songs for the Society of Mystic Animals—and even elicit some exotic imagery, the American does not know how to make it cure him. Poetry it may be, a cure it isn't—for the tribal man, the reverse is true.[26]

130

Rarihokwats is no doubt correct, but, as his comments indicate, the primary problem may be more one of cultural difference than of a translator's omission. Rothenberg's decisions no doubt promote the Idos' playful quality at the expense of their sacredness, but in this case playfulness may be all it is realistically possible to convey to non-Indians.

A more sweeping and literary criticism came from William Bevis, who complained that Rothenberg's translations of the Idos "show little respect for Indian artistic devices such as style, form, genre, and medium."[27] The problem with Bevis's objections is that he failed to qualify them by observing that *any* translation from an oral to written form represents a fundamental violation of medium, and that form, genre, and style are likely to be distorted in the process. Rothenberg may be charged with excess in taking the liberties he did, but some distortion in itself, as our discussions of translations in the early years of the century indicated, is virtually inevitable. Rothenberg responded to Bevis's charges only in part—to the general issue of respect. He took the position that in consciously choosing not to try to translate the Idos' religiosity he was actually respecting "the sense of secrecy & localization that's so important to those for whom the songs are sacred & alive."[28] Total translation is revealed, in this case, to be actually, by conscious choice, partial translation. "Translation," Rothenberg wrote, "makes a poem in this place that's analogous in whole or in part to a poem in that place . . . [the translator is] making something present, or making something as a present—for his own time and place."[29] "Something," not the same thing, is thus his original goal. Despite the catch phrase "total translation," Rothenberg's view actually opposes the common assumption that everything can or should be somehow shared across cultures.

But the fundamental questions raised by Bevis about how far one can go in taking liberties with the originals in translating poetry are not so easily dismissed. They are not easily resolved either, for they pose a number of problems, the solution to one being often contrary to what another requires. Does the translation convey all or part of the spirit of the original? Does it work as a poem in its new language for its new audience? Is it analogous? Is it respectful? Is it accurate? Fortunately, it is not our task to unravel these knotty questions or terms.[30] Any answers can only be particular ones regarding an individual poem, an individual translator's intentions, an individual audience's needs. In Rothenberg's case, the criteria for judging his work could be multiple as is reflected in the varied responses to date: the generally positive response of the Seneca people themselves; the enthusiastic response of poets and literary critics associated with countercultural journals; or, conversely, the hostile responses of more conservative or scholarly poets and critics like Bevis.

The most successful total translations, from virtually every point of view, are those that extend the poems beyond the print medium. As with the horse songs, Rothenberg's total translation of the Idos at poetry readings took a different, less abstract tack. He chanted the poems, with total physical involvement, accompanying himself, after the model of Seneca singers, on a gourd rattle. Vocal inflections, intonations, and exhalations were closely modeled after the performance of the originals and tended to lend suggestive depth to the minimal content.

In all of his attempts at total translation, Rothenberg sought to discover and convey the presence behind the originals, the hidden meanings that other translators of Indian poetry also sought. Working orally at making the translations (in the case of the horse songs) and performing—singing and chanting—at readings represented important breakthroughs for him toward this end. As he told Kevin Power in a 1974 interview:

> Certainly the excitement for me of music, when I began to compose & then chant the Horse-Songs, was the tremendous relief I felt to be able to operate in an oral situation with a minimal reliance on meaning to carry the poems. I mean, the poems obviously *meant* something, the meaning was clearly a presence behind them, but in chanting the words & sounds (which both hid & revealed the meanings) it no longer seemed to be an encumbrance to communication.[31]

Many of his translated poems work for readers in a similar way. Only when they actually hear them or begin to chant them aloud do these works begin to have meaning. Unlike other anthologists, Rothenberg, at least, encouraged us to become more Indian-like by offering specific instructions. He advised us to begin by experiencing our language and poetry in an Indian way—by bringing it off the page and singing.

Probably the most significant aspect of total translation is found in Rothenberg's refusal to shrink Native American ritual forms and their inherent poetry down to simple, more or less conventional American poems, as all previous translators and anthologists had done. Instead, Rothenberg often took these ritual forms as poetic structures themselves, using them as models for building new American forms that extend into performance and that can extend our sense of the poem itself. For instance, an appendix to *Technicians of the Sacred* provides a description of a "Gift Event" performed at the Judson Dance Theater in New York City in 1967. The event was modeled on the Seneca Eagle Dance ceremony. As adapted, the Gift Event featured several poets who shared poems, music, and food with an audience. At its outset a speaker came forward and rapped on the floor with a big stick for attention and silence. Music and dancing then began, with everyone invited to participate. When this activity stopped, the poet rapped for silence and read a poem, after which he distributed crackers or other food from a big washtub. A second poet stepped forward, rapped with the stick for attention, and the cycle of events began again continuing into the night. The Gift Event closely followed the format of the Eagle Dance on which it is based, with poets taking the place of tribal orators and singers. As Rothenberg described the Judson Dance Theater adaptation, "except for the first piece . . . there was no attempt to be Indian or to read poems on Indian themes; indeed, the point of the event, as it related to its source, was that the carry-over was not in content but in structure: a way of being heard."[32]

The Gift Event presented a new form, or format, for the poem. Of course, the poems in that event hardly reflected the Indian notion of songs. If an Indian singer began a song, others present would take it up—one song for all—whereas in the Judson event, each poem was for the individual poet. The charge can be made that until the event itself becomes familiar and customary, such an activity is not integrating but

133

isolating, that it is not as communal or communicating in practice as in theory. An Indian powwow, for instance, represents a less formally structured activity that involves a much looser demarcation between individual and community and yet is wholly communal. But there the whole form is being directed by communal customs. In the Gift Event, the poet's sharing of food and joining in the dancing were intended to bring people together, to symbolize his oneness with the community, but, as Rothenberg reported, the gift-giving was the most radical and difficult part of the actual event for it involved "the-act-of-finding-each-other." This difficulty underscored the problematical shift from a cultural "situation where a community is taken for granted to one where the activity may finally create it."[33]

The implications of events as poems thus extend beyond the purely literary. As translations, they begin to address the real issues implicit in the use of Native American poetry and consciousness as a model by offering forms that require people to come together for a tribal experience. Such specific poetic activities designed to create community can initiate the process of reintegration that other poets who were interested in the Indian also sensed as important.

Throughout *Technicians of the Sacred* and *Shaking the Pumpkin,* Rothenberg draws on Native American ritual and ceremonial forms to create poems that are, in fact, the guidelines for events like the one just described. Lists of instructions are presented, for instance, that would enable readers to take the poem off the page and roughly simulate, in part, activities such as a Kwakiutl potlatch, a Navajo sand-painting healing ceremony, and a Sioux vision quest, among many others. A Navajo "Language Event" instructs us to:

> Have a conversation in which everything refers to water:
> If someone comes in the room, say: "Someone's floating in."
> If someone sits down, say: "It looks like someone just
> stopped floating."[34]

As with almost all the event poems, Rothenberg's commentary on the "Language Event" provides very little ethnological background information. This omission is intentional. Its purpose is to discourage imitativeness and to encourage a playfully creative approach to bringing the event alive within non-Indian cultural reality. The commentary on the "Language Event," for instance, tells us:

> Among other Navajo forms of "altered language": this one, not surprisingly, for use in the Rain ceremony. But the reader might take it from there, & see what results would follow the application of a single rule to a wider series of situations.[35]

Though the lack of interpretive notes in the case of these events may result in a distorted sense of their original meanings and uses, Rothenberg made it clear that conveying such knowledge is not his main interest. Instead, he was interested in translating events as rich sources of usable forms that can extend our culture's sense of the poem into new, participatory dimensions. The skeletal instructions that comprise the event poem on the page, he argued, serve to call attention to the form of the activity off the page. They are comparable in this respect, he tells us, to "seeing Greek statues without their colors."[36]

These Native American forms—the event poems—offer skeletal structures for building a new American poetry and a new communal context and consciousness. But they require us to respond actively and creatively as "[ritual] participants." For the Native American skeleton must be fleshed out by the cooperative and creative efforts of Americans, based on the reality of contemporary American cultural conditions: what's needed and what's possible here, now. The Native American, Rothenberg's work suggests, cannot ultimately give us what we seek, but he can offer us the forms and the direction to find our way, each other, and ourselves. Only when such a reintegrative process is initiated can we begin to realize the gift that Olson, Austin, Rothenberg, and others sensed that the model of Indian poetry and consciousness holds for Americans: connectedness and community, the basis for true communion.

# ♦ 6 Gary Snyder:
## The Lessons of Turtle Island ♦

> If civilization
>    is the exploiter, the masses is nature
>       and the party
>       is the poets.

from Gary Snyder, "Revolution in the Revolution
in the Revolution"

Gary Snyder is the poet who is best known today for his presentation of the Indian and, more broadly, "the primitive" as important models and sources for the modern world. If Jerome Rothenberg is the contemporary poet who explores to their current limits the implications of Native American forms for a new American poetry, Snyder does the same in making claims for the implications and applications of Native American consciousness for American life. In Snyder's work we can find the culmination of many of the efforts of earlier American poets who sought in Indian cultures alternatives to the fragmented, materialistic culture of modern America and to the cynical, detached irony of its "crafted" poetry. Snyder's poetry and essays develop several of the key themes already discussed: relationship to place and to inner and outer nature, holistic awareness as a means to psycho-spiritual health, and, to a lesser extent, the development of a new American poetry based on Native American and other tribal models.

A look at Snyder's poetry should perhaps begin with mention of the fact that his collection of poems and essays, *Turtle Island,* received a Pulitzer Prize in 1974. Its title revives the name for the American continent derived from Native American creation stories. A recurrent theme among its poems and essays is the need for modern Americans to return to the perception of the earth as a living organism to whom we are related; we must break through geopolitical abstractions, he tells us in *Turtle Island,* and begin to see as it actually is "this continent of watersheds and life communities—plant zones, physiographic provinces, culture areas; following natural boundaries." The most important implication of such a renewal of natural perception, Snyder has written, is that it will ultimately enable us to "see ourselves more accurately."[1]

The task of achieving an intimate knowledge of the land for the sake of psycho-spiritual health, of achieving chthonic being, is important to poets like Mary Austin, Vachel Lindsay, Hart Crane, William Carlos Williams, and Charles Olson, but it is crucial to Gary Snyder. For him, it represents a commitment both in poetic stance and life-style. This commitment is reflected in his writing, in his longtime practice of Buddhist meditation techniques, and in his back-to-nature approach to living in California's Sierra Nevada. Through all this, Snyder has never become a recluse like the most influential West Coast literary figure of the previous generation who "went Indian," poet-anthropologist Jaime de Angulo, "the legendary hermit of Big Sur." Instead, Snyder has remained steadfastly concerned in literature and life with the development of an alternative *community*.

Snyder's sense of community includes not just humans, but all living things. Of the poets just mentioned, only Williams approached Snyder's precise attentiveness to beasts and plants as direct sources of the desired chthonic knowledge. Snyder's poems look closely at trout, deer, quail, dolphins, manzanita, mushrooms, and berries and, like Williams's poems on flowers, trees, and animals, Snyder's reflect an acute awareness of living nature, a sense of an intelligence to be found there, and a respectful, observant, participatory relationship with it akin to the Native American's.[2] "You should really know what the complete natural world of your region is and what all its interactions are and how you are interacting with it yourself," Snyder says in an interview. "This is just part of the work of becoming who you are, where you are."[3]

In his best poems Snyder seems to be inside nature, interacting with it, rather than outside talking about it. In "A Walk" (*The Back Country*, 1968), for instance, he takes us with him on a hike, through a sequence of shared impressions that keep reader and poet in the middle of the experience:

> . . . Hopping on creekbed boulders
> Up the rock throat three miles
> > Piute Creek—
> In steep gorge glacier-slick rattlesnake country
> Jump, land by a pool, trout skitter,
> The clear sky. Deer tracks.
> Bad places by a falls, boulders big as houses,
> Lunch tied to belt,
> I stemmed up a crack and almost fell
> But rolled out safe on a ledge
> > and ambled on.
> Quail chicks freeze underfoot, color of stone
> Then run cheep! away, hen quail fussing.

The poem is structured to seem unstructured, a stream of words reflecting a stream of sensations with occasional reflections or realizations, self-glimpses among the views of nature; it moves fast from perception to perception. In its way, this is the kind of writing that Olson called for in "Projective Verse." It "enacts" rather than "describes." The poem ambles, slips, and slides its way along, mimetically re-creating the hike. Its creatures act, but as with the trout and quail in the previous passage, their actions are not elaborately or analytically described but are "snap-said" with a speed and immediacy that re-creates the original sensory impression. The poem's "I" moves easily and casually between his senses and his memories, his reflections and their outer natural environment. The poem ends at a natural stopping point—when the hiker stops for lunch. Despite its carefully plain language and cleverly random structure, "A Walk" works convincingly as a poem because it accurately registers impressions in a language appropriate to their immediacy and in a form that synthesizes the natural rhythms of voice, sense, and the experience in nature that is the poem's subject. In this deceptively simple poem, Snyder wrote, as Olson would have described it, with *participation mystique* and he realized what Austin gropingly projected in her concept of the "landscape line": a poem in touch with the interacting rhythms of body, mind, and place.

Elsewhere, Snyder's poems often take the broad view of nature instead of the immediate, close-up look, registering the human interaction with place as continent not as locality. He tried for a "scientific myth," as in "What Happened Here Before" *(Turtle Island,* 1974), where he traces the evolution of the West Coast region of the Continent beginning 300 million years ago. Indians enter the chronological map that organizes the poem at the 40,000-year mark:

> And human people came with basket hats and nets
> winter houses underground
> yew bows painted green,
> feasts and dances for the boys and girls
> songs and stories in the smoky dark

The white man enters the picture only 125 years ago:

Then came the white man: tossing up trees and
   boulders with big hoses,
     going after that old gravel and the gold.
horses, apple orchards, card-games,
     pistol-shooting, churches, county jail.

The poem is written from the continent's point of view and re-counts the evidence of its ceaseless changes. It hopes to broaden its readers' perspective on who we are and where we are by familiarizing us with the historical depth of American life and with the variety of geological, plant, animal, and human forces that have evolved. It presents characteristic images reflecting how human groups have interacted with the land as Olson had planned in "Red, White, and Black": we see the red people in their "winter houses underground" nurtured in the womb of the earth itself, whom they regard as their mother; in contrast, the white man, "tossing up trees and boulders with big hoses," violently, phallically exploiting the land for its wealth of natural resources. The land is presented as a living, growing, changing thing unto itself:

First a sea: soft sands, mud, and marls
   —loading, compressing, heating, crumpling,
     crushing, recrystalizing, infiltrating,
several times lifted and submerged.

Though set in a geological rather than a human time frame, passages in "What Happened Here Before," as in "A Walk," pay close attention to detail and present the interacting elements of nature with precision and immediacy:

sea-bed strata raised and folded,
   granite far below.
warm quiet centuries of rains
   (make dark red tropic soils)
   wear down two miles of surface,
lay bare the veins and tumble heavy gold
   in steambeds
     slate and schist rock-riffles catch it—
volcanic ash floats down and dams the streams,
   piles up the gold and gravel—

Turtle Island is thus presented to us as a vital thing, vaster and longer-lived than man or any of its other species. When we achieve an understanding and an appreciation of the depth and scope of its life, the poem's implicit message states, we can begin to come into proper relationship to our land. To achieve the proper and necessary respect, we must realize, the poem tells us, that "the land belongs to itself," not to us. Only then can we approach a relationship of harmony and balance with the nature around us and begin to develop fully our own inner harmony and a healthy human and American identity. The poem addresses the question posed toward its conclusion by Snyder's sons: "Who are we?" It suggests that we ask ourselves the same question and that its answer requires realizing whether we hear our true voice in the military jets roaring overhead every dawn—the contemporary extension of the early white man uprooting trees, boulders, and people—or in the sounds of the land and its creatures, the nature to which we too belong, whose voice we hear in the poem's final line, "Bluejay screeches from a pine."[4]

Identification with nature—belonging without possessing—is central to Snyder's work. His writing extends the treatment of place found in earlier poets who were interested in the Indian by showing the tangible ecological consequences of our psychological and spiritual alienation from nature. Its main subject is the land itself, but not treated as mere landscape. Snyder's concept of land holds that the development by Americans of a harmonious relationship with their environment is necessary not just for psychological and spiritual health but also for actual survival, physically as well as spiritually. Crane, Williams, and Olson saw from afar the ultimate self-destructiveness inherent in contemporary culture's alienation from nature, but Snyder's camera shows that the whirlwind is nearly upon us as he reports on the exploding ecological crises of the sixties, seventies, and eighties. Snyder's attitudes on this subject, usually implicit in his poetry are more explicitly developed in his essays. In "The Wilderness," an essay in *Turtle Island,* Snyder wrote "We are beginning to get non-negotiable demands from the air, the water, the soil."[5] In "Four Changes," another of *Turtle Island's* essays, Snyder defined and proposed social and political solutions to the four interrelated ecological problems of overpopulation, pollution, consumption, and "transformation." In the latter discussion he summarizes the situation and solution:

> Civilization, which has made us so successful a species, has overshot itself and now threatens us with inertia. There also is some evidence that civilized life isn't good for the human gene pool. To achieve Changes we must change the very foundations of our society and our minds.[6]

In such urgent need, the Native American becomes in Snyder's work a model for "mind" and for living stably, respectfully, and nonexploitatively with a natural environment. In *The Old Ways* (1977), a collection of six essays exploring relationship to place, Snyder cited the example, as described in ecologist Eugene Odom's paper "The Strategy of Ecosystem Development," of certain Native American societies' relationship to their environment, as contrasted with that of contemporary white America. Odom suggested that exploitative and exhaustive use of land, as found in the United States, was characteristic of a "young" ecosystem culture. Snyder, in "The Politics of Ethnopoetics,"[7] extended Odom's discussion by tracing the exploitative tendency back to early civilizations and to the development of a centralized state in cities like Babylon and Rome, which spread their economic support systems far enough that they could afford to wreck one local territory's ecology and keep moving on. The development of America, he suggested, through the gradual settlement of an ever-expanding frontier, has followed a similar pattern.[8] In a relatively early poem, "Oil" *(The Back Country,* 1968), Snyder likened the ultimately self-destructive reliance on nonrenewable resources characteristic of this process to the self-demeaning behavior of an addict. He described the oil tanker he was a laborer on:

> bearing what all these
> crazed, hooked nations need:
> steel plates and
> long injections of pure oil

Older Native American cultures, he suggested, represented a historical alternative. Snyder pointed to Indian societies in general, and to traditionally sedentary ones like the still viable Pueblo tribes in the Southwest in particular, as models of human organization that do not self-destruct by exploiting and exhausting their resources. In Odom's terms, they are "mature" ecosystem cultures. Their relationship to the land is characterized by protection rather than production, by stability rather than growth, by a concern for quality rather than quantity. Snyder proposed this model as a guide to America's ecological survival. The radical shift that it implies is to a relationship of stewardship rather than exploitation and to a regional rather than a global approach to resource usage, particularly of energy resources.

Though dismissed as unrealistic by many, Snyder's position is that such an approach, however drastic, is necessary and imperative given the crisis we face; the "poet's" analysis agrees with those of prominent ecologists ("scientists") who, like Odom and Barry Commoner, draw similar conclusions.[9] Thus, the importance of the Native American model becomes even more urgent in Snyder's work than in that of his poetic predecessors: for those predecessors, the message was that reform of the spirit was necessary to our salvation, but Snyder showed the hell into which our present path will shortly lead us. Previous poets told us that to recover Eden we must become as Indians. Snyder asserted that unless we become true Native Americans we will make America hell on earth.

Snyder, of course, is no mere doomslinger. His poems and essays point to models of the kind of respectfully knowing attitude toward nature that would ensure survival in a good land. One such model is found in "Prayer for the Great Family" (Turtle Island), his adaptation of a traditional Mohawk prayer:

Gratitude to Mother Earth, sailing through night and day—
and to her soil: rich, rare, and sweet
*in our minds so be it.*

Gratitude to Plants, the sun-facing light-changing leaf
and fine root-hairs; standing still through wind
and rain; their dance is in the flowing spiral grain
*in our minds so be it.*

Gratitude to Air, bearing the soaring Swift and the silent
Owl at dawn. Breath of our song
clear spirit breeze
*in our minds so be it.*

145

As Olson instructed in "Projective Verse," "Prayer For the Great Family" is objective," concerned as it is with relationships, and with conveying a distinctly process-conscious "stance toward reality."

Like other poets discussed ealier in this book, Snyder believed that renewed understanding of ourselves and our land can come from communing with Indian peoples, whose traditional relationship to nature and whose techniques for meditative and visionary explorations offer hope for the deeply disturbed earth/body and spirit/mind of modern man. "The primitive world," he told me in a 1979 interview, "measures us in terms of final physical and psychological health." Further, it can lead us to take "the next great step of mankind . . . to step into the nature of his own mind," to answer "the real question . . . just what is consciousness?"[10] Native American cultures, Snyder suggested, have been dedicated to exploring this question for thousands of years, and through they have not developed a technology comparable to the West's, they have exceeded us in developing as "technicians of the sacred."[11] Poets like Snyder, Rothenberg, Olson, Williams, and Austin, who espoused or practiced an organic, relativistic poetics, sought a similar type of development: contact with the truly spiritual, truly poetic consciousness to be found in the human mind and the "mind" of nature. Snyder suggested that "very simple cultures who are really trying to find out what the possibilities of the mind are" often are far more physically and psychologically stable than more technologically advanced societies. Like most of the writers we have discussed, Snyder's work challenges the Western myth of progress through the industrial and technological development associated with civilization. Snyder went so far as to wonder aloud if "all civilization is just a very recent and somewhat eccentric sidegrowth that will find itself at a dead end likely, and then come back to the main line again."[12]

## "Original Mind"

Snyder views the study of Native American cultures and their literature as a way for poets to reconnect with this "main line" and with the shamanic roots of their own craft. To the degree that poets can integrate the perspective that they find in their study of Indian peoples into their own minds and lives, they can feed it back to their own culture through their work. Native American sources, if so employed, Snyder says provide "an exercise in locating yourself concretely in the world, and . . . an exercise in getting deeper down into your own mind."[13] But Snyder does not advocate in his poetry and prose, as many of his critics believe, nostalgic return to a past that is forever gone. Like Olson, he is an avid student of modern science and the closing informational circle of the twentieth-century world. Beginning with the essays collected in *Earth House Hold* (1969), he has been tracing the development of a new set of attitudes and assumptions in the West as our culture draws on ancient Asian and Native Americn models of reality as well as the discoveries by our own physical and environmental scientists. In "Four Changes," Snyder wrote that we must "master the archaic and primitive as models of basic nature-related cultures—as well as the most imaginative extensions of science—and build a community where these two vectors cross."[14]

Ultimately, Snyder envisioned an interpenetration of primitive and civilized states of mind that will return modern man, at least periodically, to the experience spoken of by the Buddhists as "original mind"; this is roughly equatable with the intelligence found in all nature, which ecologists call "biomass." Snyder has been interested in the point where these correspondences between exterior and interior landscapes merge.[15] Many of his poems strive for an image or a voice that can capture this interpenetration. In "Magpie's Song" *(Turtle Island,* 1974), for instance, Snyder described a sudden, magical encounter with a magpie and recorded the message that the bird communicated:

> *"Here in the mind, brother*
> *Turquoise blue.*
> *I wouldn't fool you.*
> *Smell the breeze*
> *It came through all the trees*
> *No need to fear*
> *What's ahead*

*Snow up on the hills west*
*Will be there every year*
*be at rest.*
*A feather on the ground—*
*The wind sound—*

*Here in the Mind, Brother,*
*Turquoise Blue."*

The capitalized "Mind" in the next to the last line suggests the "original" or "biomass" mind. The poem itself should be seen as a modern attempt at a "shaman song" that tries to put us into contact with that "Mind." It brings back from the mystical experience the voice of the nonhuman or extrahuman and shares it with the community, as has been the practice of shamans over the centuries.[16] Though Snyder refrained from claiming that title, this is one of the few poems that he literally sang at public readings, using the musical and inflective power of his voice to convey the poem's strange otherworldliness and power, much as a shaman would. As Snyder told Gene Fowler in a 1964 interview: "A reading is a kind of communion. I think the poet articulates the semi-known for the tribe. This is close to the ancient function of the shaman. It's not a dead function."[17] "Magpie's Song" is one of Snyder's most purely "primitive" poems. Paradoxically, it represents an evolution from the "Shaman songs" found in the early work, *Myth and Texts* (1960). There, the shamanic experience was filtered through the interpretive commentary of the poet-speaker. Here, the experience is sung directly, as if from its original source, nature itself. Such "direct treatment of the thing itself," as Ezra Pound put it in 1913, represents one of the important convergences of primitive and modern poetics.

In "Poetry and the Primitive" *(Earth House Hold,* 1969), Snyder quoted the anthropologist Claude Lévi-Strauss, who predicted the further development in the twentieth century of a type of consciousness "which is neither the mind of savages nor that of primitive or archaic humanity, but rather mind in its untamed state as distinct from mind cultivated or domesticated for yielding a return."[18] Snyder compared this untamed state to a wilderness area, calling it "wild mind."[19] The poet,

148

he said here and elewhere, was its apt spokesman, for from the beginnings in Neolithic shamanism down through the works of specific poets in the Western tradition the poet's role has been to represent the hidden forces of nature within and without. In our own age, characterized by dissociation, alienation, and a destructiveness toward nature of unprecedented proportions, the need for this "wilderness" consciousness, Snyder suggested, was more acute than ever. His poem "What You Should Know to be a Poet" *(Regarding Wave,* 1970) speaks to its reacquisition. Snyder recommended that the aspiring poet learn "all you can about animals as persons," as well as the names of trees, flowers, weeds, and stars; planetary and lunar movements; dreams; the darkness within; human love; the six senses, including the intuitive sense; the ecstasy of the dance; and the "enstasy"[20] of "silent solitary illumination." These elements represent keys to recovering holistic awareness and the "original mind" within each of us, which can counteract the dissociative tendencies inherent in modern society. Snyder's work suggests many doors into this holistic consciousness: through the formal discipline of meditation; through the types of total involvement and attention required by hunting or other forms of nonalienating work; through the investigations of surrounding and interior landscapes demanded by poetry itself. The poet is, by profession, Snyder said, a representative of nature and of "original mind." The poet who returns to his archaic shamanic roots actively seeks this original mind, and when he or she finds it, tries to speak from it to the rest of us, and to speak to it as it exists within the rest of us.

Snyder, like a number of other poets in this century, has come to believe that this "original mind" was open to and sung through the Native Americans on this continent, speaking for all of us to nature and the cosmos, and speaking to us from nature also. This, of course, sounds vague and maybe even silly. But before we dismiss it, let us consider a poem of the contemporary Native American writer Simon Ortiz, "Speaking," which seems to me to do exactly what I have just described, that is, what Snyder suggested was done by Native American shaman-poet. Here, in its entirety, is "Speaking":

I take him outside
under the trees,
have him stand on the ground.
We listen to the crickets,
cicadas, million years old sound.
Ants come by us.
I tell them,
"This is he, my son.
This boy is looking at you.
I am speaking for him."

The crickets, cicadas,
the ants, the millions of years
are watching us,
hearing us.
My son murmurs infant words,
speaking, small laughter
bubbles from him.
Tree leaves tremble.
They listen to this boy
speaking for me.[21]

The poem is notable for its simplicity and its lack of flashy rhetoric. It depicts a shared communion between father and son and the things alive in nature and in time. The father in the poem is, in effect, initiating the son into the "original mind" in nature and in himself by having the boy stand in its midst—"on the ground"—and listen to its voice in the timeless sound of the crickets and cicadas. The poem seeks to contact in its readers a similar sense of the community and continuity of life within time. It concludes with the infant boy's "small laughter"—an expression of his "original mind"—speaking both to and from nature, and for the poet.

This book has attempted to reveal how a similar sense of the community and continuity of life has struck poets in this century as lacking in our culture yet as being vitally necessary. Often independently of one another, these poets have sought to translate and interpret the Native American in ways designed to begin the process of returning the American mind to a fullness that would connect us to where we are and restore a holistic awareness that would enable us to feel, once again, holy and whole. Snyder's work is all directed toward this restoration of inner and outer unity. At times it contains a trenchant critique of American and Western civilization, but this is intended as a "Control Burn," after the Indian practice, as Snyder maintained in a poem of that title in *Turtle Island*. Its purpose, as that poem suggests, is to allow the manzanita seed buried under the razed foliage—that is, the human spirit and spirit of place underneath civilization—to come into flower.

In "Through the Smoke Hole" (*The Back Country*, 1968), Snyder contemplated the smoke hole of the ceremonial kiva of the Pueblo peoples as an image of the ultimate sort of unity that we need to seek. The metaphor is not original with Snyder. He had in fact adapted the metaphorical dimensions the kiva holds for Indian peoples—its living poetry—to the printed page. In Pueblo cultures the smoke hole atop the kiva represents the passage between worlds, the unity of time and timelessness, wordly and spiritual beings, life and death:

> Out of the kiva come
> masked dancers or
> plain men.
> > plain men go into the ground.

The masked dancers referred to here are the spirit beings (kachinas) depicted by ceremonial dancers. But the word *or* in this passage is significant, for the Hopi and other Pueblo tribes believe that the masked dancer is literally transformed into the kachina that his mask represents. His identity as man or spirit is a fluid one. The last line of the quoted passage—"plain men go into the ground"—describes the descent of the dancers into the kiva preparatory to the dance, but at the same time it emphasizes the fact of death. "Through the Smoke Hole" drifts with apparent randomness, like smoke itself, from one image sequence to another—from descriptions of cave paintings depicting the magical figures of tribal myth, to descriptions of actual, earthy women deemed equally magical, to

> thirty million years gone
> > drifting sand
> cool rooms pink stone
> worn down fort floor, slat sighting
> > heat shine on jumna river

dry wash, truck tracks in the riverbed
ciold sand pinyon

    seabottom
    riverbank
    sand dunes
the floor of a sea once again.

The poem, as this characteristic passage suggests, establishes the depth of time and its circularity, senses of which form the foundation of the Native American view of life.[22] "Through the Smoke Hole" itself ends with a line that completes a circle: "Plain men come out of the ground." Here the emphasis is not on death, but on emergence and rebirth. The normal, linear time process has been meaningfully reversed. For the poem has shown us that in the timelessness within which time exists all things occur and recur, shift identities from one reality to another like smoke drifting from the world below of the kiva to the world above. The two planes of existence are revealed as interpenetrating and one.

We exist as "plain men" within this same ticking timelessness on this same living, shifting landscape. Snyder, in this poem and elsewhere, points us to Indian cultures that, like the shamanism he urges poets to emulate, can heal us of our social, psychological, and spiritual ills by helping to restore the unity of life that has been shattered. He reads various attempts by poets in this century to translate the Indian as a fortuitous linkage, an expression of the "antennae of the race," of our need to "reconnect." In "Why Tribe" *(Earth House Hold,* 1969), he wrote of the importance of contemporary poets' interest in Indians and shamanism: "we have almost unwittingly linked ourselves to a transmission of a gnosis, a potential social order, and techniques of enlightenment surviving from prehistoric times."[23]

# ◆ 7 Snyder and the Emergence of Indian Poets: Restoring Unity ◆

> My son touches the root carefully,
> aware of its ancient quality.
> He lays his soft, small fingers on it
> and looks at me for information.
> I tell him: wood, an old root,
> and around it, the earth, ourselves.
>
> Simon Ortiz, "Canyon de Chelley"

Though it is not within the purview of this book to predict future literary trends, it will aid our understanding of today and tomorrow to review quickly the course of literary interest in the Indian during the last fifteen years. Such a review should suggest the intensity and scope of readers' and publishers' attraction to the Indian as well as the context that this activity formed for the appreciation of Gary Snyder's poetry and for the simultaneous emergence of many talented Native American poets.

In the late sixties and early seventies, interest in the Indian reached fad-like proportions. One literary event that contributed to this development was the issuing of the mass-paperback edition of *Black Elk Speaks* by Pocket Books in 1971. Its wide circulation, following John G. Neihardt's appearances on the "Dick Cavett Show," quickly established it as a modern classic. Other ethnographically sound books from earlier in the century began reappearing in paperback editions, among them Charles A. Eastman's *Indian Boyhood,* Luther Standing Bear's *My People the Sioux,* and *Geronimo's Story of His Life,* edited by S. M. Barrett. New Indian autobiographies were also released during this period, most prominent among them *Lame Deer: Seeker of Visions* (1972) and Leonard Crow Dog's *Cante Ishta: The Eye of the Heart* (1977)—both "as told to" Richard Erdoes—N. Scott Momaday's *The Way to Rainy Mountain* (1969) and *The Names: A Memoir* (1976), and Leslie Marmon Silko's *Storyteller* (1981).[1] But other, more dubious and controversial books representing Indian life, philosophy, and culture were also being published and read in startling numbers. The most notorious of these books were usually by non-Indian authors: Carlos Castaneda's *The Teachings of Don Juan: A Yaqui Way of Knowledge* (1968) and its numerous and increasingly fantastic sequels,[2] Hyemeyohsts Storm's *Seven Arrows* (1972), Doug Boyd's *Rolling Thunder* (1976),[3] and, most recently, Ruth Beebe Hill's *Hanta Yo* (1979). This list names only the best, most publicized, or most widely read works of each type. That they are only a sampling of a very large body of recently published Native American literature is indicative of American publishers' sense that Indian consciousness is a highly marketable commodity.

The reasons why Americans in the seventies were so attracted to the Native American tend to be complex. Vine Deloria, Jr., for instance, proposed that a historical pattern of "cycles of interest" in books about Indians had evolved in twentieth-century publishing in which every twenty years or so a flurry of books by whites appears and one or two Native American writers are permitted to emerge: for example, Charles Eastman and Pauline Johnson were popular around 1910; Luther Standing Bear around 1930; D'Arcy McNickle around 1950; and Ortiz, Silko, Momaday, and Deloria himself around 1970.[4] But publishing cycles should be considered only one contributing factor. More specific indications of why Americans in increasing numbers investigated the Indian in the seventies can be found in the cultural conditions of the period. Just as the development of Native American literature had been earlier accelerated by the general cultural disillusionment following World War I, the Vietnam War exerience contributed significantly to the literary surge of the seventies. Americans who were uneasy with the cultural assumptions that had led us into an unpopular and unjust war were hungry for the alternative spirituality, norms, and values presented in these Indian books. Much of the identification with the Indian that took place in the late sixties was based on a political opposition to the war and a sense that Indians were indigenous peoples who had been long overlooked and similarly wronged. Repelled philosophically and politically by the Vietnam experience, many people transferred their sympathy for the Vietnamese people to the American Indian, who had seen their cultures disrupted by American military might, their peoples displaced and beggared in barren reservations and instant agency villages (BIA rather than CIA). Tom Hayden's widely read *The Love of Possessions Is a Disease with Them* (1972) makes a compelling analysis of such parallels, showing how what was done to both the Vietnamese and the Indians stemmed from the same alienation from place, nature, and other people that has been a central concern of most of the American poets we have discussed in this book.

In the later stages of the Vietnamese War and its aftermath (1970–77), however, when its opponents in considerable numbers were withdrawing from the political consciousness and activism of the protest period (1964–70) and were rejecting traditional American materialism as unfulfilling in itself, many of them turned with typical American energy and dogged self-centeredness to look for enlightenment in the Indian books being published then. These books, which spoke to their need for new sources of spirituality and to a simultaneous resurgence of interest in the occult, reaped plentiful profits for America's paperback publishers.

In the poetry being published during this time (1974–77 or thereabouts), we can see a similar widespread interest in the Indian. Some poets came to Indian materials with respect and a deeply felt need to discover the alternative philosophical, social, and spiritual lessons that might help them locate and explore their own senses of self and Americanism. Other poets, however, came to Indian cultures as exploiters or consumers, tasting the latest popular product in the spiritual supermarket, in search of subject matter that would enable them to get published in the numerous literary magazines publishing Indian poems written by non-Indian writers.

Partially in response to this widespread interest by white readers and writers, a different and very powerful new force also emerged during this time: literature written in English by Indian people themselves. This literary activity paralleled a new Indian consciousness and assertiveness in politics, which culminated in the Wounded Knee protest in 1973. It was also, however, a reaction to the literary popularization, cooptation, and distortion of their heritage, identity, and consciousness. Native Americans, of course, could write of these things from authentic personal knowledge. They did not have to work to get there because they had been there. Deloria, Momaday, Silko, and Ortiz (among others) came to the forefront of a very active literary movement that is reflected on the lists of national publishers, like Harper & Row, and even more so in the evolving of Native American and "Third World" literary magazines and small presses. These presses and magazines had risen in response to a new interest in the sixties and seventies in "ethnic" literature. At first, in the sixties, this referred mainly to black and Jewish writers, but gradually it came to include

Native Americans, Asian Americans, Chicanos, Poles, Italians, and other groups. The melting-pot concept that had endured for so long was giving way to a new sense of America as a multicultural society with a literature to match.

Probably the most influential publication in spreading a national Indian consciousness in the late sixties and early seventies was *Akwesasne Notes,* a Native American newspaper published on the Mohawk reservation in upstate New York. *Notes'* editor during most of this period was Jerry Gamble, a Jewish American whose interest in Indians led him to the Mohawk reservation and kept him there during the same years that Jerome Rothenberg was in residence among the nearby Seneca. Rather than simply taking from the people he had settled among, Gamble got involved with the local community by sharing with it his considerable organizational and journalistic skills as he acquired an understanding of Indian lifeways and problems. Gamble was later adopted into the tribe and given the Mohawk name Rarihokwats. *Akwesasne Notes* featured detailed coverage of important issues for Indian peoples around the nation, in Canada, and in Latin America. The protests at Alcatraz and Wounded Knee, fishing-rights disputes in the Northwest, uranium mining and strip-mining in the Southwest, pollution-related illness on reservations in the Northeast all received the sort of investigative coverage in *Akwesasne Notes* that was unavailable elsewhere. *Akwesasne Notes* featured articles on Native American spirituality, history, and traditions; book reviews; and a back page regularly devoted to poetry. This last feature was influential in reviving the practice of writing poetry in Indian communities. It helped to establish poetry, for many young Indians, as a powerful means of expressing identity, solidarity, and commitment.

The literary assertiveness of Indian peoples in the seventies can also be accounted for in part by the fact that more Native Americans than ever before were attending colleges and universities, where many became active in creative-writing programs. At the universities of Oklahoma, New Mexico, Arizona, and South Dakota, especially, they made their presence felt, often receiving the aid of sympathetic whites. At the University of Arizona in Tucson, Larry Evers and his Indian students founded the Native American literary magazine

*Suntracks*. Kenneth Rosen, a teacher-editor at the University of New Mexico, began collecting the works of young Indian writers like Ortiz and Silko. His efforts resulted in two widely read anthologies: one of short stories, *Man to Send Rainclouds;* and one of poetry, *Voices of the Rainbow*. At the University of South Dakota, John Milton, editor of the *South Dakota Review,* also began taking an interest in and publishing Indian writers in his magazine and in subsequent anthologies. *Akwesasne Notes, South Dakota Review, Suntracks, Wassaja,* and *Scree;* "Third World" multicultural journals like *The Greenfield Review* in the East, *Y'Bird* in the West, and *River Styx* in the Midwest; and presses like Maurice Kenny's Strawberry Press and the Blue Cloud Quarterly Press, directed by the Benedictine monk Benet Tvedten, have published the work of many young Indian writers. Poets like Peter Blue Cloud, Ray Young Bear, Wendy Rose, Paula Gunn Allen, Carter Revard, Maurice Kenny, Duane Niatum, Joy Harjo, Diane Burns, and Joseph Bruchac have published widely in such small-press outlets and subsequently made the pages of national anthologies such as Milton's two-volume *The American Indian Speaks* (1969 and 1971) and *Four Indian Poets* (1974), Walter Lowenfels's *From the Belly of the Shark* (1973), Dick Lowie's *Come to Power* (1974), Robert K. Dodge and Joseph B. McCollough's *Voices from Wah'Kon-Tah* (1974), Duane Niatum's *Carriers of the Dream Wheel* (1975), Rosen's *Voices of the Rainbow* (1975), James White's *The First Skin around Me* (1976), and Geary Hobson's *The Remembered Earth* (1979).

It was in this atmosphere of intense interest in the Indian by whites and intense literary activity by Indian writers that Snyder's *Turtle Island* was published and won the Pulitzer Prize for 1974. For Snyder, the book culminated more than twenty years of work in which the Indian had been a central influence, dating back to his undergraduate thesis, a study of Haida myth recently published by Grey Fox Press as *He Who Hunted Birds in His Father's Village* (1979). Nevertheless, many Indian writers perceived Snyder's acclaimed book as part of a new cavalry charge into their territory by wild-eyed neo-romantics seeking to possess not merely their land, as had the invaders of the previous century, but their very spirit. Silko and Hobson responded to Snyder's book (and to his winning the Pulitzer Prize, no doubt) with critical broadsides in Ishmael Reed's multicultural journal *Y'Bird,* staking claim by dint of prior use to their literary territory and thereby raising important issues that pertain to many of the writers covered in this book.

Silko, in "An Old Time Indian Attack" (1975), and Hobson, in "The Rise of the White Shaman as a New Version of Cultural Imperialism" (1976), challenged as racist two assumptions that are central to many American poets' exploration and use of Indian subject matter. First, they questioned the assumption that chants, prayers, and stories "weaseled" out of Indian groups by white ethnologists were public property to be reused and often rewritten for use outside of their intended cultural circle. Hobson, for instance, challenged "the assumption . . . that one's 'interest' in an Indian culture makes it okay for an invader to collect 'data' from Indian people, when, in effect, this taking of the essentials of cultural lifeways, even in the name of Truth or Scholarship or whatever, is as imperialistic as those simpler forms of theft such as the theft of homeland by treaty."[5] This challenge speaks to the arrogance and insensitivity often reflected in the display of sacred materials outside their proper context. The printing of a translated chant in a book or its performance by a poet at a reading is, from this point of view akin to the display of medicine bundles under glass in a museum. In each case a power object is reduced to a curiosity or an artifact of a dead culture. What interest and, more important, *whose* interest does this serve? Certainly, Hobson and Silko have argued, it is not that of the people and purpose for which the poem or power object were intended.

But even among Indian peoples themselves, such an argument raises issues that, for many, are relative and not absolute. The attitude, sensitivity, and understanding with which Indian material is used by whites are often perceived by Native Americans as the crucial factor in rendering judgments about the value of such activity. Some Indian groups, the Hopi, for instance, hold that their teaching and responsibility is for the whole world. Black Elk, among the Sioux, shared a similar impulse. Within contemporary Indian societies the issue of openness is the subject of an ongoing debate. Given the exploitative history of Indian people's relationships with even well-meaning and friendly whites, it is understandable that there is resistance to sharing what is ultimately their most precious possession—their identity, based as it is on centuries of accumulated wisdom. Nevertheless, many Indians, the respected Vine Deloria among them, feel that it is in the interest of everyone on the continent that certain areas of Native American consciousness and knowledge be shared with sincere and respectful whites.[6]

The second challenge posed by Silko and Hobson speaks directly to this issue of sincerity and respectfulness. Silko, for instance, has questioned "the assumption that the white man, through some innate cultural or racial superiority, has the ability to master the essential beliefs, values, and emotions of persons from Native American communities." Such an assumption, she continued, "flourishes among white poets and writers who romanticize their 'power' as writers to inhabit souls and consciousness far beyond the realm of their knowledge or experience." Silko quoted Louis Simpson, for instance, talking glibly in an interview of "the poem which you wrote like an Indian, where you understood how he thought, his magic, his values." Hobson quoted a lesser contemporary poet, Gene Fowler: "Everyone of us is part Indian, y'know."[7] The cultural arrogance implicit in these typical statements is not restricted to contemporary writers. Hart Crane, for instance, was writing of the red man to Otto Kahn in a 1927 letter: "I think I really succeed in getting under the skin of this glorious and dying animal, in terms of expression, in symbols, which he himself could comprehend."[8] Such assumptions, as Silko has pointed out, reflect attitudes that are peculiarly American. She asserted, for instance, that no Indian person would assume that he or she could experience the world in the way that a white American does.[9] Further, the American desire to inhabit the soul of another people reflects a spiritual dis-ease, an insecure sense of self:

> Ironically, as white poets attempt to cast-off their Anglo-American values, their Anglo-American origins, they violate a fundamental belief held by the tribal people they desire to emulate: they deny their history, their very

161

origins. The writing of imitation "Indian" poems then,
is pathetic evidence that in more than two hundred years,
Anglo Americans have failed to create a satisfactory iden-
tity for themselves.[10]

This failure of identity is, of course, a point we have found
ourselves returning to again and again in our discussions of
poets throughout the century. It has been my position, how-
ever, that such a search for fulfilling American identity need
not be viewed exclusively as pathetic, though certainly it
can be viewed that way and has been by several American
writers, including Hart Crane. For many Indians and whites
alike, however, the interest in Indian things is interpreted as a
healthy sign, one indicating recognition of the need to make
contact with place, nature, and people in new-old ways that
are not destructive and self-destructive. Poets like Snyder,
Rothenberg, Williams, and Olson share with each other and
with Native American medicine people such as Hiamovi at
the turn of the century,[11] Black Elk and Luther Standing Bear
in the thirties, and Lame Deer, Leonard Crow Dog, and the
Hopi elders of recent year an acceptance of the reality that many
different peoples now, for better or worse, make up the hu-
man family inhabiting the American continent. They feel, in
the face of Euro-Americans' destructive stance toward nature,
if the common human experience here is to be for the better,
that Indian peoples should be looked to for their knowledge
with the respect and attention due to grandparents or teachers.
In such an acceptance there lies a hope that transcends pathos,
that a unity of consciousness can be restored to the New World
that we inhabit and create.

All of this is not to say that Hobson's and Silko's criti-
cisms are easily dismissed. They contain a good deal of truth.
Cultural arrogance, neo-romanticism, literary careerism, and
a failure to recognize and respect the Indian's contemporary
reality have been part and parcel of American writers' interest
in the Indian throughout the century. Many poets, like Vachel
Lindsay, have sought an appropriation of Indian identity rather
than a creative synthesis of some sort. They have often been
obsessed with the very un-Indian notion of possessing the
land. Other writers, however, have been less self-centered,

more sensitive, more open. Snyder, Rothenberg, Olson, Williams, and Lawrence do not, in theory, advocate becoming Indians. Rather they seek a creative synthesis of the best and most usable features of Native American and Euro-Christian consciousness. But even in their writings we can discover passages that reflect cultural excesses.

With the popularization of Indian consciousness in recent years, such excesses have become more prevalent; with the upsurge in Indian identity among Indian peoples and the corresponding appearance of many articulate Native American writers, resentment of these excesses has become outspoken. Silko and Hobson polemically shook their fists at Snyder for being the best-known contemporary popularizer of poetic interest in the Indian, but it is clear from their writing that they regarded Snyder's followers, not Snyder himself, as their main problem. These followers include many lesser poets—"second raters," or "the bastard children of Snyder," as Hobson has referred to them—whose concerns are more superficial and whose claims to be "white shamans" are more extravagant and egocentric. The works of these neo-romantic writers not only misrepresent the Indian but also create false norms for "Indian literature" with which Native American writers themselves must compete. As Hobson noted:

> Since the American public has already become accustomed to seeing the Jerome Rothenberg "translations," the poetry of "white shamans" such as Gary Snyder, Gene Fowler, Norman Moser, Barry Gifford, David Cloutier, to name a few, and other neo-romantic writers posing as Indians and/or Indian experts/spokesmen, such as Carlos Castaneda, Hyemeyohsts Storm, Tony Shearer, Doug Boyd, the Baha'i influenced "Indian" works of Naturegraph Publications, contemporary Indian writers are often discounted or ignored since they are not following or conforming to the molds created by these "experts."

Such writers, Hobson complained, "too often perceive Indian cultures through not only the rose-colored glasses of a white, Anglo-Saxon Protestant viewpoint, but the day-glo spectacles of a hastily assumed Oriental (Buddhist-Taoist, etc.) outlook."[12] His and Silko's main objection is to the ease with

which white American writers "slough off the old conscious-
ness" of European identity, to borrow Lawrence's metaphor,
and assume a new skin. They urge American poets—and Sny-
der is specifically named—to follow the Indian example and
deal more closely and directly with their own heritage, to do
more to come to grips with and accept this part of their actual
identity.

Such advice is well given. Snyder has written of his own
ancestry sparingly, usually indirectly, and has almost always
rejected it, cursing or turning away. His typical viewpoint is
found in poems like "A Curse on the Men of the Pentagon"
or in "Dusty Braces" *(Turtle Island),* where he wrote:

> you bastards . . .
>
> my fathers
>     and grandfathers, stiff-necked
> punchers, miners, dirtfarmers, railroad men
> killed off the cougar and the grizzly.

The question is still open as to whether Snyder will ever ex-
plore his ancestry in some depth and ever find anything worth
holding onto there as he has in exploring his kinship with Bud-
dhist sages and Native Americans. Interestingly, Rothenberg
emerged from his period of intense involvement with Indian
poetry and cultures to explore somewhat exhaustively his own
roots as a European Jew and an avant-garde poet, as has been
reflected in his subsequent publications: *Poland: 1931* (1970),
*Revolution of the Word* (1974), *America, a Prophecy* (1976), and
*A Big Jewish Book* (1978). In Rothenberg's total work for the
last fifteen years, which includes these texts, his tribal anthol-
ogies, and *Seneca Journal* (1978) with its poems like "Cokboy"
and "The Serpent," in which both Indian and Western influ-
ences come into play, we can see a movement toward a crea-
tive synthesis of the sources in both time and space that
contribute to his present American identity. Such a synthesis
of temporal and spatial sources of identity and kinship is not
inconsistent with what poets like Snyder, Olson, and others
have groped for, with varying degrees of success, in their work.
Nor is it inconsistent with the work of Silko, Ortiz, and other

Native American writers who have explored the temporal depth of their heritage within the spatial context of contemporary American culture.

Ultimately, Silko and Hobson have not denied American poets the possibility of meaningfully and legitimately drawing on Indian cultures to form a viable outlook on who they are and where they are. Hobson, in fact, cited Snyder's early "shaman songs" in *Myths and Texts,* the very poems that he described as inadvertently starting the "white shaman" phenomenon, as containing "great vitality" and representing "sincere efforts to incorporate an essential part of American Indian philosophy into his work." But Silko and Hobson also wrote from the point of view of the contemporary Indian writer, whose indigenous literary territory they felt they must protect from exploiters, distorters, and invaders. They were concerned, as Hobson put it, "for the great need Indian people have to speak for themselves, of being the ones to define themselves and their culture."[13]

*Native American Consciousness*

Indian writers have been speaking for themselves in the seventies, but not only of and with the holistic awareness celebrated by white poets and represented in Ortiz's poem "Speaking." We also find in much of their work a strong sense of the fragmentation and loss that results in the poverty, alcoholism, and despair that have been very much a part of the Native American heritage in this century. In the work by contemporary Native American poets depicting this depressing reality, we often find that the bar rather than the ceremonial kiva or longhouse has become the main setting for the expression of spiritual truths. James Welch, of Blackfoot and Gros Ventre descent, is one of the best mappers of this terrain. In his "Harlem Montana: Just Off the Reservation," we can quickly sense the oppressive inner and outer atmosphere:

> We need no runners here. Booze is law
> and all the Indians drink in the best tavern.
> Money is free if you're poor enough.
> Disgusted, busted whites are running
> for office in this town.[14]

In Welch's work we find an environment full of hopelessness, hatred, despair. His characters tend to lack both worldly and spiritual power and to be anguished about it. His Indians are not noble savages but poor, desperate human beings with only the vaguest and bitterest sense of their own rich heritage:

> Harlem, your hotel is overnamed, your children
> are raggedy-assed but you go on, survive
> the bad food from the two cafes and peddle
> your hate for the wild who bring you money.
> When you die, if you die, you will remember
> the three young bucks who shot the grocery up,
> locked themselves in and cried for days, we're rich,
> help us, oh God, we're rich.

A number of meanings coalesce in this final image: the desperation that Indian people feel in their poverty; the despair of being separated—having "locked themselves in"—from both the white and Indian worlds; and the inability to use the riches of either of these worlds. This is heavy stuff, far from the jolly Indians of Lindsay's "Dr. Mohawk." Welch's Indians often hate themselves and, in a perverse way, also hate the Indian past they cannot connect with. In "D-Y Bar," for instance, where "the tune is cowboy, the words sentimental crap," Welch depicts the humiliation of the Indian futilely trying to come to grips with his heritage in the midst of the local bar's sleazy, squalid, mocking surroundings:

> In stunted light, Bear Child tells a story
> to the mirror. He acts his name out,
> creeks muscling gorges fill his glass
> with gumbo. The bear crawls on all fours
> and barks like a dog. Slithering snake-wise
> he balances a nickel on his nose. The effect
> a snake in heat.

Bear Child's attempt to contact his own identity by psychologically or perhaps even literally acting out his Indian name results in a pathetic charade. He succeeds only in depicting his own confused and oppressed condition as he barks like a dog, slithers like snake, and balances a coin on his nose like a circus animal. In the D-Y Bar, where, Welch's narrator ironically tells us, "We all know our names," Bear Child cannot find himself, let alone the traditional wisdom and power of his bear namesake and totem. Welch leaves the poem's hero at the bar, "head down, the dormant bear."

We find similar disintegration and despair in the powerful poems of Marnie Walsh, a Sioux. In her "Vicki Loans Arrow," we encounter another trapped, depressed Indian character in a bar:

> this morning
> me and my cousin
> charlene lost nation
> are in to bobby simons bar
> and charlene say
> i tired of living
> there ain't nothing in it
> and bobby simon
> behind the bar
> goes ha ha ha
> when she fall off
> the stool
> i'm laughing too
> she so drunk
> she funny[15]

Charlene, whose name "lost nation" represents the dissociation felt by many Indians, has given up on life. As with Welch's Bear Child, her plight is pictured in tragicomic terms. But the comedy leaves the poem when, toward its end, the narrator finds Charlene sitting in a corner of the rest room, bloody from a self-inflicted wound:

> she looks at me
> and i see the knife
> sticking out between her teeth
> and remember what that means
> and i know shed like to die
> but cant
> so she killed her tongue
> instead.

Charlene's mutilated tongue "speaks" her inability to discover and express her true self. Her condition as a contemporary Indian lost between Native American and American cultures stifles her sense of who she really is. And so we find her drinking away her mornings and presumably the rest of her days, hopelessly, barely alive. "Vicki Loans Arrow" ends with the speaker, Charlene's drinking companion, shaken by what she's seen and heard and initiated into her cousin's despairing view:

> i leave her there
> i go out the door
> and down the street
> and the yellow wind
> make me shiver and sweat
> because now i believe her
> but wont never say so

These passages represent only a few of many possible example of poems by Indian writers that approach what Ortiz has observed as

> . . . the yet unseen translation
> where Indians have been backed up into
> and on long liquor nights, working
> in their minds, the anger and madness
> will come forth in tongues and fury.[16]

The bar is an apt setting for these works, for it is literally the place where Indian people often go to fill the emptiness they feel. But the desolation of these poems is not restricted to the barroom or its habitués. It is found everywhere contemporary Indian people are. Ortiz, for instance, who is from Acoma Pueblo, set one of his most moving poems, "Blessings," "at a civil rights function in 1969." Here, the poem's speaker senses that his hosts "are getting bored with [Indians'] misfortunes." He responds to their requests for specific proposals—how much gas is needed for a tractor, and so on—thus:

> i wait for them to ask,
> "How many dreams have you spent lately?
> How many hopes?"
>
> We are not hungry for promises of money
> not for anyone to write us
> carefully written proposals.

168

> We are hungry for the good earth,
> the deserts and mountains growing corn.
> We are hungry for the conviction
> that you are our brothers and sisters
> who are willing to share our love
> and compassionate fingers in your hands.

The poem eloquently expresses the longing of Indian peoples for a harmonious relationship with people and place, which is strikingly similar to the impulse behind much of the work of the white writers we've discussed.

The anger and frustration of contemporary Native Americans are further evidenced in the poems of Maurice Kenny, a Mohawk, and in those of the poets published in his Strawberry Press chapbook series. Kenny's "Boston Tea Party," for instance, depicts the poet's clenched rage at being regarded by his rapt audience as an all-knowing "savior and warrior, priest and poet, . . . savage and prophet, angel of death and apostle of truth."[17] Kenny refuses to play the role of a guru, describing how he eludes the leading questions of a radio interviewer in search of a modern medicine man and healer:

> I revealed only the colors of the day:
> forsythia bloomed his April yard,
> magnolias striking purple against
> the Cambridge sky; the mutability
> of the State, its saccharine lies.
> I revealed the dirt between my toes,
> lice crawling my crotch, wax building
> in my ears.

Kenny comically reminds us of how the eagerness of spiritually starved whites to romanticize the Native American denies the Indian's contemporary reality and humanity, at the same time obfuscating the fact that what America has become is now our common problem:

> Again I spoke of hunger:
> A "Big Mac" would do, instant coffee,
> plastic pizza, anything but holy water.
>
> No light hung over my monk's shaped head.
> No priest hid behind my coat.

169

This same general theme of spiritual and cultural disintegration among both contemporary Indians and whites is confronted in the poetry and prose of another prominent Native American writer, Leslie Marmon Silko of Laguna Pueblo. Silko, however, depicts the restoration of the broken unity, seeking perspective, understanding, and coherence through the application of the old stories of the Native American tradition. In her critically acclaimed novel, *Ceremony* (1977), the main character, a Laguna named Tayo, is a World War II veteran whose battle experiences have left him shaken and sick. Old Betonie, a strange medicine man who lives among the skid-row Indian derelicts in Gallup, New Mexico, helps restore Tayo to health by performing a healing ceremony and by making him understand that his sickness inside is the sickness of the modern world itself, a "witchery ranging as far as this world." Tayo must confront the witchery in himself, in his fellow veterans, and symbolically, in America itself, as the book reaches its climax along the chain-link fence of a uranium mine not far from the atomic testing grounds in the American desert. Ultimately, Tayo is restored to power and health by relying on the Native American traditionalism embodied in the stories rejected by his more modern Indian friends.

The real hero of Silko's *Ceremony,* however, is not Tayo but the Native American storytelling tradition itself. As Silko wrote in "Ceremony," the poem that begins the novel:

> I will tell you something about stories,
> > he said
> They aren't just entertainment.
> > Don't be fooled.
> They are all we have, you see,
> > all we have to fight off
> > illness and death.
>
> > You don't have anything
> if you don't have the stories.

Old stories, in the form of poems to distinguish them from the novel's narrative, are woven throughout. They act as commentaries and explications of the events in Tayo's story and reveal how the storytelling tradition keeps alive old values and lends meaning to contemporary events. Tayo's struggle for sanity, identity, and inner harmony, in this context, becomes the recurrent struggle to "purify your town," which, as the old stories populated by sacred insects and animals show and continually tell us, "is not easy." (Crane, Williams, Olson, and Snyder, it should be noted, have told us much the same thing.) Tayo's personal struggle comes to be perceived as a universal and thus ennobling one, transcending barriers of time. The old stories give Tayo (and the reader) power by connecting him to the past; to the animals and insects of this place, who are revealed as involved in the same struggle against witchery; as well as to the present, which is seen as new version of an eternally recurrent tale. As Old Grandma says at the novel's conclusion, "It seems like I already heard these stories before . . . only thing is, the names sound different."[18] Silko herself has made a similar observation in response to an interviewer:

> I don't see that there has ever been any end to the stories. They just keep going on and on. So far, I haven't seen that there are any new ones. There's a need to have a multiplicity of perspectives and tellers. I tell some stories. Simon Ortiz tells others. The ones I'm looking after have always been around. It's part of a continuum.[19]

Her point is that seeing ourselves as part of this continuum lends a sense of relationship, coherence, and meaning to everyday struggles.

Silko's *Ceremony* and the work of other Indian writers like Momaday (whose novel, *House Made of Dawn,* won a 1969 Pulitzer Prize), Kenny, Walsh, and Welch show that the twentieth-century Native American combats the same disintegrative witchery as does his white counterpart:

> Then they grow away from the earth
> then they grow away from the sun
> they they grew away from the plants and animals.
> They see no life
> When they look
> they see only objects.
> The world is a dead thing for them
> the trees and rivers are not alive
> the mountains and stones are not alive.

*The deer and bear are objects.*
*They see no life.*

*They fear.*
*They fear the world.*
*They destroy what they fear.*
*They fear themselves.*[20]

This passage from *Ceremony* describes the effects of the witchery primarily on whites but also on all peoples in America. Like the works of many of the white poets discussed earlier, Silko's poem points to a separation from surrounding and inner nature as the dis-easing affliction of the modern world, one that affects, as Silko wrote, "the fate of all living things, and even the earth." Old Man Betonie, the medicine man who treats Tayo, emphasizes that the cure begins not in battling or blaming others: " 'Nothing is that simple,' he said, 'you don't write off all the white people, just like you don't trust all the Indians.' "[21] Instead, the cure begins with "a good ceremony" that aids the individual to cure the witchery in himself. "This has been going on for a long time now," Betonie tells Tayo, and we sense the generations and centuries behind his words. "It's up to you. Don't let them stop you. Don't let them finish off the world."[22] In this view, each person is responsible for himself and, through himself, for his world. The inner and the outer reality are one unity.

In essence, Betonie's comments can speak for much of the writing by poets in this century who have turned to the Indian for a symbol, a story, a basis for poetry, and a coherent view of life. These writings grow out of a similar sense of crisis as it is reflected in the realms of literature, history, and spirituality. They likewise seek to make us confront the crisis primarily by delving within ourselves and to open us up, extend us, to reconnect us with our own vital source and other living things, to make us part of the world once again and not apart from it. Silko's *Ceremony* dramatizes this struggle toward a restoration of unity that has been the primary theme implicit in the poetics, poems, and prose of so many of the white poets we have discussed. In *Ceremony,* Tayo regains his health, and his world is restored to meaning. The witchery "is dead for now."[23] The book's final chant is repeated the sacred four times, but the phrase "for now" suggests the need for continued vigilance. Tayo, we are told,

> cried the relief he felt at finally seeing the pattern, the way all the stories fit together—the old stories, their stories—to become the story that was still being told. He was not crazy; he had never been crazy. He has only seen and heard the world as it always was: no boundaries, only transitions through all distances and time.[24]

American poets in this century interested in the Indian have similarly sought this boundaryless sense of "the world as it always was." Their work represents attempts to build meaningful transitions from the American past to the American present. Like Silko's novel, their efforts can be seen as an evolving ceremony offered to those who read it and need it, to restore in us a sense of continuity, harmony, and health.

In our brief look at the work of contemporary Indian poets, we can see two striking similarities to the white writers we have examined: an anguish over man's lost unity with his fellows and with inner and outer nature, and a desire somehow to restore that unity by connecting with the Native American past. The concluding words of *Ceremony*[25] can close our discussion effectively, for they suggest what so many of the American and Native American writers we've reviewed here have sought in their attention to Indian cultures: a reality in which we are in tune with nature's cyclical rhythms and become participants in them; a reality that is coherent, bright, and hopeful—

> Sunrise,
>     accept this offering,
> sunrise.

# ♦ Notes ♦

*Preface*

1. The development of the Indian image in American literature has been traced in Albert Keiser's *The Indian in American Literature* and Elémire Zolla's *The Writer and the Shaman: A Morphology of the American Indian*, translated by Raymond Rosenthal. A good source for studying the origins of the brutish and noble savage archetypes is *The Wild Man Within: An Image in Western Thought from the Renaissance to Romanticism*, edited by Edward Dudley and Maximillian E. Novak. Undesignated quotes in the preface are from this text.

2. For an in-depth study of the image of the Indian in Puritan and other early American literature, especially in captivity narratives, see Richard Slotkin, *Regeneration Through Violence: The Mythology of the American Frontier 1600-1860*.

3. Emerson's statement is cited in Keiser, p. 205, and Zolla, p. 139. Its original source is *Life of Henry Wadsworth Longfellow*, edited by Samuel Longfellow (Boston, 1886), 2:266.

4. Arthur O. Lovejoy and George Boas, *Primitivism and Related Ideas in Antiquity*.

5. Of course, in interpreting and adopting this consciousness they run the risk of distorting it and themselves. Contemporary Indian writers Geary Hobson and Leslie Silko discuss this tendency in their attacks on the "white shaman" writings which proliferated in the 1970s. Their essays on this subject are taken up in Chapter 7. Wendy Rose, who is of Hopi-Miwok-Cornish descent, in her poem "For the White Poets Who Would Be Indian," complains of the common tendency among these writers to expect "instant and primal knowledge," to "finish [their] poem and go back" to their comfortable white ways. Something deeper than such superficialism is, of course, what's called for here. As the Acoma poet Simon Ortiz puts

it in his powerful book *From Sand Creek*, we must all dig deeper beneath the surface to "develop another strain of corn."

6. Jan Castro and Michael Castro, "Interview with Gary Snyder," pp. 40–41.

7. Michael Castro, *The Kokopilau Cycle* (Marvin, S. Dak.: Blue Cloud Quarterly Press, 1975).

*Chapter 1*

1. Natalie Curtis, *The Indians' Book*, p. xxi. Hiamovi, identified by Curtis as "High-Chief of the Cheyenne and the Dakota," wrote a preface to *The Indians' Book* in which he suggested that the book's main value was its contribution to the white man's inevitable realization of common humanity with the red man. "In this land where once were only Indians," Hiamovi wrote, "are now men of every color—white, black, yellow, red—yet all one people. That this should come to pass was in the heart of the great mystery. It is right thus. And everywhere there shall be peace."

2. For an account of Roosevelt's support of *The Indians' Book* project, see Natalie Curtis, "Mr. Roosevelt and Indian Music," pp. 399–400.

3. *Dial* (1 December 1907), p. 302.

4. N. Curtis, quoted in *American Review of Reviews* 36 (November 1907): 63.

5. The search for poetic renewal and roots through contact with the original inhabitants of a place is not unique to American poets. T. S. Eliot made a similar appeal to the British, urging them to retain the remaining vestiges of the original languages and literatures of the tribal peoples of the British Isles lest British culture stultify and decay. See T. S. Eliot, *Notes Toward the Definition of Culture.*

6. *The New York Times*, 25 February 1911, p. 8.

7. Even for those skilled in Indian languages, adequate translation, as many of them have noted, is extremely difficult. Some degree of interpretation is inevitably necessary, as is suggested by the standard ethnological practice of providing both literal and literary translations of each poem. In many instances syntactical and structural differences between Indian languages and English make literal translations awkward and incomprehensible. A given song or ceremonial chant's accompanying act or cultural context often leads to similar difficulties. Frederick Hodge, an early translator of Indian song, wrote: "The peculiarities of Indian languages and the forms in which the Indian has cast his poetic thought, particularly in song,

make it impossible to reproduce them literally in a foreign language" (quoted in A. Grove Day, ed., *The Sky Clears: Poetry of the American Indians*, p. 18.) Similarly, Ruth Underhill observed *(Singing for Power: The Song of the Papago Indians of Southern Arizona*, p. 16):

> A translator of a language so different from ours in all its devices as an Indian tongue has much to answer for. The entire way of thought is different. So are the grammatical forms and the order of words. One can hope to make a translation exact only in spirit, not in letter.

8. Mary Hunter Austin, *The American Rhythm: Studies and Re-expressions of Amerindian Songs*, p. 28.

9. In her autobiography, *Earth Horizon*, Austin described two such experiences. The first occurred while she was walking in the Illinois woods at the age of five. She recalled a sudden sense of the presence of God: of the windblown grass being alive, of a walnut tree above her reaching into the immensity of blue sky, of a bright flower and dozing bee, of a pulsing light, and "the swift, inclusive awareness of each for the whole—I in them and they in me and all of us enclosed in a warm lucent bubble of livingness" (p. 21).

10. Austin, *The American Rhythm*, p. 38.

11. Austin, *Earth Horizon*, p. 333.

12. Carl Sandburg, review of *Chippewa Music, Poetry: A Magazine of Verse* 9 (February 1917):255. The quotation from Monroe is from the same issue, p. 251.

13. Monroe, "Editorial Comment," *Poetry, A Magazine of Verse* 7 (November 1915):84.

14. It is now published as *American Indian Poetry: An Anthology of Songs and Chants*, new ed., ed. George W. Cronyn (New York: Liveright, 1970).

15. Alice Cunningham Fletcher, "The Hako," p. 324.

16. The resonant power of "the thing itself"—the image or emotion directly presented—was, of course, a basic tenet of imagism. Pound called for "direct treatment of the 'thing' whether subjective or objective" ("A Retrospect," *Literary Essays of Ezra Pound*, p. 3). Williams later established the imagist credo "No ideas but in things" *(Paterson*, Book I, p. 14).

17. For an account of her method, see Alice Corbin Henderson, "Aboriginal Poetry," *Poetry, A Magazine of Verse* 9 (February 1917):256.

18. Frances Densmore, *Chippewa Music, Part II*, pp. 109–17. Lacrosse, it should be noted, is a game laden with ceremonial significance for the Chippewa. It was played by them as part of the sum-

mer ceremonies. Carter Revard (in a private conversation, August 1981) suggested that the Chippewa song's meaning might be read by an American as "they rang his bell in the Super Bowl, but he got up and scored the winning touchdown."

19. Ibid., p. 81.

20. I have here broken into poetic lines the prose account found in Austin, *The American Rhythm*, p. 53.

21. Ezra Pound, *Gaudier-Brzeska: A Memoir*, pp. 81–84.

22. William Bevis, "American Indian Verse Translations," p. 309. See also Jeffrey F. Huntsman, "Traditional Native American Literature: The Translation Dilemma," pp. 5–9.

23. Austin, Introduction to *The Path on the Rainbow*, p. xxvi.

24. George W. Cronyn, "Indian Melodists and Mr. Untermeyer," p. 162.

25. Nellie Barnes, *American Indian Verse: Characteristics of Style*, p. 9.

26. Paula Gunn Allen, "The Sacred Hoop: A Contemporary Indian Perspective on American Indian Literature," p. 222.

27. Ibid., p. 228.

28. Northrop Frye, *The Anatomy of Criticism* (Princeton, N.J.: Princeton University Press, 1957), p. 278.

29. Margot Astrov, *The Winged Serpent: An Anthology of American Indian Prose and Poetry*, p. 23.

30. Curtis, *The Indians' Book*, p. xxv.

31. John (Fire) Lame Deer and Richard Erdoes, *Lame Deer: Seeker of Visions*, p. 96.

32. Allen, "The Sacred Hoop," p. 234.

33. Fortune and Malinowski quoted in Andrew Welsh, *Roots of Lyric: Primitive Poetry and Modern Poetics*, p. 234.

34. Welsh's *Roots of Lyric*; Jerome Rothenberg's "Pre-Face" to *Technicians of the Sacred: A Range of Poetries from Africa, America, Asia, and Oceania*; and C. M. Bowra's *Primitive Song* are good places to start surveying contemporary writers' awareness of the relationship between primitive and modern poetries.

35. Austin, *The American Rhythm*, pp. 44, 42.

36. Ibid., p. 55.

37. Ibid., p. 4.

38. Ibid., p. 8.

39. Ibid., p. 32.

40. Ibid., p. 54.

41. Ibid., p. 29.

42. Lewis Mumford, review in *New Republic*, 30 May 1923, p. 23.

43. R. M. Allen, review in *Literary Review*, 3 November 1923, p. 204.

44. Austin, *The American Rhythm*, p. 39.

45. Louis Untermeyer, "The Indian as Poet," p. 240.

46. Austin, "The Path on the Rainbow," p. 240, and "Imagism: Original and Aboriginal," p. 162.

47. Cronyn, "Indian Melodists and Mr. Untermeyer," p. 162.

48. Louis Untermeyer, "Footnotes Wanted," *Dial*, 12 July 1919, p. 30.

49. Austin, "Imagism," p. 162.

50. Alexander had edited several early collections of Indian literature, including *North American Mythology* and *Latin American Mythology*, and in 1922 he published in *Scribner's* an article entitled "American Indian Myth Poems."

51. Hartley Burr Alexander, "The Poetry of the American Indian," p. 758.

52. John Gould Fletcher, review in *Freeman*, 5 September 1923, p. 621.

53. Carl Van Doren, review in *Nation*, 18 April 1923, p. 172.

54. Alexander, "The Poetry of the American Indian," p. 757.

## Chapter 2

1. D. H. Lawrence, *Studies in Classic American Literature*, p. 56.

2. Leslie Fiedler, *The Return of the Vanishing American*, pp. 64–75.

3. See Lawrence, *Studies in Classic American Literature*, chapters 4 and 5: "Fenimore Cooper's White Novels" and "Fenimore Cooper's Leatherstocking Novels," pp. 35–64.

4. A more historically accurate and appropriate twentieth-century image of Pocahontas is found in John Barth's novel, *The Sotweed Factor* (New York: Random House, 1960). There, as Fiedler has pointed out *(Return of the Vanishing American*, p. 152), "Pocahontas' relationship to John Smith is portrayed not as an act of pure altruism and pity, but a sexual encounter so mechanical, so bestial, that it seems an assault rather than act of love—and, therefore, a truer metaphor of our actual relations with Indians than the pretty story so long celebrated in sentimental verse."

5. "Pearl" is used here as a traditional biblical and medieval symbol meaning "Kingdom of Heaven." Lindsay ignored its possible simultaneous association with material wealth, which would tinge with all sorts of bitter ironies the image of the "pearl without flaw" as the soul of America.

6. See Frank Waters, *Book of the Hopi,* and Seymour Koenig, *Hopi Clay—Hopi Ceremony.*

7. Austin, *Earth Horizon,* p. 331.

8. Nils Erik Enkvist, "The Folk Elements in Vachel Lindsay's Poetry," p. 98.

9. Crane's letter is cited in R. W. B. Lewis, *The Poetry of Hart Crane: A Critical Study,* p. 317.

10. Ibid., p. 313.

11. Hart Crane, "A Letter to Otto Kahn," 12 September 1927, in *The Complete Poems and Selected Letters and Prose of Hart Crane* (New York: Stein & Day, 1968), p. 248.

12. Lewis, *Poetry of Hart Crane,* p. 292.

13. Ibid., pp. 320, 344.

14. William Carlos Williams, "The American Background," in *Selected Essays,* p. 157.

15. Williams, "Sample Critical Statement," *Contact* 1, no. 4 [circa 1923]:18–19.

16. Williams, "The Poem as a Field of Action," in *Selected Essays,* pp. 280–91.

17. For a thorough discussion of Williams's relationship to the 291 group and to the art of the period, see Dickran Tashijan, *William Carlos Williams and the American Scene, 1920–1940.*

18. Marsden Hartley, "Tribal Aesthetics," p. 401.

19. Alan Holder, *"In the American Grain:* William Carlos Williams on the American Past," p. 241.

20. James Breslin, *William Carlos Williams: An American Artist,* p.88.

21. Williams, *In the American Grain,* p. 33.

22. Ibid., pp. 155, 157.

23. Ibid., pp. 141–42.

24. Ibid., p. 66.

25. Ibid., p. 121.

26. Ibid., p. 137.

27. Ibid., p. 138.

28. The actual character of Daniel Boone is difficult to discern, given the way fact and fancy merge in the mythological works that make up his earliest biographies, which are the main sources of more recent biographical writings. An opposing interpretation of Boone's relationship to the wilderness to the one found in *In the American Grain* might be developed from the fact that he journeyed into the woods as an agent for the Transylvania Company, in whose employ he surveyed unsettled land with the hopes of benefiting from a get-rich-quick land-speculation scheme that never quite came off,

owing to the efforts of opposing economic and political forces. For an interesting discussion of this side of Daniel Boone and the Boone legend, see Richard Drinnon, *Facing West*, pp. 147–64.

29. Williams, *Paterson*, p. 68.

30. Williams, "The Desert Music," *Pictures from Breughel*, p. 110.

31. Williams, *In the American Grain*, p. 74.

32. Lawrence, *Studies in Classic American Literature*, p. 52.

*Chapter 3*

1. This and the following quotation are from Lew Sarett, *The Box of God*, p. 77. Page references for other quotations from *The Box of God* appear in the text.

2. See Lame Deer and Erdoes, "The Circle and the Square," in *Lame Deer: Seeker of Visions*, pp. 96–107.

3. Uncatalogued letter in the Western Manuscripts Collection of the State Historical Society of Missouri, located in the Ellis Library at the University of Missouri–Columbia.

4. Lucille F. Aly, *John G. Neihardt: A Critical Biography*, p. 34.

5. Vine Deloria, Jr., Introduction to *Black Elk Speaks*, by John G. Neihardt, p. xi.

6. John G. Neihardt, *Patterns and Coincidences*, p. 99.

7. Ibid., p. 36.

8. Ibid., p. 40.

9. John G. Neihardt, *The River and I*, p. 6.

10. The first quotation is from a taped lecture by Neihardt at the University of Missouri–Columbia in 1964. The second is from a taped interview conducted there in 1964 by John Thomas Richards. Both tapes were courtesy of Bob Dyer, a poet and film maker who taught at the University of Missouri during this period and in 1973 produced and directed the short film about Neihardt and Black Elk, *Performing the Vision*.

11. John G. Neihardt, "The Book That Would Not Die," p. 228.

12. From *Epic America*, Lecture 5. These are unpublished lectures comprised in a videotaped course at the University of Missouri–Columbia. Tapes are available at the Audio-Visual Center, University of Missouri–Columbia.

13. All quotes in this paragraph are from an undated letter Neihardt wrote to Julian T. House cited in Aly, *John G. Neihardt: A Critical Biography*, p. 168.

14. Sally McCluskey, "Black Elk Speaks, and So Does John G. Neihardt," p. 240.

15. Ibid., p. 238.

16. Unpaged transcript of Neihardt's 1931 interviews with Black Elk, Western Manuscripts Collection, State Historical Society of Missouri, Ellis Library, University of Missouri–Columbia (hereafter cited as Transcript 1931).

17. *Epic America*, Lecture 5.

18. Neihardt, *Black Elk Speaks* (University of Nebraska Press ed.), pp. 42–43. All quotations from *Black Elk Speaks* are from this edition.

19. Transcript 1931.

20. The circle-within-circle imagery of Black Elk's Great Vision as rewritten by Neihardt echoes and suggests as an influence the great vision near the end of Dante's *Paradiso*, Canto XXX, trans. John Ciardi (New York: New American Library), 1970, p. 331:

> There in Heaven, a lamp shines in whose light
> the Creator is made visible in His creature,
> whose one peace lies in having Him in sight.
>
> That lamp forms an enormous circle, such
> that its circumference, fitted to the sun
> as a bright belt, would be too large by much.
>
> It is made up entirely of the reflection
> of rays that strike the top of the first-moved sphere,
> imparting to it all its power and motion.
>
> And as a slope shines in the looking glass
> of a lake below it, as if to see itself
> in its time of brightest flower and greenest grass;
>
> So, tier on tier, mounting within that light,
> there glowed, reflected in more than a thousand circles,
> all those who had won return to Heaven's height.
>
> And if so vast a numbers can be bound
> within its lower tier, what then must be
> the measure of this rose at its topmost round?

21. Transcript 1931, Folder NR20, p. 18.

22. Neihardt, "The Book That Would Not Die," p. 229.

23. Neihardt, *Black Elk Speaks*, pp. 31–32.

24. Transcript 1931, Folder NR20, p. 7.

25. Neihardt, *Black Elk Speaks*, p. 42.

26. Transcript 1931, Folder NR20, p. 20.

27. Ibid., p. 27.

28. Ironically, uranium is now being mined in the Black Hills of South Dakota.

29. Transcript 1931, Folder NR20, p. 24.

30. Ibid., Folder NR21, p. 24.

31. Deloria, Introduction to *Black Elk Speaks*, p. xiv.

32. Pocket Books acknowledged sales of better than 350,000 through 1978. In addition, a University of Nebraska Press edition has sold well; it has been translated into German, Flemish, Italian, Dutch, and Serbo-Croatian.

33. For an excellent discussion of the theme of giving, see Roger Dunsmore's "Nikolaus Black Elk—Holy Man in History."

34. Jerome Rothenberg, "Pre-face," *Technicians of the Sacred*, p. xxii.

## Chapter 4

1. This phrase was coined by Donald M. Allen in his anthology *The New American Poetry*, an important collection of poems and statements on poetics by Beat Generation, Black Mountain, and other poets with an anti–New Critical stance.

2. D. H. Lawrence, *Selected Literary Criticism*, p. 86.

3. William Carlos Williams, "How to Write."

4. See "Projective Verse," Chapter 50 in *The Autobiography of William Carlos Williams* (New York: New Directions, 1951), pp. 329–34.

5. The evolution of this never-completed project is traced through Olson's notes in *Olson: The Journal of Charles Olson Archives* 5 (Spring 1976). A sense of Olson's broad range of interests and readings in Native American subjects can be gleaned from the listing of books in his personal library compiled by George Butterick, this journal's editor, and published in its first six issues.

6. Olson contributed a scholarly article on this subject: "Introductory Notes to the Sutter Marshall Lease with the Yalesumney Indians for Monopoly of the Gold Bearing Lands," published in *Letters of the Gold Discovery* 2 (February 1948).

7. See Creeley's introduction to Olson's *Mayan Letters*.

8. Guy Davenport, "Scholia and Conjectures for Olson's 'The Kingfishers,' " p. 250.

9. Carol Kyle, "The Mesoamerican Cultural Past and Charles Olson's 'The Kingfishers,' " p. 70.

10. Guy Davenport, "Olson," p.83.

11. "The Kingfishers," *Selected Writings of Charles Olson*, p. 172. Other page references to this poem appear in text.

12. Davenport, in his essay "Olson" in *The Geography of the Imagination* (pp. 95–96) cites Pound in the *Guide to Kulchur:* "It is my intention . . . to COMMIT myself on as many points as possible, that means I shall make a number of statements few men can AFFORD to make, for the simple reason that such taking sides might jeopard their incomes (directly) or their prestige or 'position' in one or other of the professional 'worlds.' Given my freedom, I may be a fool to use it, but I wd. be a cad not to." The echoing of Pound here is complex. In one sense Olson wished to emulate the commitment and courage of a poet he regarded as a kinsman. In another, the "primitive" and Native American emphasis in "The Kingfishers" represents a rebuttal of Pound's expatriatism and his search for renewal amid the cultural ruins of Europe and China.

13. Olson quoted Rimbaud in "The Kingfishers"—"Si j'ai du gout, ce n'est gueres / Que pour la terre et les pierres." These lines from both "Fêtes de la faim" (1872) and *Une Saison en enfer* (1873) translate literally, "If I have any taste, / It is for earth and stone." Davenport, in "Olson", pp. 97–98, suggests that the line introduces an important theme for "The Kingfishers" and for modern literature in general: the ticklish question of just what is alive. Olson in "The Kingfishers" and elsewhere sided with primitive man on this issue, answering firmly—"Everything!"

14. James Dickey, "Charles Olson," in *Babel to Byzantium: Poets and Poetry Now*, pp. 136–39.

15. Benjamin Lee Whorf, "An American Indian Model of the Universe," in *Language, Thought, and Reality: Selected Writings of Benjamin Lee Whorf*, pp. 59–60.

16. Olson, *Proprioception*, p. 2. See William Blake's *The Marriage of Heaven and Hell* for his analysis of Western Man's error of separating the body from the soul. See also D. H. Lawrence's *Fantasia of the Unconscious.*

17. Whorf, *Language, Thought, and Reality*, p. 263.

18. Olson, "Projective Verse," *Selected Writings*, p. 24.

19. Sherman Paul cites "live in your body" as one of Olson's basic "injunctions" *(Olson's Push*, p. 77).

20. Olson, "Projective Verse," p. 25.

21. Olson, "Human Universe," *Selected Writings*, p. 54.

22. Whorf, *Language, Thought, and Reality*, pp. 263, 63.

23. Creeley, Introduction to Olson's *Mayan Letters*, p. 6.

24. Olson, "Mayan Letters," *Selected Writings*, pp. 92–93.

25. Mayan hieroglyphics were to Olson what Chinese characters had been to Pound: an early poetry that reflected and projected fresh and clear ways of seeing. Like Pound, Olson projected much

into them that scholars would dispute. The quoted passage is from Charles Olson, "Human Universe," in *Human Universe and Other Essays*, p. 8. An almost identical passage is found in *The Mayan Letters*.

26. Olson, *Causal Mythology*, p. 5.

27. Olson, "Letter to Elaine Feinstein," *Selected Writings*, p. 28.

28. Ekbert Faas, "Charles Olson," *Towards a New American Poetics: Essays and Interviews*, p. 48.

29. Olson, "Letter to Elaine Feinstein," p. 28.

30. Robert Duncan, Introduction to Olson's *Special View of History*, p. 11.

## Chapter 5

1. In addition to his association with the Deep Image group during the sixties, Rothenberg's activities included translations of modern German poets, including the concrete poet Eugen Gomringer; translation of Rolf Hochhuth's play *The Deputy;* and the publishing of an English translation of the dadaist Tristan Tzara's own translations into German of African tribal poetry.

2. Ezra Pound, "A Retrospect," *Literary Essays of Ezra Pound*, p. 4.

3. Biographical information presented here is based on an interview I had with Jerome Rothenberg at the University of Missouri–Kansas City, 22 March 1979.

4. Rothenberg, "Pre-face," *Technicians of the Sacred: A Range of Poetries from Africa, America, Asia, and Oceania*, p. xxii.

5. Ibid., p. xxiii.

6. See Barbara Tedlock, "The Clown's Way," pp. 105–18.

7. Dennis Tedlock and Barbara Tedlock, eds., *Teachings from the American Earth*, pp. 112–15.

8. Neihardt, *Black Elk Speaks*, pp. 188–93.

9. Carl Jung, "On the Psychology of the Trickster Figure," in Paul Radin, *The Trickster: A Study in American Indian Mythology*, pp. 195–211.

10. Rothenberg, "Pre-face" to a Symposium on Ethnopoetics, *Alcheringa: Ethnopoetics*, n.s. 2, no. 4(1976):4.

11. Rothenberg, *Technicians of the Sacred*, p. xxiv.

12. Ibid., p. xxii.

13. Ibid., p. 360. Rothenberg's source is Knud Rasmussen, *The Netsilik Eskimos* (Copenhagen, 1931), p. 321.

14. Rothenberg, *Technicians of the Sacred*, p. 359. Rothenberg's source is Bronislaw Malinowski, *Argonauts of the Western Pacific* (New York: E. P. Dutton & Co., 1961), pp. 408–9.

15. Rothenberg, *Shaking the Pumpkin: Traditional Poetry of the Indian North Americas*, p. 23.

16. Rothenberg, "Total Translation," pp. 297–98.

17. Ibid., p. 301.

18. Ibid., p. 303.

19. Ibid.

20. See C. M. Bowra, *Primitive Song*.

21. "The Thirteenth Horse-Song of Frank Mitchell," trans. Jerome Rothenberg, *Alcheringa: Ethnopoetics*, 2 (Summer 1971):pp. 94–95.

22. Jerome Rothenberg and Dennis Tedlock, "Statement of Intent," *Alcheringa: Ethnopoetics* 1 (Autumn 1970):1.

23. Rothenberg, "Total Translation," p. 295.

24. Rothenberg, *Shaking the Pumpkin*, p. 404.

25. Rothenberg, "Total Translation," p. 299.

26. Rarihokwats, "Tribal Poetry and Tribal Lifeways," p. 115.

27. William Bevis, "American Indian Verse Translations," p. 319.

28. Rothenberg, "Total Translation," p. 299.

29. Ibid., p. 307.

30. For a more thorough discussion of these issues, see Jeffrey F. Huntsman, "Traditional Native American Literature: The Translation Dilemma," pp. 5–9. See also the quote from Bevis cited in Chapter 1.

31. Kevin Porter, "A Conversation with Jerome Rothenberg," *Vort* 3, no. 1 (1975):150.

32. Rothenberg, *Technicians of the Sacred*, pp. 376–82.

33. Ibid., p. 280.

34. Rothenberg, *Shaking the Pumpkin*, p. 191.

35. Ibid., p. 436.

36. Rothenberg, *Technicians of the Sacred*, p. 450.

## Chapter 6

1. Gary Snyder, *Turtle Island*, p. 1.

2. There are many sources that provide a sense of how important knowing and observing nature were to Indian peoples. One excellent place to start would be with Charles A. Eastman's *Indian Boyhood*, especially the chapter entitled "An Indian Boy's Training." In this chapter, Eastman, a Santee Sioux, recounts how his uncle, who was responsible for his education until he was fifteen, would send him out into the woods early in the day with the injunction, "Look closely at everything you see." When Eastman returned in

the evening, his uncle would test him for an hour on what he had observed and learned. "He did not expect a correct reply at once to all the voluminous questions that he put to me on these occasions," Eastman wrote, "but he meant to make me observant and a good student of nature."

3. Interview with Gary Snyder in *Road Apple* (1969–1970) by Doug Flaherty, reprinted in Gary Snyder: *The Real Work: Interviews and Talks 1964–1979*, p. 16.

4. As Carter Revard observed in a May 1981 conversation, for Whitman, America's first great poet who tried to express the "voice of the continent," both voices are "ours." Snyder took only half of Whitman's territory, at most.

5. Snyder, "The Wilderness," *Turtle Island*, p. 108.

6. Snyder, "Four Changes," ibid., p. 99.

7. Snyder originally delivered "The Politics of Ethnopoetics" as a talk at the first annual Ethnopoetics Conference, a gathering of scholars, ethnologists, poets, and native songmen and -women organized by Jerome Rothenberg and Dennis Tedlock at the University of Wisconsin–Milwaukee in the spring of 1975. The essay also appears in *The Old Ways*.

8. For a cogent analysis of this process and of the image making and militarism associated with it, see Richard Drinnon, *Facing West: The Metaphysics of Indian Hating and Empire Building*.

9. See Barry Commoner, *The Politics of Energy* (New York: Alfred A. Knopf, 1979). Commoner, after studying the energy problem from many angles over many years, recommends conversion to self-renewing solar-energy sources. He cites "the importance of the most distinctive feature of solar energy—that it is diffusely spread across the surface of the entire planet....This means that the present pattern of building huge, centralized power stations is inherently uneconomical if it is applied to solar energy" (p. 44).

10. See Castro and Castro, "Interview with Gary Snyder."

11. This term, which Rothenberg borrowed for the title of his anthology of tribal poetry, was coined by Mircea Eliade to describe the shaman. See Eliade, *Shamanism: Archaic Techniques of Ecstasy*.

12. Castro and Castro, "Interview with Gary Snyder," p. 38.

13. Ibid., p. 41.

14. Snyder, "Four Changes," p. 102.

15. See *The Real Work*, p. 5. For a good discussion of the intelligence in nature from the point of view of a contemporary scientist, see Lewis Thomas, "Debating the Unknowable," *Atlantic Monthly*, July 1981, pp. 49–52. Thomas writes here of the contemporary scientific debate of such issues as animal intelligence, cooperative intelli-

gence between animals and between animals and plants, and the "Gaia Hypothesis" of Lovelock and Margulis, "which is, in brief, that the earth is itself a form of life."

16. This is not to suggest that the words of Snyder's poem represent what he literally heard in his encounter with the magpie. As Kenneth Lincoln, editor of the *American Indian Culture and Research Journal*, has written in his essay "Native American Literatures: 'old like hills, like stars,' " pp. 108–9,

> There seems to be consensus among holy men, scholars, and translators that the visionary truth of the other world, regardless of time or culture, can enter this world only through the special concentration of dream images, a language of many tongues speaking in one, and a fleeting sense of witnessing more than the ordinary mind can see or comprehend or tell. John Neihardt, Black Elk's intermediary, remembers "half seeing, half sensing" the blind man's story, translated across languages, cultures, and time itself, as if he were seeing "a strange and beautiful landscape by brief flashes of lightning." The dreamer's language remains sacred and symbolic, *wakan* the Lakota say, and not to be understood as ordinary words.

17. *The Real Work*, p. 5.

18. Quoted in "Poetry and the Primitive," *Earth House Hold*, p. 118.

19. Castro and Castro, "Interview with Gary Snyder," p. 53.

20. The term *enstasy* was apparently coined by Snyder to mean "within a condition of stasis or balance." The word has intentional overtones of ecstasy, for meditative enstatic communion can involve a calm yet ecstatic experience.

21. Simon Ortiz, "Speaking," *A Good Journey*, p. 52.

22. Black Elk said, "The Power of the World always works in circles, and everything tries to be round" (Neihardt, *Black Elk Speaks*, p. 164). Lame Deer: "I point my peace pipe toward all these directions. Now we are one with the universe, with all living things, a link in the circle which has no end" (Lame Deer and Erdoes, *Lame Deer: Seeker of Visions*, p. 107).

23. Snyder, "Why Tribe," *Earth House Hold*, p. 116.


## Chapter 7

1. Silko's and Momaday's works are noteworthy for their skillful application of Native American literary traditions and techniques to Western autobiography. The narrative line in their books mixes prose anecdote, poetry, story, myth, and visual images to

tell what emerges as more the story of a people than a person, an approach that is more tribal than individualistic, more Indian than Western. Vine Deloria, Jr., interviewed in *Suntracks*, called on Indian writers to take analogous approaches—to move beyond the limitations of white literary expectations and conventions and to develop forms and styles that reflect in new ways their old Native American traditions and cultures. Deloria went so far as to praise the controversial *Seven Arrows* for succeeding in doing just that, writing of Hyemeyohsts Storm and his book:

> what I like about *Seven Arrows* is that the guy says basically, "You can take a whole new format and express the essence of what people are, using different language, using psychedelic shields, Jungian mandalas, everything, it is the emotional essence of a people that has to be captured, and not a strict adherence to what Robert Lowie and Grinnell say is true about the Crow or the Northern Cheyenne or anybody." . . . I think that the book is extremely important because an Indian dared to break out of the genre in which people had put Indian literature, and just say, "I'm going to write a story that destroys chronological time, that uses visual means to center your attention on the page, that intersperses humans and animals, that violates the standards of white society for writing about Indians." Steve Crum, "A Conversation with Vine Deloria," *Suntracks: An American Indian Literary Magazine*, no. 4 (Tucson: University of Arizona Press, 1978), pp. 80–88.

2. The authenticity of Castaneda's works has been at issue since they first appeared, especially since the first Don Juan book, *The Teachings of Don Juan: A Yaqui Way of Knowledge* (1968), earned him a Ph.D. in anthropology at UCLA. For a thorough and convincing analysis of Castaneda's ingenious "fiction," see Richard De Mille, *Castaneda's Journey: The Power and the Allegory* (Santa Barbara, Calif.: Capra Press, 1976).

3. The cultural pervasiveness of these works is suggested by Bob Dylan's naming his "Rolling Thunder Review" tour after this book.

4. See Crum, "Conversation with Vine Deloria," p. 81.

5. Hobson's and Silko's articles have both been republished and are currently available in Hobson's excellent anthology of Indian writings *The Remembered Earth: An Anthology of Contemporary Native American Literature.*

6. Deloria's *God is Red* is one such attempt. For Deloria's response to the question, "Who do you write for?" see Crum's interview with him.

7. Silko, "An Old-Time Indian Attack Conducted in Two Parts," *The Remembered Earth*, pp. 211, 212; Hobson, "The Rise of the White Shaman as a New Version of Cultural Imperialism," ibid., p. 105.

8. Crane, *Complete Poems and Selected Letters and Prose*, p. 251.

9. Such an assertion is, of course, open to question. As Carter Revard has observed (conversation, May 1981), whether or not the Indian person is able to experience the world the way a white person does may be the chief question facing nontraditional progressive factions in Native American societies.

10. Silko, "An Old-Time Indian Attack," p. 213.

11. Hiamove, whom Natalie Curtis designated as "Chief among the Cheyennes and the Dakotas," wrote in his foreword to *The Indians' Book:*

> There are birds of many colors—red, green, yellow—yet it is all one bird. There are horses of many colors—brown, black, yellow, white—yet it is all one horse. So cattle, so all living things—animals, flowers, trees. So men: in this land where once were only Indians are now men of every color—white, black, yellow, red—yet all one people. That this should come to pass was in the heart of the Great Myster. It is right thus. And everywhere there shall be peace.

12. Hobson, "The Rise of the White Shaman," p. 103.

13. Ibid., pp. 105, 103.

14. This and subsequent quoted passages of Welch's poetry are from James Welch, *Riding the Earthboy 40*.

15. Marnie Walsh's "Vicki Loans Arrow" is quoted from Dexter Fisher, ed., *The Third Woman: Minority Women Writers of the United States*, p. 116.

16. This passage is from "Irish Poets on Saturday Night and an Indian," published in Simon J. Ortiz, *A Good Journey*. Other passages from Ortiz's work quoted in the text are from this same book.

17. All the quotations from Maurice Kenny are from *Boston Tea Party*.

18. Silko, *Ceremony*, p. 260.

19. Dexter Fisher, "Stories and Their Tellers: A Conversation with Leslie Marmon Silko," in Fisher, ed., *The Third Woman*, p. 20.

20. Silko, *Ceremony*, p. 135.

21. Ibid., p. 128.

22. Ibid., p. 152.

23. Ibid., p. 261.

24. Ibid., p. 246.

25. Ibid., p. 262.

# ✦ Bibliography ✦

Alexander, Hartley Burr. "American Indian Myth Poems." *Scribner's Magazine* 71 (January 1922):112–14.

———. "Indian Songs and English Verse." *American Speech* 1 (1926): 571–75.

———, ed. *Latin American Mythology*. Boston: Marshall Jones & Co., 1920.

———, ed. *North American Mythology*. Boston: Marshall Jones & Co., 1916.

———. "The Poetry of the American Indian." *The Nation*, December 13, 1919, pp. 757–59.

Allen, Donald M., ed. *The New American Poetry*. New York: Grove Press, 1960.

———, ed. *The Poetics of the New American Poetry*. New York: Grove Press, 1973.

Allen, Paula Gunn. *Coyote's Daylight Trip*. Albuquerque: La Confluencia, 1978.

———. "The Sacred Hoop: A Contemporary Indian Perspective on American Indian Literature." In *The Remembered Earth*, edited by Geary Hobson, pp. 222–39. Albuquerque: Red Earth Press, 1979. Reprint. Albuquerque: University of New Mexico Press, 1981.

Aly, Lucille F. *John G. Neihardt*, Boise, Idaho: Boise State University, 1976.

———. *John G. Neihardt: A Critical Biography*. Amsterdam: Rodolophi, 1977.

———. "The Word Sender: John G. Neihardt and His Audiences." *Quarterly Journal of Speech* 43, no. 2 (1957):151–54.

Anderson, Edgar. *Plants, Life, and Man*. Berkeley and Los Angeles: University of California Press, 1971.

Armstrong, Virginia Irving. *I Have Spoken: American History Through the Voices of Indians*. Chicago: Swallow Press, 1971.

Artaud, Antonin. *The Peyote Dance*. Translated by Helen Weaver. 1936. Reprint. New York: Farrar, Straus and Giroux, 1976.

Astrov, Margot, ed. *The Winged Serpent: An Anthology of American Indian Prose and Poetry*. 1946. Reprint. New York: Fawcett, 1973.

Austin, Mary Hunter. *The American Rhythm: Studies and Re-expressions of Amerindian Songs*. 1923. Reprint. Boston: Houghton Mifflin Co., 1930.

————. *The Arrow-Maker: A Drama in Three Acts*. Rev. ed. Boston: Houghton Mifflin Co., 1915.

————. *The Children Sing in the Far West*. Cambridge, Mass.: Riverside Press, 1928.

————. *Earth Horizon*. Cambridge, Mass.: Literary Guild, 1932.

————. "Imagism: Original and Aboriginal." *Dial*, 23 August 1919, pp. 162–63.

————. Introduction to *The Path on the Rainbow: An Anthology of Songs and Chants from the Indians of North America*, edited by George W. Cronyn. New York: Liveright, 1918. Reprint. New York: Liveright, 1934.

————. "John G. Neihardt's Expression of the West." *Southwest Review* 13 (January 1928):255–58.

————. *One Smoke Stories*. Cambridge, Mass.: Riverside Press, 1934.

————. "The Path on the Rainbow." *Dial*, 8 March 1919, pp. 240–41.

Bandelier, Adolph. *The Delight Makers*. 1890. Reprint. New York: Harcourt Brace Jovanovich, 1971.

Barnes, Nellie. *American Indian Love Lyrics and Other Verse*. Foreword by Mary Austin. Boston: Houghton Mifflin Co., 1925.

————. *American Indian Verse: Characteristics of Style*. Bulletin of the University of Kansas Humanistic Studies 2, no. 4. Lawrence: University of Kansas, 1921.

Barnett, Louise. *The Ignoble Savage: American Literary Racism, 1790–1890*. Westport, Conn.: Greenwood Press, 1975.

Barrett, S. M., ed. *Geronimo, His Own Story*. 1906. Reprinted as *Geronimo's Story of His Life*. New York: Corner House, 1973.

Benedict, Ruth F. *Patterns of Culture*. Boston: Houghton Mifflin Co., 1934.

Bevis, William. "American Indian Verse Translations." In *Literature of the American Indians: Views and Interpretations*, edited by Abraham Chapman, pp. 308–23. New York: New American Library, 1975.

Bierhorst, John. *In the Trail of the Wind: American Indian Poems and Ritual Orations*. New York: Dell, 1975.

Black, W. E. "Ethic and Metaphysic: A Study of John G. Neihardt." *Western American Literature* 2 (Fall 1967):205–12.

Blue Cloud, Peter. *Back Then Tomorrow*. Brunswick, Maine: Blackberry Press, 1978.

———. *Turtle, Bear and Wolf*. Preface by Gary Snyder. Ithaca, N.Y.: Akwesasne Notes Press, 1976.

Boas, Franz. "Chinook Songs." *Journal of American Folklore* 7 (1894): 45–50; 10 (1897):109–15.

Boer, Charles. *Charles Olson in Connecticut*. Chicago: Swallow Press, 1975.

Borges, Jorge Luis. "The Oral Poetry of the Indians." In *Literature of the American Indians: Views and Interpretations*, edited by Abraham Chapman, pp. 276–77. New York: New American Library, 1975.

Bowra, C. M. *Primitive Song*. New York: World Publishing Co., 1962.

Boyd, Doug. *Rolling Thunder*. New York: Dell, 1976.

Breslin, James. *William Carlos Williams: An American Artist*. New York: Oxford University Press, 1970.

Brinton, Daniel G. *Aboriginal American Authors*. New York: David McKay Publishers, 1883.

———. "Native American Poetry." In *Essays of an Americanist*, pp. 284–304. Philadelphia: David McKay Publishers, 1890.

Brooks, Van Wyck. *Three Essays on America*. New York: E. P. Dutton, 1934.

Brown, Joseph Epes. *The Sacred Pipe*. 1953. Reprint. Baltimore: Penguin Books, 1971.

Bruchac, Joseph. "Native American Poetics . . . In 'The Idea of Ancestry.'" *Contact II* 1, no. 5 (1977):33–43.

Burroughs, William, and Ginsberg, Allen. *The Yage Letters*. San Francisco: City Lights, 1971.

Burton, Frederick Russell, *American Primitive Music; with Especial Attention to the Songs of the Ojibways*. 1909. Reprint. Port Washington, N.Y.: Kennikat Press, 1969.

Butterick, George, ed. *Olson: The Journal of the Charles Olson Archives*, nos. 1–8. Storrs, Conn., 1974–79.

Bynner, Witter. *Indian Earth*. New York: Alfred A. Knopf, 1929.

Capps, Walter Holder. *Seeing with a Native Eye: Essays on Native American Religion*. New York: Harper & Row, 1976.

Cardenal, Ernesto. *Homage to the American Indians*. Translated by Monique and Carlos Altschul. Baltimore: Johns Hopkins University Press, 1973.

Castaneda, Carlos. *The Teachings of Don Juan: A Yaqui Way of Knowledge*. Berkeley and Los Angeles: University of California Press, 1968. Paperback edition. New York: Pocket Books, 1974.

Castro, Jan, and Castro, Michael. "Interview with Gary Snyder." *River Styx* 4 (1979):35–59.

Chamberlain, Alexander F. "The Poetry of American Aboriginal Speech." *Journal of American Folklore* 9 (1896):43–47.

————. "Primitive Woman as Poet." *Journal of American Folklore* 16 (1903):205–21.

Chapman, Abraham, ed. *Literature of the American Indians: Views and Interpretations*. New York: New American Library, 1975.

Charters, Ann. *Olson/Melville: A Study in Affinity*. San Francisco: Oyez, 1968.

Chowka, Peter Barry. "The Original Mind of Gary Snyder." *Eastwest* 77, no. 6 (1977):24–39; 77, no. 7 (1977):34–48.

Cloutier, David. *Spirit, Spirit: Shaman Songs, Incantations*. Providence, R.I.: Copper Beech, 1973.

Coles, Robert. *William Carlos Williams: The Knack of Survival in America*. New Brunswick, N.J.: Rutgers University Press, 1975.

Corrigan, Matthew, ed. "Charles Olson: Essays, Reminiscences, Reviews," *Boundary 2* 2, no. 2 (1973–74).

Crane, Hart. *The Complete Poems and Selected Letters and Prose*. Edited by Brom Weber. Garden City, N.Y.: Doubleday, 1966.

Creeley, Robert. *Contexts of Poetry: Interviews, 1961–1971*. Edited by Donald Allen. San Francisco: Four Seasons Foundation, 1973.

————. Introduction to *The Mayan Letters* by Charles Olson. Mallorca: Divers Press, 1953.

————. *A Quick Graph: Collected Notes and Essays*. Edited by Donald Allen. San Francisco: Four Seasons Foundation, 1970.

Cronyn, George W., ed. *American Indian Poetry: An Anthology of Songs and Chants*. New ed. New York: Liveright, 1970.

————. "Indian Melodists and Mr. Untermeyer." *Dial* (August 23, 1919):162–63.

————, ed. *The Path on the Rainbow: An Anthology of Songs and Chants from the Indians of North America*. Introduction by Mary Hunter Austin. 1918. Reprint. New York: Liveright, 1934.

Curtis, Edward S. *The Portable Curtis*. Edited with an introduction by Barry Gifford. Berkeley, Calif.: Creative Arts Book Co., 1976.

Curtis, Natalie. *The Indians' Book*. 1907. Reprint. New York: Dover, 1968.

————. "Mr. Roosevelt and Indian Music." *Outlook* (March 5, 1919):399–400.

Cushing, Frank. "Outlines of Zuni Creation Myths." *Thirteenth Annual Report of the Bureau of American Ethnology.* Washington, D.C.: Smithsonian Instituation, 1896.

Davenport, Guy. "Olson." In *The Geography of the Imagination: Forty Essays by Guy Davenport.* San Francisco: North Point Press, 1981.

———. "Scholia and Conjectures for Olson's 'The Kingfishers.' " *Boundary 2,* vol. 2, nos. 1 and 2 (Fall 1973 and Winter 1974): 250–62.

Davie, Donald. "In the American Grain." In *William Carlos Williams: A Critical Anthology,* edited by Charles Tomlinson, pp. 233–39. Baltimore: Penguin Books, 1972.

Day, A. Grove. *The Sky Clears: Poetry of the American Indians.* 1951. Reprint. Lincoln: University of Nebraska Press, 1964.

———. "Types of North American Indian Poetry in English Translation." Ph.D. diss., Stanford University, 1943.

De Angulo, Jaime. *A Jaime De Angulo Reader.* Edited by Bob Callahan. Berkeley, Calif.: Turtle Island, 1979.

Deloria, Vine, Jr. *Behind the Trail of Broken Treaties: An Indian Declaration of Independence.* New York: Dell, 1974.

———. *Custer Died for Your Sins.* New York: Avon, 1969.

———. *God is Red.* New York: Dell, 1973.

———. Introduction to *Black Elk Speaks,* by John G. Neihardt. Lincoln: University of Nebraska Press, 1979.

———. *We Talk, You Listen: New Tribes, New Turf.* New York: Dell, 1970.

De Montaigne, Michel. "Of Cannibals." In *Essays.* Translated with an introduction by J. M. Cohen, pp. 105–18. Harmondsworth, England: Penguin Books, 1958.

Densmore, Frances. *Chippewa Music, Part I.* Bureau of American Ethnology Bulletin no. 45. Washington, D.C.: Smithsonian Institution, 1910.

———. *Chippewa Music, Part II.* Bureau of American Ethnology Bulletin no. 53. Washington, D.C.: Smithsonian Institution, 1913.

———. *Teton Sioux Music.* Bureau of American Ethnology Bulletin no. 61. Washington, D.C.: Smithsonian Institution, 1918.

Dickey, James, ed. *Babel to Byzantium: Poets and Poetry Now.* New York: Farrar, Straus and Giroux, 1968.

Dodge, Robert K., and McCullough, Joseph B. *Voices from Wah'Kon-Tah: Contemporary Poetry of Native Americans.* New York: International Publishers, 1974.

Dorn, Edward. *Recollections of Gran Apacheria.* San Francisco: Turtle Island Foundation, 1974.

Dorsey, Owen J. "Ponka and Omaha Songs." *Journal of American Folklore* 1 (1888):65, 209; 2 (1889):271–76.

Drinnon, Richard. *Facing West: The Metaphysics of Indian Hating and Empire-Building.* New York: New American Library, 1980.

Dudley, Edward, and Novak, Maximillian E., eds. *The Wild Man Within: An Image in Western Thought from the Renaissance to Romanticism.* Pittsburgh: University of Pittsburgh Press, 1972.

Dunsmore, Roger. "Nikolaus Black Elk—Holy Man in History." *Kuksu: Journal of Backcountry Writing,* no. 6 (1977), pp. 4–29.

Eastman, Charles A. *From the Deep Woods to Civilization.* 1916. Reprint. Lincoln: University of Nebraska Press, 1977.

———. *Indian Boyhood.* New York: McClure & Philips, 1902.

———. *The Soul of the Indian.* Boston: Houghton Mifflin Co., 1911.

Eliade, Mircea. *The Myth of the Eternal Return; or, Cosmos and History.* Princeton, N.J.: Princeton University Press, 1971.

———. *Shamanism: Archaic Techniques of Ecstasy.* Trans. Willard R. Trask. New York: Pantheon Books, 1964.

Eliot. T. S. *Notes Toward the Definition of Culture.* New York: Harcourt Brace & Co., 1949.

Emerson, Ralph Waldo. "Nature." In *The Selected Writings of Emerson,* edited by Brooks Atkinson, pp. 3–44. New York: Random House, 1950.

———. "The Poet." In *The Selected Writings of Emerson,* edited by Brooks Atkinson, pp. 319–41. New York: Random House, 1950.

Enkvist, Nils Erik. "The Folk Elements in Vachel Lindsay's Poetry." In *Profile of Vachel Lindsay,* edited by John T. Flanagan, pp. 93–107. Columbus, Ohio: Charles E. Merrill Publishing Co., 1970.

Evers, Lawrence J. "Native American Oral Literatures in the College English Classroom: An Omaha Example." *College English* 36 (1975):649–62.

Faas, Ekbert. *Towards a New American Poetics: Essays and Interviews.* Santa Barbara, Calif.: Black Sparrow Press, 1978.

Farb, Peter. *Man's Rise to Civilization.* New York: Avon, 1969.

Fenollosa, Ernest. *The Chinese Written Character as a Medium for Poetry.* Edited by Ezra Pound. San Francisco: City Lights, 1968.

Fiedler, Leslie. *The Return of the Vanishing American.* New York: Stein & Day, 1968.

Fisher, Dexter, ed. *The Third Woman: Minority Women Writers of the United States.* Boston: Houghton Mifflin Co., 1980.

Flanagan, John T. "John G. Neihardt, Chronicler of the West." *Arizona Quarterly* 21 (Spring 1965):7–20.

————, ed. *Vachel Lindsay: A Profile.* Columbus, Ohio: Charles E. Merrill Publishing Co., 1970.

Fletcher, Alice Cunningham. "The Hako, A Pawnee Ceremony." *Twenty-second Annual Report of the Bureau of American Ethnology.* Washington, D.C.: Smithsonian Institution, 1904.

————. "Indian Song and Music." *Journal of American Folklore* 11, no. 16 (1898):85–105.

————. "Poetry." In *Handbook of American Indians*, Part II. *Thirtieth Annual Report of the Bureau of American Ethnology.* Washington, D.C.: Smithsonian Institution, 1910.

Fox, Hugh. *First Fire: Central and South American Indian Poetry.* Garden City, N.Y.: Doubleday, 1978.

Frank, Waldo D. *Our America.* New York: Boni and Liveright, 1919.

Frye, Northrop. *The Anatomy of Criticism.* Princeton, N.J.: Princeton University Press, 1957.

Garland, Hamlin. *The Book of the American Indian.* Illustrated by Frederick Remington. New York: Harper Brothers, 1923.

Geneson, Paul. "An Interview with Gary Snyder." *Ohio Review* 18, no. 3 (1977):67–105.

Gilman, B. I. "Hopi Songs." *Journal of American Ethnology and Archaeology* 1 (1891).

Ginsberg, Allen. *Allen Verbatim: Lectures on Poetry, Politics, Consciousness.* Edited by Gordon Ball. New York: McGraw-Hill, 1974.

————. *Improvised Poetics.* Buffalo, N.Y.: ANONYM Press, 1971.

Grossinger, Richard, ed. *The Mediterranean.* An Olson-Melville Sourcebook, vol. 2. Plainfield, Vt.: North Atlantic Books, 1976.

————, ed. *The New Found Land.* An Olson-Melville Sourcebook, vol. 1. Plainfield, Vt.: North Atlantic Books, 1976.

Hamilton, Charles. *Cry of the Thunderbird: The American Indian's Own Story.* Norman: University of Oklahoma Press, 1972.

Hartley, Marsden. "Tribal Aesthetics." *The Dial*, 16 November 1918, pp. 399–401.

Hayden, Thomas. *The Love of Possessions Is a Disease with Them.* New York: Holt, Rinehart and Winston, 1972.

Hazard, Lucy. *The Frontier in American Literature.* New York: Thomas Y. Crowell Co., 1927.

Hill, Ruth Beebe. *Hanta Yo.* Garden City, N.Y.: Doubleday, 1979.

Hobson, Geary. "The Rise of the White Shaman as a New Version of Cultural Imperialism." In *The Remembered Earth: An Anthology of Contemporary Native American Literature*, pp. 100–108. Albuquerque: Red Earth Press, 1979. Reprint. Albuquerque: University of New Mexico Press, 1981.

————, ed. *The Remembered Earth: An Anthology of Contemporary Na-*

*tive American Literature.* Albuquerque: Red Earth Press, 1979. Reprint. Albuquerque: University of New Mexico Press, 1981.

Hodge, Frederick. *Handbook of American Indians North of Mexico.* 1909. Reprint. New York: Pageant Books, 1960.

Holder, Alan. *"In the American Grain:* William Carlos Williams on the American Past.*"* In *William Carlos Williams: A Critical Anthology,* edited by Charles Tomlinson, pp. 239–58. Baltimore: Penguin Books, 1972.

Hougland, Willard, ed. *Mary Austin: A Memorial.* Santa Fe, N.Mex.: Laboratory of Anthropology, 1944.

House, Julius T. *John G. Neihardt, Man and Poet.* Wayne, Nebr.: F. H. Jones & Sons, 1920.

Hundley, Patrick D. *Three Native American Poets: Norman H. Russell, Lance Jenson, Jim Weaver Barnes.* Marvin, S. Dak.: Blue Cloud Quarterly Press, 1978.

Huntsman, Jeffrey F. "Traditional Native American Literature: The Translation Dilemma." *Shantih* 4, no. 2 (Summer-Fall 1979):5–9.

Inman, Will. *The Wakers in the Tongue.* Marvin, S. Dak.: Blue Cloud Quarterly Press, 1977.

Jackson, Helen Hunt. *A Century of Dishonor.* Boston: Roberts Brothers, 1881.

————. *Ramona: A Story.* Boston: Roberts Brothers, 1884.

Jacob, John. "Simon J. Ortiz, *Going for the Rain.*" *ASAIL Newsletter* 2 no. 2 (1978):2–25.

Jones Llewellyn. "Indian Rhythm." *The Bookman* 51 (August, 1923): 647–48.

Keats, John. *Complete Poems and Selected Letters.* Edited by Clarence D. Thorpe. New York: Odyssey Press, 1935.

Keiser, Albert. *The Indian in American Literature.* New York: Oxford University Press, 1933.

Kenny, Maurice. *Boston Tea Party.* San Francisco: Soup Books, 1982.

————. *I Am the Sun.* Buffalo, N.Y.: White Pine Press, 1979.

————. *Kneading the Blood.* New York: Strawberry Press, 1981.

————. *North: Poems of Home.* Marvin, S. Dak.: Blue Cloud Quarterly Press, 1977.

Kern, Robert. "Clearing the Ground: Gary Snyder and the Modernist Imperative." *Criticism* 19, no. 2 (1977):158–77.

Kluckhohn, Clyde, and Wyman, Leland C. *An Introduction to Navajo Chant Practice.* Memoirs of the American Anthropological Association 53 (1940).

Koenig, Seymour. *Hopi Clay—Hopi Ceremony.* Katonah, N.Y.: Katonah Gallery, 1976.

Kopit, Arthur. *Indians*. New York: Bantam Books, 1971.

Kyle, Carol. "The Mesoamerican Cultural Past and Charles Olson's 'The Kingfishers.' " *Alcheringa: Ethnopoetics*, n.s. 1, no. 2 (1975): 67–79.

La Farge, Oliver. *Laughing Boy*. 1937. Reprint. New York: Pocket Books, 1969.

Laird, Carobeth. *Encounter with an Angry God*. New York: Ballantine Books, 1975.

Lame Deer, John (Fire), and Erdoes, Richard. *Lame Deer: Seeker of Visions*. New York: Simon and Schuster, 1972. Paperback edition. New York: Pocket Books, 1976.

Lawrence, D. H. "American Heroes." Review of *In the American Grain*, by William Carlos Williams. In *William Carlos Williams: A Critical Anthology*, edited by Charles Tomlinson, pp. 89–91. Baltimore: Penguin Books, 1972.

———. *Fantasia of the Unconscious* and *Psychoanalysis and the Unconscious*. Harmondsworth, England.: Penguin Books, 1971.

———. *Mornings in Mexico* and *Etruscan Places*. Harmondsworth, England: Penguin Books, 1971.

———. *The Plumed Serpent*. 1926. Reprint. Harmondsworth, England: Penguin Books, 1950.

———. *Selected Essays*. Harmondsworth, England: Penguin Books, 1968.

———. *Selected Literary Criticism*. Edited by A. Beal. New York: Viking Press, 1956.

———. *Studies in Classic American Literature*. 1923. Reprint. New York: Viking Press, 1964.

Lewis, R. W. B. *The Poetry of Hart Crane: A Critical Study*. Princeton, N.J.: Princeton University Press, 1967.

Liebowitz, Herbert. *Hart Crane: An Introduction to the Poetry*. New York: Columbia University Press, 1968.

Lincoln, Kenneth. "Native American Literature: 'Old like hills, like stars.' " In *Three American Literatures: Essays in Chicano, Native American, and Asian-American Literature for Teachers of American Literature*. New York: Modern Language Association, 1982.

Lindsay, Vachel. *Collected Poems*. New York: Macmillan, 1946.

———. *Earth Man and Star Thrower*, with an essay by Robert F. Sayer. New York: Eakins Press, 1968.

Lomakema, Milland, and Lomayestewa, Mark. *Two Hopi Song Poets of Shungopavi*. Edited by Mike Kabotie. n.p., 1978.

Long, Haniel. *The Marvelous Adventure of Cabeza de Vaca, also Malinche*. London: n.p., 1972.

Longfellow, Henry Wadsworth. *The Song of Hiawatha*. Boston: Ticknor and Fields, 1855.

Lovejoy, Arthur O., and Boas, George. *Primitivism and Related Ideas in Antiquity*. Baltimore: Johns Hopkins University Press, 1935.

Lowell, Robert. "Patterson, Book Two." *The Nation*, June 19, 1948, pp. 692–94.

Lowenfels, Walter. *From the Belly of the Shark*. New York: Random House, Vintage Books, 1973.

Lummis, Charles F. *The Man Who Married the Moon, and Other Pueblo Folk-Stories*. New York: Century Co., 1894.

Lyday, Jo W. *Mary Austin: The Southwest Works*. Austin, Tex.: Steck-Vaughn Co., 1968.

McCluskey, Sally. "Black Elk Speaks, and So Does John G. Neihardt." *Western Literature* 6, no. 4 (1972):231–42.

———. "Image and Idea in the Poetry of John G. Neihardt." Ph.D. diss., Northern Illinois University, 1973.

McCord, Howard. "Some Notes to Gary Snyder's *Myths and Texts*." Berkeley, Calif.: Sand Dollar Books, 1971.

Malanga, Gerard. "The Art of Poetry, XII: Charles Olson." (Interview.) *The Paris Review* 13, no. 49 (1970):177–204.

Marriott, Alice, and Rachlin, Carol K. *American Indian Mythology*. New York: New American Library, 1968.

Massa, Ann. *Vachel Lindsay: Fieldworker for the American Dream*. Bloomington: Indiana University Press, 1970.

Matthews, Washington. "The Mountain Chant, a Navajo Ceremony." In *Fifth Annual Report of the Bureau of American Ethnology*, pp. 379–468. Washington, D.C.: Smithsonian Institution, 1887.

Mazzaro, Jerome. *Profile of William Carlos Williams*. Columbus, Ohio: Charles E. Merrill Publishing Co., 1971.

Metcalf, Paul. *Apalache*. Berkeley, Calif.: Turtle Island Foundation, 1976.

Momaday, N. Scott. *The Gourd Dancer*. New York: Harper & Row, 1976.

———. *House Made of Dawn*. New York: Harper & Row, 1968.

———. *The Names: A Memoir*. New York: Harper & Row, 1976.

———. "Native American Attitudes toward the Environment," in *Seeing With a Native Eye*, edited by Walter Holden Capps, pp. 79–85. New York: Harper & Row, 1976.

———. *The Way to Rainy Mountain*. Albuquerque: University of New Mexico Press, 1969.

Monroe, Harriet. *A Poet's Life*. New York: Macmillan, 1938.

————. "What of Mr. Neihardt?" *Poetry, A Magazine of Verse* 30 (May 1927):99–104.

Mooney, James. *The Ghost Dance Religion and Wounded Knee.* 1896. Reprint. New York: Dover, 1973.

————. "The Sacred Formulas of the Cherokees." In *Seventh Annual Report of the Bureau of American Ethnology*, pp. 301–97. Washington, D.C.: Smithsonian Institution, 1891.

Mumford, Lewis. *The Golden Day: A Study in American Literature and Culture.* Boston: Beacon Press, 1957.

Neihardt, John G. *All Is But a Beginning.* New York: Harcourt Brace Jovanovich, 1972.

————. *Black Elk Speaks*, 1932. Reprint. New York: Pocket Books, 1972.

————. *Black Elk Speaks.* Introduction by Vine Deloria, Jr. Lincoln: University of Nebraska Press, 1979.

————. "The Book That Would Not Die," *Western American Literature* 6, no. 4 (Winter 1972):227–30.

————. *Indian Tales and Others.* New York: Macmillan, 1926.

————. "The Interpretation of Poetry." *Quarterly Journal of Speech* 38, no. 1 (1952):74–78.

————. *Laureate Address.* Chicago: Bookfellows, 1921.

————. *The Mountain Men.* Volume 1 of *The Cycle of the West.* Lincoln: University of Nebraska Press, 1971.

————. *Patterns and Coincidences.* Columbia: University of Missouri Press, 1978.

————. *Poetic Values.* New York: Macmillan, 1925.

————. *The River and I.* Lincoln: University of Nebraska Press, 1968.

————. *The Twilight of the Sioux.* Volume 2 of *The Cycle of the West:* Lincoln: University of Nebraska Press, 1971. Includes *The Song of the Indian Wars* and *The Song of the Messiah.*

————. *When the Tree Flowered.* Lincoln: University of Nebraska Press, 1954.

Newcomb, Franc Johnson. *Hosteen Klah: Navajo Medicine Man and Sandpainter.* Norman: University of Oklahoma Press, 1966.

Niatum, Duane. *Ascending Red Cedar Moon.* New York: Harper & Row, 1974.

————. *Digging Out the Roots.* New York: Harper & Row, 1977.

————. *Taos Pueblo.* Greenfield Center, N.Y.: Greenfield Review Press, 1973.

————, ed. *Carriers of the Dream Wheel.* New York: Harper & Row, 1975.

Norman, Howard A. *The Wishing Bone Cycle: Narrative Poems from the Swampy Cree Indians*. Translated by Howard A. Norman; preface by Jerome Rothenberg. New York: Stonehill, 1976.

Olson, Charles. *Archaeologist of Morning*. New York: Grossman, 1970.

————. *A Bibliography on America for Ed Dorn*. San Francisco: Four Seasons Foundation, 1964.

————. "Cabeza de Vaca (An Idea for an Opera)." In *New World Journal* 1, no. 1 (1975).

————. *Call Me Ishmael: A Study of Melville*. San Francisco: City Lights, 1947.

————. *Causal Mythology*. San Francisco: Four Seasons Foundation, 1969.

————. *Charles Olson and Ezra Pound: An Encounter at St. Elizabeth's*. Edited by Catherine Seeleye. New York: Grossman, 1975.

————. *Human Universe and Other Essays*. Edited by Donald Allen. New York: Grove Press, 1967.

————. *In Cold Hell, in Thicket*. San Francisco: Four Seasons Foundation, 1967.

————. *Letters for Origin: 1950–1955*. Edited by Albert Glover. London: Cape Goliard Press, 1970.

————. *The Maximus Poems*. New York: Jargon Corinth Books, 1960.

————. *The Maximus Poems, III*. Edited by Charles Boer and George Butterick. New York: Viking/Compass, 1975.

————. *The Maximus Poems, IV, V, VI*. New York: Grossman; London: Cape Goliard Press, 1968.

————. *The Mayan Letters*. Mallorca: Divers Press, 1953.

————. *New Man and Woman*. Gloucester, Mass.: Millenia Foundation, n.d.

————. *Pleistocene Man*. Buffalo, N.Y.: Institute for Further Studies, 1968.

————. *Poetry and Truth: The Beloit Lectures and Poems*. San Francisco: Four Seasons Foundation, 1971.

————. *Proprioception*. San Francisco: Four Seasons Foundation, 1965.

————. *Reading at Berkeley*. Transcribed by Zoe Brown. San Francisco: Coyote Books, 1966.

————. *Selected Writings of Charles Olson*. Edited with an introduction by Robert Creeley. New York: New Directions, 1966.

————. *The Special View of History*. Edited by Ann Charters. Berkeley, Calif.: Oyez, 1970.

————, and Sauer, Carl O., "The Correspondences: Charles Olson and Carl Sauer." In *New World Journal* 4. (Spring 1979):136–68.

Oppen, George. *Primitive*. Santa Barbara, Calif.: Black Sparrow Press, 1978.

Ortiz, Simon J. *Fight Back: For the Sake of the People for the Sake of the Land. INAD Literary Journal* 1, no. 1. Albuquerque: University of New Mexico, 1980.

———. *From Sand Creek*. Oak Park, New York: Thunder's Mouth Press, 1981.

———. *Going for the Rain*. New York: Harper & Row, 1976.

———. *A Good Journey*. Berkeley, Calif.: Turtle Island, 1977.

Osborn, Chase Salmon. *Schoolcraft, Longfellow, Hiawatha*. Lancaster, Pa.: Jacques Cattell Press, 1942.

Packard, William. "Craft Interview with Gary Snyder." *New York Quarterly*, no. 22 (1978), pp. 13–28.

Paul, Sherman. *The Music of Survival: A Biography of a Poem by William Carlos Williams*. Urbana: University of Illinois Press, 1968.

———. *Olson's Push* (Baton Rouge, La., Louisiana State University Press, 1978).

Pearce, Roy Harvey. *The Savages of America: A Study of the Indian and the Idea of Civilization*. Baltimore: Johns Hopkins University Press, 1953.

Pearce, Thomas M. *The Beloved House*. Caldwell, Ohio: Caxton Publishers, 1940.

———. *Mary Hunter Austin*. New York: Twayne Publishers, 1965.

Perkins, George, ed. *American Poetic Theory*. New York: Holt, Rinehart and Winston, 1972.

Peterson, Elmer. *Tristan Tzara: Dada and Surrational Theorist*. New Brunswick, N.J.: Rutgers University Press, 1971.

Pound, Ezra. *Gaudier-Brzeska: A Memoir*. 1916. Reprint. New York: New Directions, 1960.

———. *Literary Essays of Ezra Pound*. New York: New Directions, 1968.

Pound, Louise. "The Beginnings of Poetry." *Publications of the Modern Language Association of America* 32, no. 2 (1917):201–22.

———. *Poetic Origins and the Ballad*. New York: Macmillan, 1921.

Prescott, William H. *The Conquest of Peru*. New York: New American Library, 1961.

Proctor, Edna Dean. *The Song of the Ancient People*. Boston: J. R. Osgood, 1893.

Radin, Paul. *Primitive Man as a Philosopher*. New York: Dover, 1957.

———. *The Trickster: A Study in American Indian Mythology*. New York: Schocken Books, 1956.

Rarihokwats. "Tribal Poetry and Tribal Lifeways." *Alcheringa: Ethnopoetics*, no. 4 (Autumn 1972), pp. 114–17.

Revard, Carter. *My Right Hand Don't Leave Me No More*. St. Louis: EEDIN Press, 1970.

————. *Ponca War Dancers*. Norman, Okla.: Point Riders Press, 1980.

Rexroth, Kenneth. "American Indian Songs." In *Literature of the American Indian: Views and Interpretations*, edited by Abraham Chapman, pp. 278–91. New York: New American Library, 1975.

Richter, Hans. *Dada, Art and Anti-Art*. New York: McGraw-Hill, 1965.

Rosen, Kenneth, ed. *The Man to Send Rain Clouds*. New York: Random House, 1974.

————, ed. *Voices of the Rainbow: Contemporary Poetry of American Indians*. New York: Viking Press, 1975.

Rothenberg, Jerome. *A Book of Testimony*. San Francisco: Tree Books, 1971.

————. "Changing the Present, Changing the Past: A New Poetics." In *Talking Poetics from Naropa Institute*, vol. 2. Boulder, Colo.: Shambala Publications, 1978.

————. *The Notebooks*. Milwaukee: Membrane Press, 1976.

————. *Poems, 1964–1967*. Los Angeles: Black Sparrow Press, 1968.

————. *Poems for the Game of Silence, 1960–1970*. New York: Dial Press, 1971.

————. *Poland: 1931*, with photomontage by Eleanor Antin. Santa Barbara, Calif.: Unicorn Press, 1970.

————. *Poland: 1931*. New York: New Directions, 1974.

————. "Postscript to Tzara." *Alcheringa: Ethnopoetics* 2, no. 1 (1976):114.

————. *A Seneca Journal*. New York: New Directions, 1978.

————. "Total Translation." In *Literature of the American Indians: Views and Interpretations*, edited by Abraham Chapman, pp. 292–307. New York: New American Library, 1975.

————, ed. *A Big Jewish Book: Poems and Other Visions of the Jews from Tribal Times to the Present*. Garden City, N.Y.: Doubleday, 1978.

————, ed. *Shaking the Pumpkin: Traditional Poetry of the Indian North Americas*. Garden City, N.Y.: Doubleday, 1972.

————, ed. *Technicians of the Sacred: A Range of Poetries from Africa, America, Asia, and Oceania*. Garden City, N.Y.: Doubleday, 1969.

————, and George Quasha, eds. *America, a Prophecy: A New Reading of American Poetry from Pre-Columbian Times to the Present*. New York: Random House, 1974.

Rothwell, Kenneth S. "In Search of a Western Epic: Neihardt, Sandburg, and Jaffe as Regionalists and 'Astoriadists.' " *Kansas Quarterly*, no. 2 (Spring 1970), pp. 53-63.

Ruland, Richard. *America in Modern European Literature.* New York: New York University Press, 1976.

Sahlins, Marshall David. *Stone Age Economics.* Chicago: Aldine-Atherton, 1972.

Sanders, Thomas E., and Peek, Walter W. *Literature of the American Indian.* Beverly Hills, Calif.: Glencoe, 1973.

Sandoz, Mary. *Crazy Horse: The Strange Man of the Oglalas.* Lincoln: University of Nebraska Press, 1961.

Sapir, Edward. "Song Recitative in Paiute Mythology." *Journal of American Folklore* 23 (1910):455–72.

Sarett, Lew. *The Box of God.* New York: Henry Holt & Co., 1922.

———. *Many, Many Moons.* New York: Henry Holt & Co., 1920.

———. *Slow Smoke.* New York: Henry Holt & Co., 1925.

Sauer, Carl O. *Land and Life: A Selection from the Writings of Carl Ortwin Sauer.* Edited by John Leighly. Berkeley and Los Angeles: University of California Press, 1963.

Sayer, Robert. "Vision and Experience in *Black Elk Speaks.*" *College English* 32, no. 5 (1971): 509–35.

Schoolcraft, Henry Roe. *Indian Legends from Algic Researches.* Edited by Mentor L. Williams. East Lansing: Michigan State University Press, 1956.

Silko, Leslie Marmon. *Ceremony.* New York: Viking Press, 1977.

———. *Laguna Woman.* Greenfield Center, N.Y.: Greenfield Review Press, 1975.

———. "An Old-Time Indian Attack Conducted in Two Parts." *Yardbird Reader* 5 (1976):77–85.

———. *Storyteller.* New York: Seaver Books, 1981.

Skinner, Constance Lindsay. "Aztec Poets." *Poetry, a Magazine of Verse* 26 (June 1925):166–68.

———. *Songs of the Coast Dwellers.* New York: Coward-McCann, 1930.

Slotkin, Richard. *Regeneration Through Violence: The Mythology of the American Frontier, 1600–1860.* (Middletown, Conn.: Wesleyan University Press).

Snyder, Gary. *The Back Country.* New York: New Directions, 1968.

———. *Earth House Hold.* New York: New Directions, 1969.

———. *He Who Hunted Birds in His Father's Village: The Dimensions of a Haida Myth.* Bolinas, Calif.: Grey Fox Press, 1979.

———. *Myths and Texts.* New York: Totem Press, 1960.

———. *The Old Ways.* San Francisco: City Lights, 1977.

———. *The Real Work: Interviews and Talks 1964–1979.* New York: New Directions, 1980.

————. *Regarding Wave*. New York: New Directions, 1970.

————. *Six Sections from Mountains and Rivers without End Plus One.*. San Francisco: Four Seasons Foundation, 1970.

————. *Turtle Island*. New York: New Directions, 1974.

Spicer, Edward H. *Cycles of Conquest: The Impact of Spain, Mexico, and the United States on the Indians of the Southwest, 1533–1960*. Tucson: University of Arizona Press, 1974.

Spinden, Herbert Joseph, "American Indian Poetry." *Natural History* 19 (1919):301–8.

————. *Songs of the Tewa*, with an essay on American Indian Poetry. 1933. Reprint. New York: W. W. Norton, 1976.

Standing Bear, Luther. *Land of the Spotted Eagle*. 1933. Reprint. Lincoln: University of Nebraska Press, 1978.

————. *My People the Sioux*. Edited by E. A. Brinistool. 1928. Reprint. Lincoln: University of Nebraska Press, 1975.

Steiner, Stan. *The New Indians*. New York: Dell, 1968.

Storm, Hyemeyohsts. *Seven Arrows*. New York: Ballantine Books, 1972.

Street, Alfred B. *Frontenac; or, The Atoharto of the Iroquois*. New York, 1849.

Sutton, Walter. *American Free Verse: The Modern Revolution in Poetry*. New York: New Directions, 1973.

Swanton, John R. *Haida Texts and Myths*. Bureau of American Ethnology Bulletin no. 29. Washington, D.C.: Smithsonian Institution, 1905.

Tashijan, Dickran. *William Carlos Williams and the American Scene, 1920–1940*. Berkeley and Los Angeles: University of California Press, 1978.

Tedlock, Barbara. "The Clown's Way." In *Teaching from the American Earth: Indian Religion and Philosophy*, edited by Dennis Tedlock and Barbara Tedlock, pp. 105–18. New York: Liveright, 1975.

————, and Dennis Tedlock, eds. *Teachings from the American Earth: Indian Religion and Philosophy*. New York: Liveright, 1975.

Tedlock, Dennis. "On the Translation of Style in Oral Narrative." *Journal of American Folklore* 82 (1969): 313–28.

————, trans. *Finding the Center. Narrative Poetry of the Zuni Indians*. Lincoln: University of Nebraska Press, 1972.

Todd, Edgeley W. "The Frontier Epic: Frank Norris and John G. Neihardt." *Western Humanities Review* 13 (Winter 1959):40–45.

Toelken, Barre. "The Demands of Harmony: An Appreciation of Navajo Relations." *Parabola* 2, no. 4 (1979):74–81.

————. "Seeing with a Native Eye: How Many Sheep Will It Hold?" In *Seeing With A Native Eye*, edited by Walter Holden Capps, pp. 9–24. New York: Harper & Row, 1976.

Tomlinson, Charles, ed. *William Carlos Williams: A Critical Anthology*. Baltimore: Penguin Books, 1972.

Turner, Frederick W. *The Portable North American Indian Reader*. New York: Viking Press, 1975.

Tzara, Tristan. *Approximate Man and Other Writings*. Translated by Mary Ann Caws. Detroit: Wayne State University Press, 1973.

————. "Poèmes Nègres." Translated by Pierre Joris. In *Alcheringa: Ethnopoetics* 2, no. 1 (1976):76–114.

Ude, Wayne. *Buffalo and Other Stories*. Amherst, Mass.: Lynx House Press, 1975.

Underhill, Ruth. *Singing for Power: The Song Magic of the Papago Indians of Southern Arizona*. Berkeley and Los Angeles: University of California Press, 1938.

Untermeyer, Louis. "The Indian as Poet." Review of *The Path on the Rainbow*, by George W. Cronyn. *Dial*, 8 March 1919, pp. 240–41.

Villaseñor, David. *Tapestries in Sand: The Spirit of Indian Sandpainting*. Healdsburg, Calif.: Naturegraph, 1966.

Vogel, Virgil J. *This Country Was Ours: A Documentary History of the American Indians*. New York: Harper & Row, 1974.

von Hallberg, Robert. "Olson's Relation to Pound and Williams." *Contemporary Literature* 15, no. 1 (1974):15–48.

Walton, Eda Lou. *Dawn Boy*. Introduction by Witter Bynner. New York: E. P. Dutton, 1926.

————. "Navajo Verse Rhythms." *Poetry, a Magazine of Verse* 24 (April 1924):40–44.

Waters, Frank. *Book of the Hopi*. New York: Viking Press, 1963.

Weaver, Mike. *William Carlos Williams: The American Background*. Cambridge: Cambridge University Press, 1971.

Welch, James. *The Death of Jim Loney*. New York: Harper & Row, 1979.

————. *Riding the Earthboy 40*. New York: Harper & Row, 1976.

————. *Winter in the Blood*. New York: Harper & Row, 1974.

Welsh, Andrew. *Roots of Lyric: Primitive Poetry and Modern Poetics*. Princeton, N.J.: Princeton University Press, 1977.

Weltfish, Gene. *The Lost Universe: Pawnee Life and Culture*. Lincoln: University of Nebraska Press, 1977.

Whitman, Walt. *An American Primer*. Edited by Horace Traubel. San Francisco: City Lights, 1970.

————. *Leaves of Grass*. Edited by Scully Bradley and Harold W. Blodgett. New York: W. W. Norton, 1973.

Whitney, Blair. *John G. Neihardt*. Boston: Twayne Publishers, 1976.

Whittemore, Reed. *William Carlos Williams: Poet from Jersey*. Boston: Houghton Mifflin Co., 1975.

Whorf, Benjamin Lee. *Language, Thought, and Reality: Selected Writings of Benjamin Lee Whorf*. Edited by John B. Carroll. Cambridge: M.I.T. Press, 1956.

Williams, William Carlos. *The Autobiography of William Carlos Williams*. New York: New Directions, 1951.

————. *The Collected Earlier Poems*. New York: New Directions, 1938.

————. *The Collected Later Poems*. New York: New Directions, 1963.

————. "How to Write." *New Directions in Prose and Poetry*, no. 1 (1936).

————. *Imaginations*. New York: New Directions, 1970.

————. *In the American Grain*. New York: New Directions, 1956.

————. *I Wanted to Write a Poem*. New York: New Directions, 1958.

————. *Paterson*. New York: New Directions, 1963.

————. *Pictures from Brueghel*. New York: New Directions, 1963.

————. *Selected Essays*. New York: New Directions, 1954.

————. *The Selected Letters of William Carlos Williams*. Edited by John C. Thirlwall. New York: New Directions, 1957.

————. *Spring and All*. 1923. Reprint. New York: Frontier Press, 1970.

————, ed. *Contact: Nos. 1–5, 1920–1924*. New York: Kraus Reprint Corp., 1967.

Winters, Yvor. *Primitivism and Decadence: A Study of American Experimental Poetry*. New York: Haskell House, 1969.

Wyman, Leland C. *The Sacred Mountains of the Navajo*. Flagstaff: University of Northern Arizona, 1967.

Zolla, Elémire. *The Writer and the Shaman: A Morphology of the American Indian*. Translated by Raymond Rosenthal. New York: Harcourt Brace Jovanovich, 1973.

The Zuni People. *The Zuñis: Self-Portrayals*. Albuquerque: University of New Mexico Press, 1972. Paperback edition with an afterword by Robert Coles. New York: New America Library, 1974.

## Selected Periodicals

*Akwesasne Notes*. (Rooseveltown, N.Y.: Mohawk Nation), Rarihokwats, ed., circa 1968–1978.

*Alcheringa: Ethnopoetics.* (Boston: Boston University), Jerome Rothenberg and Dennis Tedlock, eds., circa 1969–1976.

*ASAIL Newsletter.* (New York: Association for the Study of American Indian Literatures, Columbia University), Karl Kroeber and LaVonne Ruoff, eds.

*Black Mountain Review.* (Black Mountain, N.C.: Black Mountain College), Robert Creeley, ed.

*The Blue Cloud Quarterly.* (Marvin, S.Dak.), Benet Tvedten, ed.

*Boundary 2: Charles Olson: Essays, Reminiscences, Reviews*, Special Issue 2, nos. 1 and 2 (Fall 1973–Winter 1974) (State University of New York at Binghampton), Matthew Corrigan, ed.

*Contact.* (New York), William Carlos Williams, ed.

*Contact II.* (New York), Maurice Kenny, ed.

*Greenfield Review.* (Greenfield Center, N.Y.), Joseph Bruchac, ed.

*Kuksu: A Journal of Backcountry Writing.* (Nevada City, Calif.), Dale Pendell, ed.

*New America.* (Albuquerque: University of New Mexico), jointly edited by graduate students.

*New World Journal.* (Berkeley, Calif.: Turtle Island Foundation), Bob Callahan, ed.

*Olson: The Journal of the Charles Olson Archives.* (Storrs, Conn.: University of Connecticut), George Butterick, ed.

*Poems from the Floating World.* (New York), Jerome Rothenberg, ed.

*Poetry, A Magazine of Verse.* (Chicago), Harriet Monroe, ed.

*River Styx.* (St. Louis: Big River Association), Michael Castro and Jan Castro, eds.

*Shantih*: Native American Issue 4, no. 2. (New York), Roberta Hill and Brian Swann, eds.

*The South Dakota Review.* (Vermillion, S. Dak.), John Milton, ed.

*Suntracks, a Magazine of Native American Literature.* (Tucson: University of Arizona), Larry Evers, ed.

*Y'Bird.* (Berkeley, Calif.), Ishmael Reed, ed.

# ◆ *Permission Acknowledgments* ◆

# ✦ Index ✦

Abnaki, the, 64
*Aboriginal American Authors,* 8
Acoma Pueblo, 168
*Akwesasne Notes,* 130, 158,
   159
Alberti, Carl, 118
*Alcheringa: Ethnopoetics,* 129
Alexander, Hartley Burr,
   44–45
Allen, Paula Gunn, 33, 34, 36,
   159; "The Sacred Hoop,"
   33–34
Allen, R. M., 43
*America, a Prophecy: A New*
   *Reading of American Poetry*
   *from Pre-Columbian Times to*
   *the Present* (Rothenberg),
   164
*American Poetry from the*
   *Beginning to Whitman*
   (Untermeyer), 44
*The American Review of*
   *Reviews* (quoted), 11
*The American Rhythm* (Austin),
   3, 5, 6, 15, 21, 32, 38,
   41–43, 68
*America's Coming of Age*
   (Brooks), 62

Anderson, Sherwood, 41
Angulo, Jaime de, 140
Antin, David, 118
Appleseed, Johnny (John
   Chapman), 53
arrogance, cultural, 161, 162
*The Arrow Maker* (Austin), 13
Astrov, Margaret, 32, 35,
   102, 118
Auden, W. H., 117
Austin, Mary Hunter, 5–7,
   12–17, 19–22, 24, 25,
   27–33, 35, 38–45, 59, 69,
   73, 81, 101, 103, 111, 113,
   117, 120, 122–24, 135, 139,
   141, 146; "Glyph," 27;
   "Prayer to the Mountain
   Spirit," 28–30; quoted, 3,
   15, 21, 40, 42
*The Autobiography of William*
   *Carlos Williams,* 103,
awareness, holistic, defined, 5

*The Back Country* (Snyder),
   140, 144, 151
Bandelier, Adolph, 13
Barnes, Nellie, 32–36, 78
Barrett, S. M., 13, 155

Beat poets, 108, 117, 120,
121; West Coast, 102
Beauty Way, 29, 35
Bevis, William, 131, 132;
quoted, 30
Big Eagle, 13
*A Big Jewish Book* (Rothen-
berg), 164
Black Elk, 14, 82–96, 121,
160, 162; Great Vision of,
85, 89–94; quoted, 83,
88–94
*Black Elk Speaks,* 79, 80,
82–97, 155
Black Mountain College, 113,
125
Black Mountain School (of
poetry), 102
Blake, William, 108, 119, 121
Blue Cloud, Peter, 159
Bonnin, Gertrude (Zitkala-Sa),
13
*Book of Changes,* 120
Boone, Daniel, 64–65
"Boston Tea Party" (Kenny),
169
Bowra, C. M., 128
*The Box of God* (Sarett),
73–78
Boyd, Doug, 155, 163
breath, 107–9
Breslin, James, 61; quoted, 62
Breton, André, 118
brevity, 35
Brinton, Daniel G., 8, 43
Brown, Joseph Epes, 86
Bruchac, Joseph, 159
Buffalo Bill's Wild West
Show, 85
Bureau of American
Ethnology, 118
Burns, Diane, 159
Burr, Aaron, 64

Cabeza de Vaca, Álvar
Núñez, 104, 106
Caillois, Roger, 118
*Cante Ishta: The Eye of the
Heart* (Crow Dog), 155
Castaneda, Carlos, 155, 163
Cavett, Dick, 96, 155
Celan, Paul, 118
*A Century of Dishonor*
(Jackson), 12
*Ceremony* (Silko), 170–173
Chippewa, the, 25–27
*Chippewa Music* (Densmore)
7, 18
Cloutier, David, 163
clown, sacred *(heyoka),* 121
Commoner, Barry, 145
*Contact,* 19, 59–61
Cooper, James Fenimore, 51
Cortez, Hernando de, 62, 106
Crane, Hart, 16, 19, 49,
55–59, 68–69, 73, 76, 101,
139, 143, 161, 162, 171;
"The Bridge," 55–59;
"National Winter Garden,"
59
*Creation Myth of the Zunis*
(Cushing), 18
Creeley, Robert, quoted, 110
Cronyn, George W., 19, 21,
31–32, 43–44
Crow Dog, Leonard, 155, 162
Cummings, E. E., 103
Curtis, Natalie, 8–12, 14;
quoted, 35
Cushing, Frank Hamilton, 18
*The Cycle of the West*
(Neihardt), 80–81, 83, 84

Davenport, Guy, 104; quoted,
105
Day, A. Grove, 32, 102, 118
Deep Image, 102, 118

*The Delight Makers* (Bandelier), 13

Deloria, Vine, Jr., 95, 156, 157, 161; quoted, 95

Densmore, Frances, 7, 18, 20, 25–26, 39; "The Deer and the Flower," 22; "Healing Song," 23, 24; "On the Bank of a Stream," 26; "Songs from the North and South," 20; "They Are Playing a Game," 25, 26; "The Water Bug and the Shadows," 22

*The Dial,* 43–44

Dickey, James, 107

Duncan, Robert, 113

Eagle Dance, Seneca, 133

*Earth House Hold* (Snyder), 147, 148, 152

Eastaway, Edward, 17

Eastman, Charles A. (Ohiyesa), 13, 155, 156

Eliot, T. S., 104, 117; "The Waste Land," 104

Enkvist, Nils Erik, 54–55

Erdoes, Richard, 155

ethnic literature, 157–58

Evers, Lawrence J., 158–59

Faas, Ekbert, 112

Fiedler, Leslie, 50

*Finding the Center: Narrative Poetry of the Zuni Indians* (Tedlock), 32

Fire, John. *See* Lame Deer.

Flaming Rainbow. *See* Peyta-Wigimou-Ge.

Fletcher, Alice Cunningham, 7, 20; "The Hako: A Pawnee Ceremony," 20

Fletcher, John Gould, 45

Flying Hawk, 83

forms of poetry: avant-garde, 119; event, 133–35; experimental, 119; free verse *(vers libre),* 17; haiku, 23; Ido, 129–32; imagist, 22–23, 25, 28, 118; performance, 54, 117, 119; postlogical, 120; postmodern, 117; projective verse, 102–4, 107–13, 117, 119; surrealist, 118, 121

Fortune, R. F., 37

Fowler, Gene, 161, 163

Frank, Waldo, 19, 62

Franklin, Benjamin, 62–63

*From a Shaman's Notebook* (Rothenberg), 119

*From the Deep Woods to Civilization* (Eastman), 13

Frye, Northrop, 35

Gallery 291, 60

Gamble, Jerry (Rarihokwats), 130–31, 158; quoted, 130

Garland, Hamlin, 19

genres, poetic. *See* forms of poetry

*Geronimo, His Own Story (also: Geronimo's Story of His Life),* 13, 155

Ghost Dance religion, 33, 83, 85

*The Ghost Dance Religion* (Mooney), 7

Gifford, Barry, 163

Ginsberg, Allen, 37, 110

*The Golden Day* (Mumford), 62

*Goodbird the Indian* (Wilson), 13

Gordon, Frank S., 17, 20, 31

Grass, Gunter, 118

Great Vision. *See* Black Elk.
*The Greenfield Review,* 159
Griffis, Joseph K., 13
Grinnell, George Bird, 13

haiku, 23
Hamilton, Alexander, 63
*Hanta Yo* (Hill), 155
Harjo, Joy, 159
Hartley, Marsden, 19, 60;
    "Tribal Aesthetics," 60
Hayden, Thomas, 156
*He Who Hunted Birds in His
    Father's Village: The
    Dimensions of a Haida Myth*
    (Snyder), 159
healing chants, 23–24, 28–30
Henderson, Alice Corbin, 17,
    20, 25–27; "Where the
    Fight Was," 26–27
*heyoka. See* clown, sacred.
Hiamovi, 162
Hill, Ruth Beebe, 155
Hobson, Geary, 32, 159–63,
    165; quoted, 163; "The Rise
    of the White Shaman as a
    New Version of Cultural
    Imperialism," 160
Holder, Alan, 61
holistic awareness, defined, 5
hoop, sacred, 88–90, 92
Hopi, the, 160, 162; language,
    108, 109–10
*House Made of Dawn*
    (Momaday), 171
Houston, Sam, 64
*Howl* (Ginsberg), 37

imagery, body-related, 120–21
*In the American Grain*
    (Williams), 47, 61–67
*Indian Boyhood* (Eastman), 13,
    155

*Indian Love Song* (film), 31
"Indian poetry" defined, 7
*Indian Tales and Others*
    (Neihardt), 80
*The Indians' Book* (Curtis),
    8–12, 14, 35

Jacataqua, 64
Jackson, Helen Hunt, 12
Jimeson, Avery, 126; "Fidelia,"
    126
John, Richard Johnny, 130
Johnson, Pauline (the
    "Mohawk warbler"), 20,
    31–32, 156
Jung, Carl, 96, 121

*Kaddish* (Ginsberg), 37
Kelly, Robert, 118
Kenny, Maurice, 159, 169,
    171
Kokopilau (Kokopelli), 53
Kwakiutl potlatch, 134
Kyle, Carol, 104–5

LaFlesche, Francis, 7
Laguna Pueblo, 33, 170
Lamantia, Philip, 118
Lambert, Jean, 118
Lame Deer (John Fire), 162;
    quoted, 36
*Lame Deer: Seeker of Visions,*
    155
landscape line, 39, 40, 141;
    defined, 40
Lawrence, D. H., 18, 19, 49,
    62, 73, 103, 111, 120, 163,
    164; quoted, 49, 69
Leatherstocking Tales
    (Cooper), 51
Lévi-Strauss, Claude, 148
Lewis, R. W. B.: quoted, 55,
    56, 58–59

Linderman, Frank S., 13
Lindsay, Vachel, 19, 41, 49–55, 58, 59, 68–69, 73, 76, 101, 139, 162; "The Babbitt Jamboree," 51; "Doctor Mohawk," 52–53, 166; "The Ghost of the Buffaloes," 51–52; "The Hunting Dogs," 51; "In Praise of Johnny Appleseed," 53–54; "Our Mother Pocahantas," 49–51, 53; "The Statue of Andrew Jackson," 55
*The Literary Review,* 43
Little Big Horn, 85
Little Bull Buffalo. See Tae-Nuga-Zhinga.
*The Lonesome Trail* (Neihardt), 80
*The Love of Possessions Is a Disease with Them* (Hayden), 156
Lowell, Robert, 117
Lummis, Charles F., 13

McAllester, David, 125, 128
McCluskey, Sally, 86, 87
McLow, Jackson, 118
McLuhan, Marshall, 119
McNickle, D'Arcy, 156
Malinowski, Bronislaw, 37
*The Man to Send Rainclouds* (Rosen), 159
*Many, Many Moons* (Sarett), 73
Maquokeeta, 57–58
Mather, Cotton, 62
Matthews, Washington, 7, 28, 30; "Invocation to Dsilye N'eyeani," 28
*Maximus Poems* (Olson), 99, 110, 112, 113

Mayan influence, 105, 106, 111
*The Mayan Letters* (Olson), 104, 111
media, mixed, 120, 125
Melville, Herman, 74
Midewiwin Society, 24
Milton, John, 159
Mitchell, Frank, 127–28; "Horse Songs," 127–29
Mohawk, the, 145, 158, 169
"Mohawk warbler," See Johnson, Pauline.
Momaday, N. Scott, 155, 156, 157, 171
Monroe, Harriet, 18, 25
Mooney, James, 7
*Mornings in Mexico* (Lawrence), 18
Morton, Thomas, 62
Moser, Norman, 163
Mountain Men books, 81
Mumford, Lewis, 43, 62
*My People the Sioux* (Standing Bear), 155
*Myths and Texts* (Snyder), 148, 165

*The Names: A Memoir* (Momaday), 155
*The Nation,* 44
Navajo, the, 28–30, 35, 127–128, 134
Neihardt, John G., 14, 15, 69, 73, 79–97, 101, 124, 155; quoted, 71, 79, 80, 82, 87
Neruda, Pablo, 118
"New American Poetry," defined, 102
New Criticism, 102, 117, 118
*The New Poetry,* 25
*The New Republic,* 43
Niatum, Duane, 159

objectism, defined, 109
Odom, Eugene, 144–45
Ohiyesa. *See* Eastman, Charles A.
O'Keeffe, Georgia, 19, 60
*Old Indian Legends* (Bonnin), 13
*The Old Ways* (Snyder), 144
Olson, Charles, 15, 16, 99, 101–13, 117, 119, 120, 122–24, 135, 139, 141, 143, 146, 147, 162–64, 171; quoted, 99, 110, 111; "Human Universe," 107, 109, 111; "The Kingfishers," 104–7, 112; "Letter to Elaine Feinstein," 107, 109; "Projective Verse," 102–4, 107–9, 110–13, 123, 124, 141, 146; "Proprioception," 108; "Red, White and Black," 103–4, 142
Omaha, the, 79–80
Ortiz, Simon, 149–50, 156, 157, 159, 164, 165, 168–69; quoted, 168; "Blessings," 168–69; "Canyon de Chelley," 153; "Speaking," 149–50
*Our America* (Frank), 62
Owens, Rochelle, 118

*Paterson* (Williams), 67
*The Path on the Rainbow: An Anthology of Songs and Chants from the Indians of North America* (Cronyn), 19–24, 28, 29, 31–34, 42–44
*Patterns and Coincidences* (Neihardt), 80
personal power chants, 25–26

Peyta-Wigimou-Ge (John G. Neihardt), 88
Picotte, Susan LaFlesche, 80
place, spirit of, 19, 21–22
Plains Indians, 33, 83
Pocahontas, 49–51, 56–59
Poe, Edgar Allan, 63
*Poems from the Floating World,* 118
*Poetry, A Magazine of Verse,* 17–19, 21, 25, 42, 73
*Poetry New York,* 102
Poets Hardware Theater, 119
*Poland: 1931* (Rothenberg), 164
Pound, Ezra, 17, 28, 106, 117, 118, 148
Pound, Louise, 38
Pueblo Indians, 144–45, 151; Acoma, 168; Laguna, 33, 170

Radin, Paul, 120–21
*Ramona* (Jackson), 12
Rarihokwats. *See* Gamble, Jerry.
Rasles, Père Sebastian, 64
*Regarding Wave* (Snyder), 149
*The Remembered Earth: An Anthology of Contemporary Native American Literature* (Hobson), 32, 33–34, 159
repetition, 34–35
*The Return of the Vanishing American* (Fiedler), 50
Revard, Carter, 159
*Revolution of the Word* (Rothenberg), 164
rhythm; bodily, 40; environmental, 39–40; poetic, influences on, 39–41

218

Rimbaud, Arthur, 106, 118, 119, 121
*River Styx,* 159
*Rolling Thunder* (Boyd), 155
Roosevelt, President Theodore, 9, 10
"rootedness, animal body," defined, 120
Rose, Wendy, 159
Rosen, Kenneth, 159
Rothenberg, Jerome, 15, 16, 32, 97, 101, 102, 116–35, 139, 146, 158, 162–64; quoted, 115, 122, 127, 130, 132, 134, 135; "Gift Event," 133–34; "Horse Songs," 127–29, 132; "Language Event," 134–35; "Seneca Women's Dance Song," 126–27

*The Sacred Pipe* (Brown), 86
Sandburg, Carl, 17–19, 22, 41, 43, 75
Sapir, Edward, 103, 109
Sarett, Lew, 14, 15, 69, 73–79, 124; quoted, 74, 76; "Iron Wind Dances," 74–75; "Medals and Holes," 76; "Thunder-drums," 74–75
*Scree,* 159
Seneca, the, 122, 125, 127, 129–30, 132, 133, 158
*Seneca Journal,* 164
*Seven Arrows* (Storm), 155
Silko, Leslie Marmon, 155–57, 159–65, 170–73; quoted, 161–62, 171; "An Old Time Indian Attack Conducted in Two Parts," 160–62

*Shaking the Pumpkin: Traditional Poetry of the Indian North Americas* (Rothenberg), 32, 117, 125–26, 129, 134
shaman, 86, 121–24, 148–49, 152
Shearer, Tony, 163
Simpson, Louis, 161
Sioux, the, 26–27, 83–92, 134
Skinner, Constance Lindsay, 17, 20, 31
*The Sky Clears: Poetry of the American Indians* (Day), 32, 102
*Slow Smoke* (Sarett), 73
Smith, John, 50
*Smoke and Steel* (Sandburg), 41
Snyder, Gary, 101, 102, 125, 139–152, 155, 159, 162–65, 171; quoted, 137, 144; "Control Burn," 151; "Dusty Braces," 164; "Four Changes," 143–44, 147; "Magpie's Song," 147–48; "Oil," 144; "Poetry and the Primitive," 148; "The Politics of Ethnopoetics," 144; "Prayer for the Great Family," 145–46; "Through the Smoke Hole," 151–52; "A Walk," 140–41, 142; "What Happened Here Before," 141–43; "What You Should Know to be a Poet," 149; "Why Tribe," 152; "The Wilderness," 143
Society of Mystic Animals, 130
soldier weed. *See* war herb.
Song Maid. *See* Tawa Mana.
*Song of Myself* (Whitman), 115

219

*The Song of the Messiah*
(Neihardt), 80, 83, 96
*The Song of the Indian Wars*
(Neihardt), 80, 96
song types, 32
*The Soul of the Indian*
(Eastman), 13
*South Dakota Review,* 159
*Spring & All* (Williams), 66
Standing Bear, Luther, 19,
155, 156, 162
Stein, Gertrude, 19, 117
Stieglitz, Alfred, 60
Storm, Hyemeyohsts, 155,
163
*Storyteller* (Silko), 155
*Studies in Classic American
Literature* (Lawrence), 49,
62, 69
*Suntracks,* 159
symbol: buffalo hide as, 84;
dark woman as, 66; eagle
feather as, 84; Elsie as,
66–67; Indian (man) as,
67–69, 73; Indian woman
as, 64; morning star as, 84
symbolism, 35–36

Tae-Nuga-Zhinga (John G.
Neihardt), 80
*Tahan: Out of Savagery Into
Civilization* (Griffis), 13
Tahirussawichi, 20
Tawa Mana (Natalie Curtis),
9
*The Teachings of Don Juan: A
Yaqui Way of Knowledge*
(Castaneda), 155
*Technicians of the Sacred: A
Range of Poetries from Africa,
Asia, America, and Oceania*
(Rothenberg), 32, 117, 119,
122–25, 133, 134

Tedlock, Barbara, 125
Tedlock, Dennis, 32, 125, 129
translation, total, defined, 126
*Trésor de la poésie universelle*
(Caillois and Lambert), 118
*The Trickster: A Study in
American Indian Mythology*
(Radin), 120–21
*Turtle Island* (Snyder), 139,
141, 143–44, 145, 147, 151,
159, 164

Untermeyer, Louis, 43–45

Van Doren, Carl, 43, 45
Vietnam War, 156–57
*Voices of the Rainbow:
Contemporary Poetry of
American Indians* (Rosen),
159

Walsh, Marnie, 167–68, 171;
"Vicki Loans Arrow,"
167–68
war herb, 93–94
Washington, George, 63
Washoe, the, 27
Washoe Sam, 27–28; "The
Magic Ribbon," 27–28
*Wassaja,* 159
*The Way to Rainy Mountain*
(Momaday), 155
Welch, James, 165–67, 171;
"D-Y Bar," 166–67;
"Harlem Montana: Just Off
the Reservation," 165–66
Wenabojo, 23–24
White Buffalo Woman, 86
Whitman, Walt, 120; quoted,
115
Whorf, Benjamin Lee, 103–4,
107–9; "An American

Indian Model of the Universe," 109
*wicasha wican,* 83
Williams, William Carlos, 16, 19, 49, 59–69, 73, 76, 101, 103, 111, 117, 120, 139, 140, 143, 146, 162, 163, 171; quoted, 47, 59, 63, 65, 66; "The American Background," 59; "The Desert Music," 67–68
Wilson, Gilbert L., 13
*The Winged Serpent: An Anthology of American Indian Prose and Poetry* (Astrov), 32, 102
Winnebago, the, 13, 23–24, 74
Wounded Knee: battle at, 85; protest at, 157, 158

*Y'Bird,* 159, 160
Young Bear, Ray, 159
Yucatán, 104, 106, 110

Zitkala-Sa. *See* Bonnin, Gertrude.